God's Plan Fulfilled

God's Plan Fulfilled

a guide for understanding the new testament

kenneth schenck

wesleyan
publishing
house

Indianapolis, Indiana

Copyright © 2009 by Triangle Publishing and Indiana Wesleyan University
Published by Wesleyan Publishing House
Indianapolis, Indiana 46250
Printed in the United States of America
ISBN 978-0-89827-378-6

Library of Congress Cataloging-in-Publication Data

Schenck, Kenneth, 1966-
  God's plan fulfilled : a guide to understanding the New Testament /
Kenneth Schenck.
    p. cm.
  Includes bibliographical references and index.
  ISBN 978-0-89827-378-6
  1. Bible. N.T.--Introductions. I. Title.

  BS2330.3.S34 2009
  225.6'1--dc22

                              2008046750

Originally published as *Jesus Is Lord: An Introduction to the New Testament*, © Triangle
Publishing, Marion, Indiana, 2003.

To Angela, Stefanie, Stacy, Thomas, and Sophia

Contents

Acknowledgments   9

Abbreviations of the Books of the Bible   11

Section 1: Introduction and Background

  1. Why Read the New Testament?   15

  2. How to Read the Bible as a Christian   19

  3. An Overview of the New Testament   33

  4. Who Chose These Books?   37

  5. Why Are there So Many Different Bibles?   45

  6. The Story Behind the Story: From Abraham to Moses   53

  7. The Story Behind the Story: From Promised Land to No Land   61

Section 2: Gospels

  8. Jewish Groups at the Time of Christ   73

  9. The Life and Teachings of Jesus: An Overview   83

  10. Jesus, the Son of David: The Gospel of Matthew   91

  11. Jesus, the Suffering Messiah: The Gospel of Mark   99

  12. The Beginnings of Jesus' Mission: The Gospel of Luke   109

  13. Stories Jesus Told: The Parables   119

  14. Jesus, the Way: The Gospel of John   129

  15. The Story of Jesus in John   139

Section 3: Acts

  16. Luke's Sequel: Acts   151

  17. Jerusalem, Judea, and Samaria: The Story of the Church in Acts Part 1   163

  18. To the Ends of the Earth: The Story of the Church in Acts Part 2   171

Section 4: Paul's Letters

19. The Life and Writings of Paul   183

20. Is God Really Faithful?: Paul's Letter to Rome   193

21. Unity Problems: The Corinthian Letters   205

22. Healing Relationships: 2 Corinthians   213

23. Paul on the Defense: Galatians   219

24. Letters from Prison: Ephesians, Philippians,
    Colossians, and Philemon   227

25. Paul's Earliest Preaching: 1 and 2 Thessalonians   239

26. Passing on the Torch: 1 and 2 Timothy, and Titus   249

Section 5: Hebrews, General Letters, and Revelation

27. Don't Give Up the Race: Hebrews   263

28. The General Letters: James, 1 and 2 Peter, 1–3 John, and Jude 275

29. Jesus Revealed! The Apocalypse   293

Epilogue: Where Do We Go from Here?   309

Notes   317

Acknowledgments

Countless individuals have had an impact on this final work. They have bequeathed this book its strengths. In my "brief" thirty-some years on the earth, I have had countless positive influences on my spiritual and intellectual understanding. I would like to go on record with thanks to my parents, broader family, and former teachers for their impact on my life.

Numerous colleagues have read one or more chapters. Dr. David Smith and Dr. Steve Lennox checked my content for plausibility and accuracy, although they did not always agree with me. David in particular read the entire manuscript. I must take responsibility for the ideas as they now stand.

Dr. Keith Drury and Dr. Bud Bence provided me with helpful spiritual and practical advice. Keith, more than anyone else, has helped me aim at always building up the body of Christ and avoiding anything that might be a stumbling block. I share his priority that our hearts are far more important than our heads. Beyond the spiritual, I also have him to thank more than anyone else for any skill I might have as a teacher. It is hard to imagine the level of pain I might still inflict on my students if his office were not next to mine!

I want to thank my students these last few years at Indiana Wesleyan University. They have labored under photocopies and loosely bound editions, oral reports, and written evaluations. They have made me a better teacher and, I trust, made this book a better introduction to the New Testament.

Bobbie Sease has done an incredible job editing the project. I have improved tenfold as a writer from her suggestions. Nathan Birky and Triangle Publishing have been models of patience and support. Graphic designers, other readers, and many other unnamed individuals deserve immense thanks.

Most of all I would like to thank my family for their incredible sacrifice of time and my attentiveness. They surrendered innumerable hours so that I could work at a computer. My wife, Angela, also waded through numerous chapters and made excellent suggestions toward making the book more helpful and readable. Stefanie, Stacy, Thomas, and Sophia lost hours of fun and play with their dad, who wasn't always patient and rested. It is to my family that I dedicate this book.

—Kenneth Schenck

Abbreviations of the Books of the Bible

Genesis	Gen.	**Nahum**	Nah.
Exodus	Ex.	**Habakkuk**	Hab.
Leviticus	Lev.	**Zephaniah**	Zeph.
Numbers	Num.	**Haggai**	Hag.
Deuteronomy	Deut.	**Zechariah**	Zech.
Joshua	Josh.	**Malachi**	Mal.
Judges	Judg.	**Matthew**	Matt.
Ruth	Ruth	**Mark**	Mark
1 Samuel	1 Sam.	**Luke**	Luke
2 Samuel	2 Sam.	**John**	John
1 Kings	1 Kings	**Acts**	Acts
2 Kings	2 Kings	**Romans**	Rom.
1 Chronicles	1 Chron.	**1 Corinthians**	1 Cor.
2 Chronicles	2 Chron.	**2 Corinthians**	2 Cor.
Ezra	Ezra	**Galatians**	Gal.
Nehemiah	Neh.	**Ephesians**	Eph.
Esther	Est.	**Philippians**	Phil.
Job	Job	**Colossians**	Col.
Psalm	Ps. (pl. Pss.)	**1 Thessalonians**	1 Thess.
Proverbs	Prov.	**2 Thessalonians**	2 Thess.
Ecclesiastes	Eccl.	**1 Timothy**	1 Tim.
Song of Songs	Song	**2 Timothy**	2 Tim.
Isaiah	Isa.	**Titus**	Titus
Jeremiah	Jer.	**Philemon**	Philem.
Lamentations	Lam.	**Hebrews**	Heb.
Ezekiel	Ezek.	**James**	James
Daniel	Dan.	**1 Peter**	1 Pet.
Hosea	Hos.	**2 Peter**	2 Pet.
Joel	Joel	**1 John**	1 John
Amos	Amos	**2 John**	2 John
Obadiah	Obad.	**3 John**	3 John
Jonah	Jon.	**Jude**	Jude
Micah	Mic.	**Revelation**	Rev.

section one

Introduction and Background

Why Read the New Testament?

Many are convinced that the Bible is the best way to find God and ultimate meaning; perhaps the only way.

The Bible has had an immense impact on the history of our world, especially on Western culture. Consider how it is used in American courtrooms. Before testifying, a witness takes an oath to tell the truth by placing his or her right hand on a Bible. The Bible has long been a symbol of honesty, truth, and the highest values of Western culture.

People read the Bible for lots of reasons. Some see it simply as classic literature. The Bible outsells all other books even in today's competitive market. One reason is that Christianity has been the dominant religion of the Western world for over fifteen hundred years. We learn about ourselves through these pages, even though they were written in another time and culture. It's amazing how often we hear the words and thoughts of the Bible in everyday circumstances, sometimes without even realizing their origin.

On the other hand, the Bible is more than a window on Western culture. People from other cultures might be surprised at how well it reflects the highest values of their world as well. Some will recognize right away what many Westerners do not—that the Bible was not actually written from the perspective of Western culture. Some read the Bible—in particular its second part, the New Testament—to learn more about Christianity. For those seeking something beyond our passing existence in this life, the New Testament is essential reading. Millions of individuals have claimed to find God on this path.

Indeed, many are convinced that the Bible is the best, perhaps even the only way to find God and ultimate meaning. For Christians, the Bible holds important keys to becoming better individuals and to finding strength beyond ordinary means to handle life's challenges. Many read the Bible when they are facing a situation beyond their control, especially death, which is perhaps the ultimate challenge of our earthly existence. In both the Old Testament—the first part of the Bible—and the New Testament, they find comfort and hope.

This book is based on the story of Jesus Christ, Christianity's founder. In one early Christian statement of faith, the Apostle's Creed, we read, "He was crucified, dead, and buried . . . On the third day he rose again from the dead." In that statement, Christians express their belief that Jesus Christ not only overcame death, but that He can help us do the same.

While we cannot begin to cover every topic, it is my hope that in this book, you will find a way to think about certain pivotal aspects of the New Testament. I invite you to view this survey of the New Testament as a collection of snapshots in a photo album. If you are already familiar with the New Testament, try to see these pictures as if you were looking at them for the first time.

Within the pages of the New Testament, you will find the ultimate concerns of humanity. Why are we here? What is the purpose of our lives? Is there anything beyond death? These are the kinds of questions the New Testament addresses; questions that are just as relevant today as they were two thousand years ago.

Questions for Study and Discussion

1. What value do you think reading the Bible might have for you?
2. What expectations do you have as you approach the New Testament, and how do you think these expectations will affect what you see there? Are you a skeptic? Do you feel you already know what the New Testament teaches? If you find that the Bible contradicts something you currently believe, how open would you be to changing your beliefs?

How to Read the Bible as a Christian

Most Christians today do not read the Bible for what it originally meant. Instead, we tend to read it for the significance it might have for us today.

The Problem

The sheer number of different churches thriving in the Western world today is mind numbing. On a random city street in America, you might find any number of different groups worshiping almost side-by-side—Roman Catholics, Orthodox, Episcopalians, Lutherans, Presbyterians, Baptists, Methodists, or any one of a host of other denominations. Walk into one of these churches and you will find that it differs significantly from the others. Even two churches in the same denomination can differ dramatically in worship style and

At a Glance

- Many Christians read the Bible *personally*, applying its ancient words directly to themselves.
- Christianity has often reinterpreted the words to have more universal meaning.
- Denominations often reinterpret the Bible's words according to their particular emphases and situations.
- The *original meaning* of the Bible is a function of how these words were used back when they were first written.
- The Bible consists of over sixty books written over a long period of time under many different circumstances.

teaching. "If the Bible is the path of ultimate truth," one might ask, "why is there so much disagreement on what it means?"

In one respect, the diversity of interpretations is easy enough to explain. Words mean different things when read in different ways. And the Bible has many, many words! It is comprised of over sixty books authored by writers from varied backgrounds over a long period of time under vastly different circumstances. Relating the ideas from so many different contexts to one another is not an easy task, especially since we often lack important information about the original contexts. And we are reading these words at least nineteen hundred years after they were written, meaning that our words usually have significantly different connotations than they did back then. When you consider all these factors, it is no wonder people often disagree over what the Bible means.

Thankfully, Christian tradition does hold many interpretations of the Bible in common, such as the belief that Jesus' death and resurrection hold the key to life. But people will always disagree to some extent over what the Bible means. Thus, it is very important that we find common ground so Christians can talk to one another profitably. This goal will require us to know what is really going on when we read the Bible.

Of course, many individuals read the Bible strictly as good literature or because of historical interest. The Bible may hold no particular authority for such people, who read it simply as historians or students of literature might read it. Others believe the Bible to have great significance for their Christian faith—they may even consider it to be inspired or divinely revealed to some extent—but may not give it absolute authority. A number of Christians believe that Christ rose from the dead, yet are not sure the writers of the New Testament were always correct in their teachings. On the other hand, many Christians believe that the entire Bible holds absolute authority. Christians often use words like *inerrant* and *infallible* when they discuss the Bible, implying that it does not have errors. Those who use the word *inerrant* often mean that the Bible has no errors of any kind, including matters of science and history. The word *infallible* usually implies that the Bible has no errors in terms of faith or doctrine, allowing for mistakes of a historical or scientific nature. As the rest of this chapter will show, these categories often start our discussions on the wrong foot and rarely lead to common ground.

For example, presuming that our categories of science and history are those of God himself is a questionable practice.[1] Yet this is exactly what some Christians subtly imply when they use the word *inerrant*. They define errors according to the standards of modern historical writing or the categories of modern science. They expect the biblical authors to speak of the world as a globe and for the book of Acts to give us something like a documentary of words and events. They fail to realize that these are the ways we talk about history and the world, not the way the first authors and readers of the Bible did. These Christians assume that modern methods of writing about science and history go about things the right way — God's way — and ignore the possibility that God might meet people of all times in their own categories.

Those who first heard the writings of the Bible, for example, no doubt understood those writings from the standpoint of their own worldviews. After all, it was God's word to them long before it was God's word to us. Their ancient worldviews thus provide us with a much more appropriate starting place for understanding the Bible's words than do our current views of the world. For these reasons, terms like *inerrancy* and *infallibility*, because they often are used in an anachronistic way, are not the best starting points for finding common ground among Christians.

One thing that is extremely helpful in reaching this common ground is the realization that the Bible basically can be read in two different ways: (1) we can read it for what it actually meant to those who first wrote and heard it, or (2) we can invest its words with some other meaning. While this distinction seems obvious and perhaps even pointless, it is extremely important because Christians today largely do not read the Bible in terms of what it originally meant. We much more often read it for the significance it might have for us today.

We might call what the Bible originally meant to its authors and first readers the *original meaning*. The meanings of words originate from how people use them at any particular time and place. While these meanings often overlap significantly from language to language and from place to place, the connotations many times do not carry across from one historical or cultural context to the next. This is one of the reasons translations of the Bible frequently render the same Greek or Hebrew sentence in significantly different ways—it is often difficult to capture the precise meaning of a sentence from one language to another. To understand the original meaning of the Bible, we will need to have extensive knowledge of the history, literature, and culture of the ancient world. In other words, we will need to understand the "dictionaries" from which the Bible's words derived their original meanings.

Needless to say, the "dictionary" from which the average reader today draws meaning will not be an "original-meaning dictionary." The dictionary of the person who knows little about Christianity will consist almost completely of what the words in his or her English Bible mean in contemporary American culture. If someone comes from some Christian tradition—perhaps they are Roman Catholic, Baptist, or Methodist—they no doubt have learned further "definitions" for the Bible's words. Is it any surprise that a person with a "Baptist dictionary" will often think the Bible clearly teaches Baptist doctrine, or that a person with a "Methodist dictionary" would think the Bible teaches the beliefs of Methodism? When we realize the difference between these approaches to the Bible's meaning and the original meaning, we can begin to find common ground for using the Bible as Christians.

Reading the Bible Personally

Growing up, one of my favorite verses was Joshua 1:9: "Be strong and courageous. Do not be terrified, do not be discouraged, for the LORD your God will be with you wherever you go." I took this verse as a promise from God directly to me—I did not need to be afraid of the circumstances of my life because God was always with me. It was one of many verses I memorized as a child for reassurance and in order to learn the basics of Christian belief. The King James Version of the Bible (KJV), the Bible I used as a child, listed every verse by number, making it easy for me to see individual verses as self-contained statements of truth.

However, it does not take much reflection to see that in its original setting, Joshua 1:9 was not written to me or to any other human being alive today. God spoke these words to a man named Joshua as he was about to conduct a military campaign in Canaan. God promised that Joshua would be victorious in battle throughout his conquest of the land. Nothing in the immediate context of Joshua 1:9 indicates that anyone else should apply that verse to his or her life. While I still believe that the meaning I drew from that verse is true for me as a Christian, I am now aware that it is not what the verse really meant.

> Christians have often taken words that were closely related to a particular ancient situation in the Bible and given them more contemporary or universal meanings for the church.

This way of interpreting the Bible gives its words a *personal* meaning. The words are brought directly from the Bible into my world and given meaning in my context without careful consideration of what they might have meant originally. Sometimes the interpretation parallels the original sense closely, as in this case; sometimes it goes quite far afield.

On the one hand, it would be easy to dismiss such interpretations, since they often have nothing to do with the actual meaning of the words when they were written. And this approach to Scripture can be extremely dangerous if you do not realize you are reading the Bible out of context. In fact, this approach to the Bible is the stuff of which cults are born—cult leaders like David Koresh and Jim Jones read the Bible this way. Since the words are not limited to their original meaning, they can come to mean almost anything, depending on who is reading them.

On the other hand, Christians are regularly programmed to read the Bible in this manner, as if they are always the "you" addressed by its words.

However, it takes little thought to realize that the immediate audiences of the Bible were the Israelites, Romans, Corinthians, Thessalonians, and others to whom it was first written. In one sense, not a word of the Bible was written to anyone alive today. While the message of God to these individuals relates to us today in an indirect way, it is often inappropriate—and can actually be contrary to God's purposes—to take its words and apply them directly to ourselves.

It does the doctor no service if his or her patient takes someone else's medicine. A person who has high blood pressure will not make the doctor happy by taking medicine prescribed for someone with low blood pressure. In the same way, it does not necessarily honor God to do what He told the ancients to do, without prayerfully and thoughtfully considering what He would say directly to our context. Could it be that in our situations God would sometimes require us to do exactly the opposite of what He commanded the ancients?

Before we completely dismiss personal interpretations of the Bible, we should remember how extensively God seems to minister to His people through this approach to the Bible's words. Since the Bible became available in nearly everyone's language, people of all stripes and backgrounds have heard God speaking to them through the words of Scripture. In a sense, Scripture has become a sacrament like baptism or communion, a divinely appointed meeting place where God can "stoop to our weakness" and meet us where we are. As ordinary bread and wine are supercharged to signify the body and blood of Jesus in communion, so the ancient words of the Bible seem to be a catalyst for God's Spirit to speak to His people—even out of context.

> When we read the Bible in terms of what it originally meant, it becomes a witness to how God has revealed himself to His people in the past—in fact, in the most important moments of all history.

Since so many Christians experience God through the Bible in this way—in fact, far more frequently than through its original meaning—we must accept personal interpretations as potentially valid ways of meeting

God through the Bible. However, it is important for those who read the Bible in this way to realize that the authority of their interpretations depends on whether or not they are truly hearing God. Like ancient prophecy, any individual's "spirit interpretation" is subject to the critique and testing of his or her fellow Christians (cf. 1 Cor. 14:32; 1 John 4:1).

Reading the Bible in Church

A visit to a few churches quickly demonstrates that different denominations often have their own unique interpretations of the Bible. While some of this diversity comes from genuine ambiguity within the pages of Scripture itself, a great deal of it also comes from reading the Bible out of context. Christianity in general has often taken words that were closely related to a particular ancient situation in the Bible and given them more contemporary or universal meanings for the church. We might call such interpretations community meanings of the Bible, because they are meanings that various Christian churches or communities see in the text.

The book of Romans is an excellent case in point. The apostle Paul, a famous early Christian, wrote this letter in part to defend his mission to those who were not Jews, that is, the Gentiles. He argued that keeping the Jewish Law by doing such things as circumcising your son would not keep anyone from destruction when God came to judge the world. God had found another way of escape; He sent Jesus Christ to pay the penalty for this breaking of the Law by both Jew and Gentile. All one needed to do was trust in what God had done through Jesus. God had not thrown the Jews away, like some said Paul taught. God had found a way not only to save the Jews, but the Gentiles as well.

If you found the previous paragraph a little boring or somewhat removed from the concerns of your life, you may find the following rendering easier: Everybody in the whole world has done wrong, so no one will get to heaven by doing good things. The punishment for doing wrong is death and hell. God loves us, though, and does not want us to go to hell, so He sent Jesus to die in our place. All you have to do is believe that all this is true, and you will go to heaven.

This last rendition is an excellent example of how churches throughout the centuries have sometimes taken the Bible just a little out of context to make its teaching more contemporary or universal in focus. Not that the second paragraph is untrue—it is, in fact, a fairly close parallel to Paul's original message. But it has subtly changed the original meaning in the process of making the message more universal in scope. This shows how the church, in attempting to address the ongoing concerns of Christians in the world, has often, without even realizing it, slightly changed the Bible's meaning.

One reason the Bible has such a *transferable* quality is that so much of it is *story*. Stories by their very nature can be told in numerous ways with differing emphases. For example, take the story of the prodigal son, which is found in Luke 15. You probably will not hear this story told in church with the specific meaning Jesus had in mind—that the characters in the story represent the various ways in which the Jews had received His message of restoration for Israel. Yet it is so easy to see this as a story about new beginnings for those who have messed up and want to start again.

In the course of this book, you will see many instances in which Christian denominations have taken biblical verses to worlds the original authors never imagined. Many of the disagreements among churches actually come from these "over-readings" of the text. These observations lead us to an important conclusion: Churches—even those that claim to be Bible-based—often use the Bible far more as a mirror to see what they already believe than as the true source of their beliefs. Realizing the implications of what it means to read the Bible according to its original meaning is the first step toward finding common ground among Christians. Reading the Bible in terms of its original message also helps tremendously in the appropriate application of its message today.

Reading the Bible for its Original Meaning

Many Christians have taken a keen interest in the original context of the Bible. In the last few decades, a lot of books have been published about the historical background of Scripture, many of which have availed themselves of these original resources. Many churches publish study guides and Sunday school material meant to help the members of their congregations move closer to the Bible's original meaning. Countless Christians have visited the Holy Land to retrace the steps of Jesus and other biblical figures. When these pilgrims return, they usually have a better appreciation of the Bible's meaning than they did before their trips.

Even with all this attention to history, however, many Christians only go part of the way toward really reading the Bible in terms of what it originally meant. The tendency to make sense of the Bible's words according to our own worldview—even our current "Christian" worldview—is strong and understandable, since the ancient significance will often seem strange and foreign to our world. Cultural differences are sometimes very subtle and easily missed, clouded as they are by the cultural glasses through which we see our own world.

> **Applying the Bible Today**
>
> *Phase One: The Bible*
> 1. What did the passage mean originally?
> 2. Why did it say what it said? What are the principles behind it or what does it say about the character of God?
> 3. What do other Scriptures say on the topic?
>
> *Phase Two: The Church*
> 1. What have Christians through the ages said about this topic?
> 2. What are my fellow Christians saying now?
> 3. What do I believe the Holy Spirit is saying?

Since the books of the Bible were God's revelation to ancient Israelites, Romans, Corinthians, and other people, it makes sense that He would reveal himself in terms they would understand. Why would He speak to ancient people using modern categories of expression? To be sure, humans hold many experiences in common: love, suffering, death, and joy, to name a few. These common human experiences that God addresses in Scripture are another reason Christians have so easily and directly applied the Bible to today's realities.

The pages of the Bible address so many issues common to human experience that its words sometimes seem to hit two birds with one stone; that is, the meanings that spoke to their concerns centuries ago seem to speak just as directly to ours today.

But we should also realize that even something as obvious as love had somewhat different connotations to the first audiences of the Bible than it has to contemporary audiences. Often these basic categories, the ones we could not imagine being different, will cause us to misread the Bible in the most subtle ways—like our understanding of sexuality, what it means to be divine, or even what defines a person. We should not be surprised that the disciples thought heaven was straight up (Acts 1:10) or that Paul pictured Paradise in the third layer of the sky (2 Cor. 12:2). Why would God present himself in the context of what we think of the universe when He was working in their context?

> **Finding Verses in the Bible**
> - The book of the Bible is listed first (e.g., **Matthew** 1:1).
> - The chapter number comes before the colon (e.g., Matthew **1**:1).
> - The verse number comes last (e.g., Matthew 1:**1**).

It is also difficult for many Christians to read the Bible as a collection of books rather than as a single book. The different authors of the Bible's books do not always use the same words in the same ways. We cannot necessarily use a verse in Paul's writings to clarify a verse in Matthew, for these two individuals used words differently. John says Jesus performed countless "signs" (John 20:30); Mark says He gave none (Mark 8:12). James says God accepts us because of "actions" [works] (James 2:24); Paul says He does not (Gal. 2:16). In these examples, the different authors are using the same words in a different sense.

The difference between reading the Bible according to its original meaning and reading it personally has quite significant implications for how we appropriate the authority of the Bible. When individuals read the Bible as a direct word from God to them or when churches universalize the Bible's message, the Bible seems to immediately take on a timeless and authoritative character. Some Christians speak of "absolute truth" or of a "biblical worldview" when referring to the Bible in this context. Many denominational statements of faith arguably refer to Scripture in this way. We should not rush to dismiss these kinds of interpretations, even if they often do take the words of Scripture out of context. Surely these are the dominant ways in which God has spoken through Scripture to His people throughout the ages. However, it is important to realize that these readings of the Bible really are God speaking through His Spirit and the church more than through the Bible itself.

Reading the Bible in terms of its original meaning changes the way we appropriate its message. Rather than a direct revelation from God to us, it becomes a witness to how God has revealed himself to His people in the past—in fact, in the most important moments of all history. When we use the Bible in this way, we cannot assume that God wishes us to do exactly what the people of the past did or to think the way they thought. Today we must look for the underlying principles of what God told them to do (in their terms) and then conceptualize these truths as they would apply to us. We do this when we look both for continuity in the character of God and for points of contact between our context and theirs.

We can apply the original meaning of the Bible today by way of a two-phase process. The first phase is the scriptural phase. Determine what the particular passage at which you are looking meant in its original context. Then ask why it said what it said. What principles are at work? What was God doing? What do other Scriptures say on the topic in their individual situations?

The second phase involves other Christians—God's church. One of the things a full understanding of the Bible's original meaning does is to help us realize just how much we need one another—as Christians listening to God's Spirit in order to work out what Christianity should be today. The Bible addresses problems similar to ours, but usually not exactly the same as ours. Bridging the distance between then and now is a bigger task than any one Christian can handle. What have Christians said on this topic throughout the centuries, and what are they saying now? What do I believe the Holy Spirit is saying to me directly? It is by prayerful and thoughtful work like this that Christians will "work out your [plural] salvation with fear and trembling, for it is God who works in you to will and to act according to his good purpose" (Phil. 2:12–13).

Questions for Study and Discussion

1. Why do you think Christians have different beliefs? After all, they are using the same Bible.
2. What does it mean to you to say that the Bible is inspired? Do you think it is appropriate to call it inerrant? Infallible?
3. Do you agree with the claim that Christians largely do not read the Bible in terms of its original meaning? Or do we mostly read its words the same way its first audiences did?
4. How do you read the Bible? Personally? Following what you have learned from your church? For its original meaning?
5. Identify the following as either a personal interpretation, a community interpretation, or an interpretation in terms of the original meaning:

- I sat by the bedside of my dying father, wondering whether it was God's will for him to die now or whether God would miraculously heal him of his cancer. As I read my Bible, I came across Acts 20:25: "Now I know that none of you . . . will ever see me again." I suddenly felt a strange peace that my father was going home to be with God. Like Paul, he was leaving on a victorious note after a life full of goodness.
- When Paul said, "[Y]our body is a temple of the Holy Spirit" (1 Cor. 6:19), he used the plural word for *you* in Greek. He was telling the Corinthian church as a whole that they together made up the body of

Christ, the temple in which God's Spirit lived. Therefore, an individual in the church who would visit a prostitute at the temple of Aphrodite not only was taking his physical body, but also was taking the "body" of Christ with him.

- My church does not allow smoking. Further, my pastor tells me it is wrong to drink too much coffee, go excessively without sleep, or get fat because 1 Corinthians 3:16 says that "you are God's temple." Why would I want to harm my body if it is the temple of God's Spirit?

An Overview of
the New Testament

The Bible is more like a library of books
than a single volume.

It is all too easy to think of the Bible as one book. In fact, some refer to it as "the Good Book." You can even buy a Bible that is titled *The Book* (NLT). But the Bible was not originally one book. The word *Bible* originally meant "little books"—over sixty-six little books when the word was first coined.

At a Glance

- The books of the New Testament are best read individually. Each author used words in a unique way to address different situations.
- The New Testament contains several different genres. The ancient genres are different from our genres today.

The Bible is actually more like a library of books than a single volume. It is divided into two sets of books called the Old Testament and the New Testament. For Protestants, the Old Testament contains thirty-nine books. The Old Testament of the Roman Catholic and Orthodox churches includes some additional documents called the Apocrypha.[1] The New Testament, in all traditions, is made up of twenty-seven books.

Initially, these writings were not bound together, but were written in different places, by different authors, for different purposes over as many as one thousand years. Eventually, they came to be grouped together in various ways and were recorded on scrolls. At some point, after all the books of the Bible had been written, Christians gathered them together into one big book—more like the Bible as we now know it.

We mentioned that the Bible is more of a library than an individual book. In a library, of course, there are many different kinds of books—novels, history books, science books, magazines, and scholarly journals to name a few. These different types of literature are called genres. No one would read a comic strip in the same way as a math book, nor would anyone read a novel in quite the same way as a history of World War II. We have learned over the years to have different expectations of a comic play and a book on the Holocaust.

The same is true of the library of the New Testament. Of its twenty-seven books, there are at least four different kinds of basic genres in use, probably more. The first four books—Matthew, Mark, Luke, and John—are called *gospels*. Each in its own unique way presents what it considers to be important events and teachings from Jesus' life on earth.

The fifth book, Acts, looks like a history book to us, although we should not assume that ancient history writing followed the same rules used by modern historians. This book takes us from Jesus' last days on earth to a time over thirty years later when Paul arrived in Rome to stand trial before the emperor.

The Formation of the New Testament Canon

The New Testament canon—the group of early Christian writings considered authoritative for Christians—took several hundred years to reach its current form. The books themselves were written in a different order than they appear in our Bibles.

Paul's letters were collected first and began circulating among churches. By the late A.D. 100s, the mainstream church had accepted four gospels—and only those four gospels—as Scripture.

Other books were debated over time as to which were to be considered Scripture. Some were accepted; others were not. The first known canon (or list) of authoritative books that corresponds to those in our Bibles today was made in A.D. 367.

There are also a number of letters (or epistles) in the New Testament. Thirteen of these have Paul's name on them. There is also an anonymous epistle named Hebrews, which may actually be an early Christian sermon. The remaining seven letters are called the "Catholic" or "General" Epistles, since they seem to have a general audience in mind.

The final book of the New Testament is of a genre completely unfamiliar to most of us. It is an apocalypse, and to many it will no doubt seem an extremely strange book. The word *apocalypse* means that the book is the revelation of hidden things, which is why it is also called the book of Revelation. We will have to learn a whole new set of expectations from the ancient world if we want to hear this book as it was first heard.

> **Basic Genres of the New Testament**
>
> **Gospels**
>   Matthew, Mark, Luke, John
> **History**
>   Acts
> **Letters/Epistles**
> • Pauline Epistles
>   ○ Romans, 1 and 2 Corinthians, Galatians, Ephesians, Philippians, Colossians, 1 and 2 Thessalonians, 1 and 2 Timothy, Titus, Philemon
> • Hebrews (possibly a sermon)
> • General Epistles
>   ○ James, 1 and 2 Peter, 1, 2, and 3 John, Jude
> **Apocalypse**
>   Revelation

As you are perhaps beginning to see, reading the Bible for what it originally meant is a lot more involved than many people think. It involves learning a whole new set of assumptions about things that seem obvious to us—like what it means to be the author of a letter. Before we are done, we will have to shift our thinking on matters as basic as what a father is or what it means to be poor. This shift is necessary if we want to have any chance of understanding what Jesus or Paul or any of the New Testament personalities were really saying.

Questions for Study and Discussion

1. What are the two parts of the Christian Bible?
2. What section do Roman Catholics and other Christian traditions include that Protestants do not?
3. What are the four basic genres in the New Testament?

4. If some artistic license were taken for the genres of ancient history or biography writing, can we consider them legitimate today?

5. Into what genre might Hebrews actually fit?

6. Which letters are included among the Pauline Epistles? Which books are included in the General Epistles? Which book was an apocalypse?

Who Chose These Books?

If God had a hand in the formation of the canon,
then He must have been directing the process
toward its final result.

Introduction

Since the Bibles we buy come as a single book, it is all too easy to assume that the group of books we call the New Testament has always been bound together. This is not the case. As we pointed out in the previous chapter, the books of the New Testament were written and circulated independently for the most part. The earliest manuscript we have that contains all the books of our New Testament comes from the A.D. 300s, and it includes other books that ultimately did not end up in the Bible. Before then smaller collections had

> **At a Glance**
>
> - The writings of the New Testament were not written in the order in which they appear in our Bibles.
> - The writing process took place over a number of decades.
> - Paul's letters were collected first.
> - By the late A.D. 100s, the four gospels were the gospels of the mainstream church.
> - With regard to the remaining Christian books in circulation, churches debated which were authoritative enough to be considered Scripture.
> - The first list of authoritative books known to correspond to our New Testament list was made in A.D. 367.

been in circulation, like Paul's writings or the four gospels. But the development of the New Testament canon—the group of early Christian writings considered to be authoritative for Christians—took several hundred years to reach its current form.

Early Christians debated which books belonged in the canon. To be sure, mainstream Christians agreed early on concerning the majority of the writings. But they were uncertain whether other books (such as Hebrews and Revelation) were authoritative enough to be considered Scripture. Similarly, some books did not make it into the canon (such as the Shepherd of Hermas or 1 Clement) that many Christians thought should be included. The discussion continued well into the A.D. 300s. The first list we have that contains exactly the same writings found in our current Bible was part of an Easter letter sent out in A.D. 367—some two and a half centuries after the last books of the New Testament were written. The Council of Carthage in A.D. 397 gave this list official approval (at least for half of the church), accepting these twenty-seven writings as the New Testament.

> Either 1 Thessalonians or Galatians was the first book of the entire New Testament to be written.

Collecting the Books

The books of the New Testament were not written in the order in which they now appear. For example, the gospels, which appear first in our New Testament, were written later than many of the other books. The writings of the apostle Paul were the earliest, although some think the letter of James was early as well. Even Paul's letters were not written in the order in which they appear in our Bibles. They were arranged by length, going roughly from longest to shortest. Either 1 Thessalonians or Galatians was the first book of the entire New Testament to be written.

Paul's writings began to circulate together rather early. The letter to the Colossians indicates that churches were sharing Paul's letters with one another within his lifetime or soon thereafter (Col. 4:16). Second Peter also shows that Paul's writings had been collected together from early on and could be read as a group (2 Pet. 3:15–16).

Aside from 2 Peter's mention of Paul's writings as Scripture, the first clear reference to a New Testament book as authoritative in this way comes in the mid-second century (about A.D. 150) in an anonymous sermon known as 2 Clement. There, a quotation from the gospel of Matthew is apparently referred to as "Scripture," that is, on the same level as the Old Testament. This trend toward creating a second body of authoritative writings alongside the Hebrew Scriptures would continue and expand in the days to come. Soon, not only the Old Testament was referred to as Scripture, but the New Testament was as well. We do not know for certain when Christians began making lists—called canon lists—of the books they considered to be authoritative Scripture. Some think the whole process was started in response to a man named Marcion, whose list was so unsatisfactory that it led more mainstream Christians to make better ones. We know that mainstream Christianity was fairly united by the end of the A.D. 100s in considering the four gospels of the New Testament to be the only ones the church should use. Many of the other writings in the New Testament were also accepted, but a discussion about the precise list would continue over the next few centuries.

We should point out that the question these Christians were debating was not necessarily whether these books were good or bad. No doubt some did object to books like Hebrews and Revelation because they thought these books taught inappropriate things (e.g., in Hebrews, the impossibility of returning to Christ after you have left Christianity). But more often than not, the issue was whether these were just

> After you have read this letter, pass it on to the church at Laodicea so they can read it, too. And you should read the letter I wrote to them.
>
> —Colossians 4:16 NLT

good books in general or whether they were authoritative Scripture. No one, for example, thought that 1 Clement was a bad letter; indeed, some thought it should be a part of the canon. In the end, it was excluded from the New Testament because the church did not think it was as authoritative as, for example, Paul's letters were.

Further, we should not think that some committee just sat down one day and took a vote on these matters. The decision of the Council of Carthage in A.D. 397 simply affirmed what had come to be the general consensus of the church at large. We should think of this process of "canonization," as it is called, as a long process of dialogue among Christians in authority around the ancient world.

What Qualified a Book as Scripture?

Several different factors came into play as the church was deciding which books were authoritative for Christianity. Who the author was, how long the book had been around, whether it taught the right things—these factors played an important role. But the process was no doubt more complicated than these questions might suggest. For example, the criteria of the second century may have been slightly different from that of the third. Group dynamics came into play as well, including tensions between groups. Such conflicts no doubt led some groups to resist books accepted by others.

> Bear in mind that our Lord's patience means salvation, just as our dear brother Paul also wrote you with the wisdom that God gave him. He writes the same way in all his letters, speaking in them of these matters. His letters contain some things that are hard to understand, which ignorant and unstable people distort, as they do the other Scriptures, to their own destruction.
>
> —2 Peter 3:15–16

If you believe that God had a hand in the formation of the canon, then He must have been in this process, directing things toward their final result. If so, was it important that the intentions and thought processes of the church be correct in order for us to accept their conclusions as legitimate? Or did God direct the process toward its ultimate conclusion despite the understandings or misunderstandings of the humans involved? These are interesting questions for Christians to ask.

The Christians of the A.D. 100s do not seem to have been as definitive as later generations would be in considering standards for what constituted a book as Scripture. Two of the gospels in our New Testament are attributed to Matthew and John, followers of Jesus while he was on earth—Jesus' disciples. The belief that Matthew and John wrote them assured these books a place in the canon; they had the right authors. Mark and Luke were not Jesus' disciples, but their gospels were connected respectively to the apostles Peter and

> And another Scripture also says, "I came not to call righteous, but sinners" [quotation of Matt. 9:13].
>
> —2 Clement 2:4

Paul. Perhaps the longstanding use of these four gospels by the church—that is, their antiquity and connection with mainstream Christianity—would have ensured their canonicity regardless of their authors. Nevertheless, a concern arose to connect them with important apostles, followers of Jesus who led the way in the spread of Christianity. This connection ensured their place in the canon.

Paul's writings were collected and used even earlier than the gospels. Indeed, we have no record of any ancient Christian debating their authority. Even in regard to 1 and 2 Timothy and Titus—the Pastoral Epistles—we have little debate, although they do not appear in the literature of Christianity until the middle of the second century (the A.D. 100s). Many scholars believe these books to have been written by a second-century Christian, perhaps to address a perceived lack of order in some churches. Using the name of a deceased authority figure as a pseudonym was a fairly common practice at that time, and some scholars believe the church of that day was open to this practice—as long as it was done by an appropriate authority with an appropriate teaching. Whether pseudonymous or not, we have no evidence that the Pastoral Epistles faced opposition by the mainstream of Christianity.

The last books of the New Testament—Hebrews, the General Epistles, and Revelation—gave rise to the most debate. It is in regard to these and other writings of the period that questions of authorship, antiquity, and orthodoxy seem to have become most important in the A.D. 200s and 300s. Nevertheless, many of these books were quickly accepted—even books like 1 John and 1 Peter.

The book of Hebrews gives us a good illustration of the factors involved in the process of canonization. Hebrews is anonymous—it nowhere names its author—although in the second century it increasingly came to be associated

> Marcion's (ca. A.D. 150) list of authoritative books included only "mutilated" versions of some of Paul's writings and the gospel of Luke, edited to his liking.

with the apostle Paul. That is, at least the Eastern Mediterranean part of the church came to believe Paul authored it. Most Christians in Rome and the Western Mediterranean considered it to be a good book, but they resisted the idea that Paul wrote it. Eventually the decision about its authorship seems to have played a role in its acceptance as Scripture. The Eastern half of the Roman world, for example, seems to have had no problem with its "canonicity." It is probably no coincidence that the Western half also accepted Hebrews into the canon at about the same time they accepted Paul as its author.

This example demonstrates some of the dynamics involved in the decision-making process. On the one hand, there was the question of authorship and the desire to link the writings of the New Testament with the original apostles. On the other hand, group dynamics were at play as East and West disagreed in part just to disagree.

> The "Muratorian Canon" at the end of the A.D. 100s included the four gospels, Acts, all of Paul's letters, James, 1 and 2 John, Jude, Revelation, and two other works—the Revelation of Peter and the Wisdom of Solomon. Hebrews, 1 and 2 Peter, and 3 John were not included.

A further issue is the question of orthodoxy or "correct teaching." This is in contrast to heresy or "incorrect teaching." Passages in Hebrews seem to teach that one cannot return to Christianity after one has committed apostasy—that is, made a definitive break with Christianity. This issue was hotly debated in the middle A.D. 200s when some Christians betrayed their communities to the government by renouncing Christ and turning in fellow Christians, some of whom were killed for their beliefs. Many did not wish to take such traitors back after the persecution died down, but others argued that God would forgive the apostates. Eventually, the church made it policy to take them back. In this light, we can see why some questioned the orthodoxy of Hebrews.

The book of Hebrews thus raises the question we asked earlier about the whole process of canonization. Authorship seems to have played an important role in the church's discussion concerning whether or not to include Hebrews in the canon. It very well may have been the belief that Paul authored it that secured its place in the canon. And yet it is nearly the unanimous verdict of scholars that Hebrews was not written by Paul. Did Hebrews get in, therefore, on the basis of a mistake? One might claim that the hearts of the early Christians knew it should be included—they simply found a way for their heads to agree, even though their thoughts were incorrect. But Hebrews raises the question of God's direction in the process. Did God work not only with the understandings of the church, but also around its misunderstandings?

> Some of the key criteria for accepting a book into the canon were authorship, antiquity, and orthodoxy. The author should be linked in some way to an original apostle, the book should be written by one of the earliest Christians, and it should teach correct ideas.

A final issue is worth mentioning. Many Christians consider the Bible to be the ultimate authority on any matter of faith and practice. But many of these same Christians downplay the significance of the church and their fellow Christians as sources of authority as well. Yet, as we can see, those who believe the Bible to be authoritative must also believe that God led the church in the right direction in the process of canonization. That is, there would be no Bible if there had been no church. What does this say about the role the church has played (and still plays) in determining the authority of Scripture for Christians?

For some readers, this whole process will seem very human. It involves personalities, groups, ideas, and traditions, all interacting with one another in a series of causes and effects. For others, this process demonstrates God's church carefully verifying the inspiration of the books it was already using as authoritative, doing so with a care and caution befitting a sincere seeking of God's will. Perhaps a third group will strike a middle position and see in this process God stooping to the weakness of His people once again, a God-directed process that worked despite whatever human politics and misunderstandings might have been involved. The important thing was the end result toward which God was working.

Questions for Study and Discussion

1. Were the books of the New Testament written in the order in which they now appear?

2. Were they written all at once or over a period of several years?

3. How long after the books of the New Testament were written did it take before someone came up with exactly the same list of authoritative books for the New Testament that we now believe is correct? Which books were most debated? What are some other books that did not make the final cut?

4. In deciding which book of the New Testament was written first, what are the top two candidates?

5. What individual's poor collection of books may have inspired other Christians to move toward an authoritative list of "canonical" books?

6. What were some of the criteria that played into the church's decisions about whether a book qualified as Scripture or not?

7. Do you think it is possible that some books of the New Testament got in on the basis of misunderstandings—e.g., did Hebrews get in because early Christians thought Paul wrote it? Does God work through human misunderstanding as well as through human understanding?

8. Which came first—the Bible as Scripture or the church? Given that Protestants often try to eliminate the role the church plays in the authority of Scripture, what do we make of the fact that it was through the church that God "created" Scripture? Does this place more authority in God's church than in the text of the New Testament?

Why Are there So Many Different Bibles?

We need not be troubled about the original wording of the Bible—scholarship has done its homework.

The *Real* Bible

It would not take long at your average bookstore to realize the incredible number of Bibles available in today's market. Not only do we have the old favorite, the King James Version (KJV), but we also have the New King James Version (NKJV), the New American Standard Bible (NASB), the New Revised Standard Version (NRSV), the New English Bible (NEB), the New International Version (NIV), and the New Living Translation (NLT). But this list just scratches the surface. There are countless other translations of the Bible in English alone, as well as

At a Glance

- We do not have the "first editions" of any New Testament book.

- The copies, or manuscripts, of the New Testament that we do have sometimes differ significantly from one another.

- Some translations, such as the King James Version, differ from other versions because they rely on different manuscripts.

- Other versions differ because they try to express the ancient words in ways we can more easily understand today.

- There is often ambiguity in the original meaning that makes possible more than one translation of the same words.

English study Bibles galore, which are Bibles equipped with all kinds of study tools for better understanding the Bible. Among these are the Serendipity Bible, the Max Lucado Bible, the NIV Study Bible, the Thompson Chain Reference Bible, and the list goes on. The uninitiated could get really confused—will the real Bible please stand up?

> The general rule for finding the original wording of a passage from the New Testament is to choose the wording that best explains how the other variations among the manuscripts would have come into existence.

If you were raised on one of these versions, like the King James Version, other surprises await you when reading a modern translation. Perhaps you grew up saying the Lord's Prayer and happen to run into it while reading Matthew 6 in a modern translation. You start quoting it aloud and are all ready to say, "for thine is the kingdom and the power and the glory forever"—until you realize it is not in the version you are reading! Perhaps you are reading Mark 16 in the NIV and suddenly come upon this bracketed comment: "The earliest manuscripts and some other ancient witnesses do not have Mark 16:9–20." And an observant reader of Acts 8 may just notice that the story goes straight from verse 36 to 38—what happened to verse 37?

Textual Criticism

These minor variations reflect one aspect of the process by which we came to have the Bible as we know it today. The New Testament was originally written in Greek. But the original manuscripts—the very first copies of such books as Matthew, Mark, Luke, and John—almost certainly disintegrated into dust long ago. We have thousands of manuscripts of the New Testament books, but these are copies of copies of copies of copies. And no two of these manuscripts have exactly the same words as the others. Most of them were copied between the years A.D. 900–1500, a thousand years after the books were first written.

It can be unsettling to hear of the diversity of manuscripts and the variations among them. This information can make those Christians who base their

Christianity on the Bible a little nervous, to say the least. Those looking for ammunition use this fact to argue against the Bible as a true authority. Others retreat into a "King James Only" stance, seeing in the more recent translations a conspiracy to corrupt the true faith.

But not to worry—scholars are actually very confident about the overwhelming majority of variations among the manuscripts we have. A branch of New Testament studies called textual criticism is devoted to the science of figuring out what the first editions likely said. Thus, there is no need to be troubled about the original wording of the Bible—scholarship has done its homework.

While most of the manuscripts we have are late, copied over a thousand years after the New Testament was written, we do have a number of very old manuscripts. For example, the oldest one is a tiny fragment of John 18 that may date as early as A.D. 125, about thirty years after the original letter was written. It is not really that unusual for the oldest surviving manuscript of an ancient work to have been copied hundreds or even a thousand years after the original. After all, do you think the letters you write would survive a thousand years? The earliest copies of Plato's writings, for example, come well over a thousand years after Plato lived, yet no one would seriously question whether these manuscripts are at least basically accurate.

Further, most of the variations among the biblical manuscripts are insignificant and have resulted from simple errors that were inevitable as each manuscript was copied by hand. Maybe two lines ended with the same word and the copyist's eye skipped from one line to the next, causing him to omit a line. Since many manuscripts were copied in halls as a reader read

> Because of the discoveries of the last century and a half, we can now determine the wording of the original Bible more accurately than ever before.

them aloud to a group of copyists, sometimes a copyist would mishear and write down the wrong word. Sometimes someone would smooth out or edit a rough or ambiguous original. Others relied on their memories rather than the text they were copying. Copyists might take comments someone had written in the margins and put them somewhere in the text. Still other copyists, faced with more than one reading in the manuscripts in front of them, combined them into one long passage.

There were countless, predictable reasons for many of the mistakes that were made. Being aware of these common ways in which variations arose, scholars can make good decisions about how the original probably read. The general rule is to choose the wording that best explains how the other readings in the manuscripts came about. Those who translated the Bible into English in the 1500s, as well as those who completed the King James Version in 1611, had only "late" copies of the New Testament at their disposal. A man named Erasmus referred to about a dozen Greek manuscripts in deciding what the New Testament originally said. However, the earliest of these had been copied in the A.D. 900s—over eight hundred years after the New Testament was written. Since the 1500s we have discovered copies of New Testament books that predate by a thousand years most of the copies he used. Modern versions are thus based on the earliest manuscripts we have available.

Why Are there So Many Different Bibles?

It might surprise you to know that there are no first editions existing of any New Testament book. The copies, or manuscripts, that we do have are not identical. In fact, sometimes they differ significantly. Some English translations differ, like the King James Version and the New International Version, because they are translated from different manuscripts.

Other versions differ because they try to express ancient words and thoughts in contemporary language. Even though the translations might be based on the same manuscript, you'll find differences in interpretation and in the way thoughts are expressed in modern English. Sometimes this is because there is ambiguity in the original meaning. Other times it's due to a difference in the perspective of the translators.

When you have grown up using a Bible like the King James Version, it is easy to think the modern versions have taken words out of the Bible. After all, some of the words you grew up with are not in these modern versions. In reality, the King James Version is based on manuscripts that added verses that were not in the first copies of the New Testament. The KJV is based on Greek manuscripts that had embellished the original text by adding words that made the New Testament clearer and smoother.

A minority of scholars still defends the Greek text behind the King James Version as being more original. This text is closely related to the Greek and Latin text the church used from the A.D. 300s on. Since most of the earliest copies of the New Testament have long since disintegrated, it is understandable that the majority of manuscripts read this way, since most of these were copied in the late Middle Ages. But scholars who defend this form of the text maintain their position based on theological reasons rather than on the evidence. They do not believe God would have allowed the majority of manuscripts to deviate from the originals, even on details that do not change the overall meaning. You may share their concerns and want to do some further research on the topic.

> Modern translations do not take words out of the Bible or change them. Rather, older versions like the King James Version were based on traditions that had embellished and added to the original text.

Therefore, one reason we have so many different Bibles is because we have different approaches to the various manuscripts available. The King James Version and the New King James Version (which updates the earlier English of the KJV) are based on the textual tradition that the church used from the 300s to the early 1800s. Other versions utilize older, more recently discovered manuscripts to recreate the original text with more accuracy.

Different Approaches to Translation

Chapter 2 of this text explains some of the reasons why just one translation is impossible when going from one language to another. Sometimes Christians assume that knowing Greek or Hebrew will clear up all questions about a verse they do not understand in English. Take the verse in which the apostle Paul says, "I thank God that I speak in tongues more than all of you" (1 Cor. 14:18). Some would say that "tongues" here means human languages, while others believe that Paul referred to angelic languages unintelligible to the human ear. The Greek does not make the meaning any clearer: the word *tongues* simply means *languages*. The Greek word does not tell us what kinds of languages are meant—or even if Paul meant the word languages to be taken literally.

As this example illustrates, it is often possible to translate the same word in different ways. Take these two translations of Romans 3:25:

New Living Translation

"God sent Jesus to take the punishment for our sins and to satisfy God's anger against us."

Contemporary English Version

"God sent Christ to be our sacrifice. Christ offered his life's blood, so that by faith in him we could come to God. And God did this to show that in the past he was right to be patient and forgive sinners."

These two versions do their best to bring out the meaning of the verse. But they have expanded the original wording and meaning to try to help us understand it.

The translations below stick more closely to the original wording. The first two of these versions no doubt leave most people wondering what "expiation" or "propitiation" means. Most English speakers do not use words like these. Yet these versions come the closest to the words of the original Greek.

Revised Standard Version

"[Christ Jesus], whom God put forward as an expiation . . ."

King James Version

". . . whom God hath set forth to be a propitiation . . ."

New International Version

"God presented him as a sacrifice of atonement . . ."

These passages reflect two basic approaches to translation. One tries to stay as close as possible to the sentence structure and words of the original Greek. These are what might be called formal equivalence translations. Versions such as the Revised Standard Version or the New American Standard Bible present the reader with a fairly good look at the way the Greek text was arranged. Yet, these versions are often difficult for today's average reader to understand.

On the other hand, dynamic equivalence translations attempt to find words that convey the spirit of the original meaning in terms we can understand in our culture. The New Living Translation and New International Version, for example, have tried their best to bring the basic meaning of the original into English. Of course, these versions can thus be somewhat deceptive, since the precise meaning of the Bible cannot be expressed exactly in our cultural terms. These versions can only approximate the spirit of the original meaning at best.

Questions for Study and Discussion

1. Do we have any of the original copies of the books of the New Testament?
2. Of the thousands of New Testament manuscripts that we have, do any agree completely with one another?
3. Which translations of the Bible do most scholars think are based on manuscripts whose wording in Greek and Hebrew comes closest to the first copies of the Bible? Would they select versions like the KJV and NKJV, or those like the NRSV, NIV, NLT, etc.?
4. Where the Greek and Hebrew texts behind the various translations are the same, which versions stick most closely to the original wording and sentence structure: formal equivalence translations like the KJV and NRSV, or dynamic equivalence translations like the NIV and NLT?
5. What is the general rule for deciding the original wording of the New Testament?

6. If God allowed the wording of the Bible to change over time—in fact, allowed the church to use a different text for over a thousand years—does this imply that God is not concerned with the exact words of Scripture, but with its overall message instead?

7. Why do you think some continue to maintain that the Greek and Hebrew texts behind the KJV are more original?

8. Why do you think so many churches and scholars today seem to locate the authority of Scripture in its original wording rather than in the text God allowed the church to use for over a thousand years? Should the story of the woman caught in adultery in John 8 stay a part of Scripture, even though it probably was not originally in John? After all, the church has used this story for over fifteen hundred years.

The Story Behind the Story

From Abraham to Moses

The early Christians did not see themselves as part of a new religion but as the true ending to the Jewish story.

Stories that Tell Who We Are

Although you may never have thought about it, we identify who we are to a great extent by the stories we tell about ourselves. Your life is one long story with numerous episodes. Some of those episodes capture who you are better than others, although our stories can be told in many different ways. We usually focus on episodes that compliment us when we are presenting ourselves to others. Someone else might focus on events that embarrass us or bring out our weak points. In either case, a person without a story is to some extent a person without an identity.

At a Glance

- The story behind the story of the New Testament begins with a man named Abraham. The twelve sons of his grandson, Israel, gave rise to twelve tribes.
- God led these twelve tribes out of slavery in Egypt to a land He had promised to their forefather Abraham.
- God made a solemn agreement—a covenant—with Israel at Mount Sinai. We refer to this covenant as the Law.
- Since God chose Israel exclusively from all the nations to be His people, they were to serve Him alone. He promised to prosper them if they would keep this agreement.

Western culture differs from other cultures in that we tell far more stories about ourselves as individuals than we do about the groups to which we belong. We want someone to judge us on our own merits, not because of what we look like or who our family is. To us, stereotypes often involve prejudice, which we consider highly inappropriate.

However, the ancients identified themselves extensively by the groups to which they belonged—by things like gender, race, and family background. This collectivist culture is still the case in most places outside the Western world today. In the world of the Bible, someone who was an independent thinker—something we prize—was a misfit, a danger to society.

It surprises some people to learn that Jesus and the first Christians were Jews. An understanding of the New Testament's original meaning is incomplete without knowing something about the Judaism that preceded it. Christianity sprang from the roots of Judaism, and the words of the New Testament constantly draw from that background. Therefore, we must know something about the Jewish story—the story that Jews of Jesus' day told to identify who they were as a group—in order to understand the New Testament appropriately. The story of the Jewish people is thus the "story behind the story" of the New Testament.

Beginnings

The story behind the identity of ancient Jews started with a man named Abraham. According to the story, God picked out Abraham from all the people of his day some two thousand years before the birth of Christ (Gen. 12:1–3). After bringing Abraham out of his home to a foreign land, God promised to make his offspring into a great nation. God even promised to give Abraham's descendants the very land in which Abraham then found himself a stranger, a land later called Palestine. Finally, God gave Abraham a special symbol of their relationship, circumcision. All of the male descendants of Abraham were to be circumcised soon after they were born (Gen. 17:1–14).

Abraham's grandson Jacob was later renamed Israel. The nation of Israel and the Jews would eventually descend from this man. Jacob himself had twelve sons, who gave rise to twelve tribes, twelve different clans of people who would eventually inherit twelve distinct regions of land in Palestine. Because of a famine, the family of Jacob migrated to Egypt where food was available (Gen. 46:1–7). At first they lived there peacefully and comfortably, but soon they found themselves slaves to the Egyptians and to Egypt's ruler, the Pharaoh.

In these early stories, the Jews found some of the most basic aspects of their identity. For example, they called themselves "Israel" after Jacob and the twelve tribes that descended from him. They also identified themselves as "sons of Abraham," even arguing among themselves at times about who the true sons of Abraham were.

Circumcision was perhaps the most important indicator that a male was a Jew. At the time of Christ, it also stood as one of the biggest obstacles for someone who was thinking about converting to Judaism. It is thus no surprise that one of the biggest debates in the early years of Christianity was whether non-Jews needed to be circumcised before they could become Christians.

The Exit from Egypt

Some of the most significant events in the Jewish story occurred when the Israelites escaped from slavery in Egypt and made their way through the desert toward Canaan, the name by which Palestine was known before Israel inhabited it. In the story, God guided them out of slavery through the leadership of an Israelite named Moses. At first Moses negotiated with Pharaoh so that Israel could offer sacrifices in the desert to Israel's God, whose name was Yahweh. But even after God brought nine plagues—including such things as frogs, lice, darkness, and blood in the drinking water—Pharaoh refused to let them go.

The tenth and final plague was the one that convinced Pharaoh. Moses instructed the Israelites to kill a lamb and place some of its blood on the doorposts of their houses. At midnight, the angel of death went through the land of Egypt, killing the firstborn sons of any house not marked in this way, including the house of Pharaoh. When the angel found a house with blood on the doorpost, he passed over that house. For this reason, Jews today celebrate a yearly feast called Passover to commemorate the fact that God saved their sons from death and rescued them from slavery.

Pharaoh finally released the Israelites, only to change his mind after they had left. Before they had traveled far, they discovered that Pharaoh's army was bearing down on them. You may be familiar with the story of how the Israelites crossed the Red Sea. God enabled Israel to cross this sea on dry ground by piling up the water on both sides of them like walls. But God allowed the army of the Egyptians to drown when he returned the waters to their original place.

> Jews thought of Moses primarily as the great lawgiver, the one through whom God made a covenant with Israel.

This departure from Egypt is known as the exodus, which basically means *exit*. For Jews, it symbolizes the power of God to deliver them out of oppression, as well as His love for them above all the peoples of the earth. Even further, it came to define Israel's attitude toward the oppressed. Some of ancient Israel's laws commanded kindness toward foreigners who might find themselves living outside their homeland (e.g., Deut. 24:17–18).

This part of the Jewish story is especially significant as it relates to the New Testament. Christianity makes an important connection between Passover and Easter, the day that Christians believe Jesus came back from the dead. Jesus died on the day of Passover. The apostle Paul even calls Jesus the "Passover Lamb" (1 Cor. 5:7). Similarly, the book of John calls Jesus the "Lamb of God who takes away the sin of the world" (John 1:29), imagery also used in the book of Revelation (e.g., Rev. 5:6).

All these passages indicate that Jesus' death prevents us from experiencing God's judgment, just as the blood on the doorposts in Egypt saved the Israelites from the angel of death. You can see how closely connected the Christian story is to the Jewish story. The early Christians did not see themselves as part of a new religion but as the true ending to the Jewish story.

The Giving of the Law

Another crucial event in the story of Israel took place just after the Israelites escaped Egypt. On Mount Sinai God presented Moses with the Law, the code of conduct by which the Israelites were to live in order to enjoy the protection and blessing of Yahweh. God and Israel made a solemn agreement, a covenant. If Israel would serve Yahweh alone as its God, God would bless Israel with a land of its own and prosper its people.

The Law was at the heart of what it meant to be a Jew. The Ten Commandments are the best-known part of the Law, including such commands as "Thou shalt not kill" and "Thou shalt not steal" (Ex. 20:13, 15 KJV). But the Law was much more than just these commands. Jews often refer to the first five books of the Old Testament — or Pentateuch — as the Law.

The Law also included a great deal of civil legislation, laws that related to successful living with one another. What would happen if your bull gored someone to death (Ex. 21:28)? Would a man have to pay a "bride-price" to the father of a virgin he seduced (Ex. 22:16)? These legal questions were a part of the Jewish Law.

There was also much concerning the appropriate offering of sacrifices and the proper maintenance of Israel's relationship with God. How were sacrifices to be made (Lev. 1–7)? In what kind of structure or sanctuary were they to be offered, and what items should the structure contain (Ex. 25–27)? When were sacrifices to be offered, and on what days was Israel to celebrate special religious feasts (Lev. 23)?

Finally, a great deal of the Law dealt with distinctions that set off Israel as a special people different from other nations; that is, as a people belonging strictly to Yahweh. This category included rules concerning the foods Israel was not allowed to eat (Lev. 11), as well as some sexual taboos (Lev. 18). As previously mentioned, circumcision was perhaps the most important practice that distinguished Jewish males from the males of many other races.

Interestingly enough, Jews at the time of Christ had several different views on what the Law meant for them. For example, a group known as the

Samaritans had a version of the Pentateuch that differed significantly from the version used by more mainstream Jews. Another group called the Pharisees followed a well-developed oral tradition that extended and supplemented the Law considerably. On the other hand, a group known as the Sadducees had a much more limited understanding of what the Law entailed. They were more conservative in their beliefs and politics than the Pharisees, who taught many things that the Law did not even mention—like the idea of resurrection. We will say more about these groups in chapter 8. Because of the diversity of Jewish views regarding the Law, we will not be surprised to find some diversity in the way the early Christians looked at the Jewish Law as well.

The importance of the Law for Judaism can hardly be underestimated: it is fundamental to what it means to be a Jew. Since Jewish tradition teaches that God delivered the Law through Moses, he is one of the most important figures in the Jewish story, if not the most important. He is known primarily as the lawgiver of Israel, the one through whom God made the covenant. It is no surprise to find that the New Testament compares Jesus to Moses as the giver of a new covenant and as one who far surpasses Moses in significance (e.g., Heb. 3:1–6).

Although Moses led the Israelites out of slavery in Egypt, he was not the one who led them into the land God had promised to Abraham—the Promised Land. Only two individuals out of all those who had escaped Egypt lived long enough to enter the land of Canaan. Even though they easily could have completed the trip in under a month, the Israelites spent forty years wandering in the desert between Egypt and Canaan. According to the story, this delay was due to their lack of trust in Yahweh to give them military success against the people that already inhabited the Promised Land. So all but two of the original participants in the exodus died without having reached their goal. Even Moses died just short of entering the Promised Land.

Here we see the basic dynamics of Yahweh's relationship with Israel, as the Jews understood that relationship. Yahweh had chosen or elected Israel out of all the nations of the world. As a result, Israel was to serve Him exclusively out of all the other gods of the earth. This service primarily consisted of keeping His commands as they were found in the Law. If they kept this covenant arrangement, Yahweh promised to bless them, not least by letting them control their land. Unfortunately, they would fail Yahweh in the years to come.

Questions for Study and Discussion

1. If you have heard this story before (from Abraham to Moses), did you learn anything new in this chapter, such as a perspective you had never heard before?

2. How do you define yourself? As an individual with certain unique characteristics, likes, and dislikes? Or as a member of various groups: a Christian, a female, an athlete, a Republican?

3. Have you ever thought seriously about how central the Law was in the Old Testament and in God's relationship with His people? Put yourself in an ancient Israelite's shoes—would you ever have expected God to change the rules?

The Story Behind the Story

From Promised Land to No Land

Most Jews probably thought of a messiah or son of God in human terms, a political ruler who would defeat the enemies of Israel, particularly Rome.

The Four Pillars

The Law, particularly the Old Testament book of Deuteronomy, presents us with what one scholar has called the "four pillars" of Judaism—four concepts that capture the heart of how many Jews at the time of Christ understood their relationship with God.[1] The passage from Deuteronomy below gives us a glimpse of all four.

The first two pillars that show up in the passage are (1) God's exclusive election of Israel and (2) the fact that Israel must serve Yahweh exclusively—monotheism. These are two sides of

---

At a Glance

- The four pillars of Judaism were monotheism, election, covenant, and land.
- King David became the ideal king for the Jews.
- King Solomon built the temple in Jerusalem.
- The New Testament titles "Son of David," "Christ," and "Son of God" are royal titles that originate in the Old Testament.
- Israel was destroyed because it did not keep the covenant.
- The Maccabees led a successful revolt against the Syrians, giving the Jews about one hundred years of freedom (165–63 B.C.).

> The LORD did not set his affection on you and choose you because you were more numerous than other peoples, for you were the fewest of all peoples. But it was because the LORD loved you and kept the oath he swore to your forefathers that he brought you out with a mighty hand and redeemed you from the land of slavery, from the power of Pharaoh king of Egypt. Know therefore that the LORD your God is God; he is the faithful God, keeping his covenant of love to a thousand generations of those who love him and keep his commands. But those who hate him he will repay to their face by destruction; he will not be slow to repay to their face those who hate him. Therefore, take care to follow the commands, decrees and laws I give you today. If you pay attention to these laws and are careful to follow them, then the LORD your God will keep his covenant of love with you, as he swore to your forefathers. He will love you and bless you and increase your numbers. He will bless the fruit of your womb, the crops of your land—your grain, new wine and oil—the calves of your herds and the lambs of your flocks in the land that he swore to your forefathers to give you.
>
> —Deuteronomy 7:7–13

the same coin: it is an exclusive pairing of Yahweh and Israel. Some modern readers, even Christian readers, may find it arrogant or presumptuous of the Jews to believe that God specifically chose them as His people over and against all the other nations of the earth. Yet this is clearly what the Old and New Testaments teach.

Of course, there are parts of the Old Testament that open up the blessings of Yahweh to other peoples as well. In the book of Jonah, for example, Yahweh blesses the Assyrians, one of the archenemies of Israel. It is important to remember that in the days of the Old Testament, people did not decide which gods to worship. Different peoples worshiped different gods. Each nation had its own patron deity, the god that looked out for the well-being and prosperity of that particular people. When two nations went to war, two gods were also going to war.

The Israelites considered themselves blessed to have the greatest of all gods as their divine patron—Yahweh. Yahweh had chosen them to be His particular people. It was only to be expected that in return they would serve Him only as their God. This relationship was captured in a covenant between the two parties, a solemn agreement that if Israel kept the Law, then Yahweh would give the Israelites prosperity.

The focus of this prosperity centered on their land. If the Israelites kept the covenant, they would control their land and be free from foreign rule. The reasoning was simple. Yahweh was the most powerful God and could beat the god of any other nation. If Israel lost a battle or became enslaved to another nation, the only possible explanation was that the Israelites had broken the covenant. Understanding this way of thinking is key to understanding the background of Christianity.

The Beginnings of a Nation

After Moses died, God used a man named Joshua to lead the Israelites into the Promised Land. Following a series of military victories, the Israelites took possession of Canaan. The next few hundred years brought a tug of war between the tribes of Israel and the surrounding peoples. Israel remained free when it served Yahweh. When the Israelites began to serve other gods, Yahweh enabled their enemies to defeat them. The Old Testament book of Judges is one of the clearest expressions of the four pillars at work in this way. It presents a constantly repeated cycle of freedom to slavery to freedom again, all on the basis of Israel's loyalty or disloyalty to Yahweh.

A little over a thousand years before Christ, Israel made the transition from a loosely connected group of tribes to a nation united under a single king. Israel's second king, David, is very important for our understanding of the New Testament. Not only did David take Jerusalem from its non-Israelite inhabitants and make it the capital of Israel, but he was the first in a dynasty of kings that would ultimately rule for over four hundred years. In keeping

> When the Most High gave the nations their inheritance, when he divided all mankind, he set up boundaries for the peoples according to the number of the sons of Israel. For the LORD's portion is his people, Jacob his allotted inheritance.
>
> —Deuteronomy 32:8–9

with the family orientation of the ancient world, David came to symbolize kingship for many Jews. He was considered the ideal king who had an ideal relationship with Yahweh. At the time of Christ, Israel was without a king. Many looked for another David—a Son of David—to come and restore their kingdom to its former glory and boundaries.

David's son Solomon also played a significant role in the story behind the New Testament. Before Solomon, Yahweh had been worshiped primarily in a portable tent or tabernacle. Solomon took on the task of building a permanent temple for Yahweh in Jerusalem. The Old Testament book of Deuteronomy implies that this temple (built on the pattern of the tabernacle) was the only legitimate place to offer sacrifices to Yahweh from that point on.

The unity of the kingdom disintegrated after the death of Solomon. For the next few hundred years, the Israelites were divided into two different kingdoms. The northern kingdom retained the name "Israel" and constituted the larger nation. The southern kingdom was largely made up of one tribe, Judah, from which we actually get the word *Jew*. This is the tribe to which David and Solomon had belonged. Thus the "Davidic dynasty" only continued to rule in the southern kingdom. It is in this southern kingdom that the story behind the New Testament continues, for the Assyrians would obliterate the northern kingdom in 722–21 B.C.

The Four Pillars of Judaism

- **Monotheism**—Yahweh was the only God Israel could worship.
- **Election**—God chose Israel out of all the nations.
- **Covenant**—an agreement between Yahweh and Israel. If the Israelites followed the Law, God would bless them. If they did not, He would curse them.
- **Land**—what God would give Israel if it followed His commands. The focus of God's presence in the land was the temple in Jerusalem.

If we are to understand the New Testament, it is important to know a few things about kingship in the Old Testament. Three of the most important titles the New Testament uses for Jesus are Christ, Son of God, and Son of David, all of which are royal titles that originate in the Old Testament. If we are unaware of this background, we will probably misunderstand the precise nuances these titles have in the New Testament.

For example, since we refer to Jesus as "Jesus Christ," it would be easy for a modern person to think that Christ was Jesus' last name, like Smith or Jones. But people did not have last names in the ancient world. The word *Christ* actually means *anointed one*, a Greek translation of the word *messiah*. In the Old Testament, the phrase *anointed one* referred to someone God had set apart for a special role or purpose, such as a king or high priest.

> Hear, O Israel: The LORD our God, the LORD is one.
>
> —Deuteronomy 6:4

It is also easy for Christians and even some Jews to believe the word *messiah* always refers to a single individual who brings definitive salvation and judgment to the earth. Christians think of Jesus as that one person who made salvation available to all. Some Jews still believe a messiah will come and usher in a new age.

But the term *anointed one* was used for different kinds of individuals in the Old Testament. In a sense, all of the kings of Judah were messiahs—they were "anointed ones" of God (e.g., 1 Sam. 24:10). The book of Isaiah even refers to a pagan king with this term (Cyrus, the Persian), using the exact word Christians would later use of Jesus to mean *Messiah* (Isa. 45:1). The Dead Sea Scrolls, Jewish literature that was written not long before Jesus was born, expected that a king-messiah would arrive and restore the political kingdom of Israel. But they also looked for the coming of an anointed priest, a priest-messiah who would restore a pure temple. Scholars now generally agree that Jews at the time of Christ used the word *messiah* in a number of different ways. Christians to a great extent would create their own unique understanding of this word.

The title *Son of God* is also easily misunderstood. In the Old Testament it is used in several different ways, the most relevant of which is as a title for the kings of Judah. Israel was not unique in considering its kings to be the sons of gods. It was very common to view kings in this way throughout the Near East and the Mediterranean world at that time. With Israel this designation meant the kings had a relationship with Yahweh, that he was the father of the king of Israel (e.g., 2 Sam. 7:14).

At one point, the Old Testament even addresses the human king as "God." Psalm 45:6 says of the king, "Your throne, O God, will last forever and ever." Because of this human king's justice and goodness, the God anointed him as the ruler or god of Israel. In the Old Testament, therefore, the title *son of God* shows that the king is in a position of authority that mirrors and represents God himself. It also means the king is in a special relationship with God like that of a son to a father. The king represented God to the people, and he represented the people to God.

Christianity would take these concepts of kingship and develop them well beyond their Old Testament meanings. For example, the Jews were primarily concerned with their own political situation rather than the world at large. Most Jews probably thought of a messiah or son of God in human terms, a political ruler who would defeat the enemies of Israel, particularly Rome. But Christianity would add yet another royal title, Lord, to the meaning of Messiah. For Christians, this term meant that Jesus was Son of David, Messiah, and Son of God—the king par excellence in terms of the nation of Israel. Lord also became a cosmic term, one that indicated that Christ was ruler of both heaven and earth, including not only all humans but all spiritual forces as well.

> The king proclaims the LORD's decree: "The LORD said to me, 'You are my son. Today I have become your Father. Only ask, and I will give you the nations.'"
>
> —Psalm 2:7–8 NLT

A Time of Waiting

In the view of the Hebrew Scriptures, the northern kingdom never served Yahweh appropriately. By setting up shrines in several places in their territory, the people did not worship Yahweh in the correct location. Further, they worshiped gods other than Yahweh. Given the dynamics of the four pillars, it was only a matter of time before God judged them.

In 722–21 B.C., the Assyrians came and obliterated the northern kingdom. Ten of Israel's twelve tribes basically disappeared from the face of the earth, although a group that traced their heritage to Israel would continue to live in the region. These were the Samaritans. Even today there are those who claim to be the descendants of this group. Jews at the time of Christ looked down on Samaritans because they were thought to be "half-breeds," tainted by mixture with other races and false beliefs.

Yet the southern kingdom, Judah, did not escape God's judgment either. Judah also failed to keep its covenant with Yahweh. The nation of Babylon destroyed Jerusalem and its temple in 586 B.C. The conquering army carried hordes of Israelites back to Babylon as slaves. Unlike the northern kingdom, however, these exiled Israelites managed to keep their identity intact in captivity. After about seventy years, a group or remnant returned to Jerusalem.

But Israel never returned to the former glory and independence it had once enjoyed. For the next few hundred years leading up to New Testament times, the Jews were bounced back and forth from one foreign power to another. The one bright spot in those years was the time of the Maccabees, a Jewish family that led a successful revolt against the foreign nation of Syria.

In the last years of the 300s B.C., the Greeks under Alexander the Great conquered all of the Middle East. This included Persia, the nation that controlled the Jews at that time. In its entire history, the earth had never been brought together under such an extensive rule and influence. The result would change the face of the world forever. For the first time, a common culture developed that cut across the boundaries of the individual nations. With regard to gods, Greek influence overcame the idea that each nation could only worship its individual gods. This influence helped integrate the nations and created a more unified world, a unity that would later facilitate the spread of Christianity.

In 175 B.C., however, some Jews believed that the Greek influence was threatening to destroy the distinctiveness of Israel and its relationship with Yahweh. For example, some Jews were participating in a Greek "gymnasia" that had been built in Jerusalem. Many underwent an operation to undo their circumcision. The ancient Greeks exercised

> "Comfort, comfort my people," says your God. "Speak tenderly to Jerusalem. Tell her that her sad days are gone and that her sins are pardoned . . ." Listen! It's the voice of someone shouting, "Clear the way through the wilderness for the LORD! Make a straight highway through the wasteland for our God."
>
> —Isaiah 40:1–3 NLT

naked, so one's Jewish identity would have been overwhelmingly obvious in that setting. Those who "erased" the marks of circumcision were thus seen as traitors of the highest degree.

The last straw came when a representative of the Syrian ruler Antiochus Epiphanes IV tried to get the father of the Maccabean family to offer an inappropriate sacrifice. When another Jew went ahead with the sacrifice, the father killed him on the spot, along with all the Syrian emissaries. Several years of guerilla warfare resulted, with the Maccabees surprisingly emerging as the victors. The Jews still celebrate the "Feast of Dedication" every year—Hanukkah—to commemorate the resumption of proper worship in the Jerusalem temple. Israel was independent of foreign rulers for about a hundred years under the Hasmoneans, the actual family name of the Maccabees.

Several aspects of this story are important for our understanding of the New Testament. For example, some think that Jews at the time of Christ never felt they had ever really returned from their exile in Babylon.[2] Although a second temple had been built, it was not as glorious as the previous one. Therefore, it is no surprise that the New Testament describes salvation by using Old Testament imagery about Israel's return from Babylonian captivity. Certain passages in the New Testament even use "Babylon" as a code word for Rome, primarily because the Romans destroyed Jerusalem in A.D. 70, just as the Babylonians had in 586 B.C.

Although we only have hints of what the early Christians thought of the Maccabees, there are at least two places where the New Testament makes an allusion to their successes. The first is in the Gospel of John, where Jesus actually attends the Feast of Hanukkah in Jerusalem, the Feast of Dedication (John 10:22). The other is in Hebrews 11:35. Many scholars believe this is an allusion to a story in which seven brothers chose to die rather than betray the covenant, a story that is set during the Maccabean revolt. However, even more important than actual references to the Maccabees is the tone they set for much of Israel in the days just preceding the New Testament. The following chapter will show how their heritage influenced Jewish thought right up to the time that Jesus walked the earth and the early church was born.

Questions for Study and Discussion

1. If you have heard this story before (from Promised Land to No Land), did you learn anything new in this chapter, such as a perspective you had never heard before?

2. What do you think about the idea that Israel is or was God's exclusive people over and against any other ethnic group? Does the Old Testament really teach this idea? Do you think modern-day Israel is the same Israel? Do you think Israel's people are still God's people and heir to all these promises?

3. What do you think about the idea that the Jews were not expecting the Messiah to be divine? How do you think they understood the Bible verses the New Testament interprets to be about Jesus? What do you think about the claim that the phrase *Son of God* did not necessarily imply someone was divine in the Old Testament? Can you think of a way to argue against this claim?

4. Were you surprised to hear that Jesus might have celebrated Hanukkah? What is your reaction to the claim that the early Christians might have found significance in some of the events and writings mentioned in the Apocrypha? If you have a strong reaction one way or the other, explain why.

section two

Gospels

Jewish Groups at the Time of Christ

Paul's language of divine predestination, his view of human sinfulness, and the cosmic scope of salvation all find their closest parallels in the Dead Sea Scrolls.

Most of the Jewish groups important for our understanding of the New Testament trace their stories in one way or another to the period in which the Hasmoneans—the descendants of the Maccabees—ruled. The story of the Maccabeans seems to have had an enormous effect on how Jews in Palestine understood themselves in Jesus' day.

Sadducees and Priests

The Hasmoneans did not descend from David, nor were they in the royal line. Rather, they descended from

At a Glance

- Most Jews in Palestine were just going about their daily lives (people of the land).
- More Jews lived outside Palestine than in Palestine (Diaspora Jews). The majority of these spoke Greek (Hellenistic Jews).
- Samaritan Jews were of mixed race and thus were despised by many other Jews.
- The aristocratic Sadducees ran the temple. They followed only things that were clearly set out in the first five books of the Old Testament.
- Pharisees not only observed the specifics of the Jewish Law carefully, they also followed many oral traditions about how to keep it.
- Essenes kept the highest standards of purity of all. Some of them became like monks in a desert place called Qumran.
- Revolutionaries occasionally tried to oust the Romans by force.

Israelite priests. Some Jews opposed their leadership in part for this reason: they were not "sons of David." Nevertheless, their descendants ruled Israel for well over a hundred years. In 63 B.C., a dispute between two brothers over who should be king led to the intervention of the Roman general Pompey, who defeated Jerusalem and brought Israel under Roman rule.

Despite the presence of the Romans in Palestine, the Hasmoneans continued as rulers until the infamous Herod the Great came to power—the one the New Testament tells us tried to kill the baby Jesus. He put to death almost all the Hasmonean descendants who might have had a claim to the throne. Then from the wealthy class he handpicked a high priest, the highest rank of priest in Judaism. Herod was careful to choose someone who would never challenge his rule.

Priests took care of the temple in Jerusalem and administered the Jewish Law in general for the people. Ideally, Israelite priests, who lived throughout the nation of Israel, traced their ancestry back to the tribe of Levi, one of the twelve sons of Jacob. The overwhelming majority of priests lived outside Jerusalem, where they often settled local disputes and served as an extension of the temple for the people in the countryside—the people of the land. In the time of Christ, there were more priests than any of the other distinct groups we will discuss in this chapter.

The priests who lived outside Jerusalem were often very poor. In addition to helping people resolve disputes, they provided most of whatever education

> "Lord, you chose David to be king over Israel, and swore to him about his descendants forever, that his kingdom should not fail before you."
>
> "But (because of) our sins, sinners rose up against us . . . Lord, raise up for them their king, the son of David, to rule over your servant Israel . . ."
>
> "Undergird him with the strength to destroy the unrighteous rulers, to purge Jerusalem from gentiles . . . to drive out the sinners from the inheritance . . ."
>
> "He will have gentile nations serving him under his yoke . . ."
>
> "And he will purge Jerusalem . . ."
>
> "And he will be a righteous king over them, taught by God . . ."
>
> "He shall be the Lord Messiah."
>
> —Psalms of Solomon 17:4–5, 21–23, 30, 32

went on among the common people. Since the temple was the focal point of Israel's land, those who were in control of it held considerable power. Local priests thus derived some authority from their connection with the Jerusalem temple.

Yet there was often a significant difference between the local priests and the Jerusalem priests, both in their status and their thinking. While the local priests were poor, the Jerusalem priests (who largely consisted of a group known as the Sadducees) tended to come from the wealthy aristocracy. After Rome took over and Herod the Great renovated the temple on a massive scale, the Sadducees found themselves having to be "buddy-buddy" with the Romans. Since many Jews considered the Romans to be their greatest enemies, no doubt many were suspicious of the Sadducees for this reason alone.

Some believe that the Sadducees only considered the first five books of the Hebrew Scriptures (the Pentateuch) to be authoritative, although this is far from certain. What is certain is that they did not follow the tradition of the elders, oral traditions that had developed over the years on how to keep the Law. Groups such as the Pharisees considered these oral traditions to be authoritative in addition to the text of the Old Testament itself. Further, Sadducees did not believe in any sort of afterlife, an idea that only clearly occurs in one or two places in the Old Testament (e.g., Dan. 12:1–3). Acts 23:8 may also imply that Sadducees did not believe in angels.

Sadducees appear several times in the pages of the New Testament. Notably, more than any other group they seem to bring about Jesus' death. As the party in power politically, they tried their best to keep relations good between the Romans and the Jews—after all, they had the most to lose. During times like Passover, when Jerusalem was filled with crowds of people, they watched carefully to keep order. The Romans reacted forcibly against any situation that might turn into a riot. Therefore, when Jesus created conflict in the temple during Passover week, He probably set in motion His eventual arrest and crucifixion (cf. Mark 11:12–19).

The Essenes

If the Sadducees inherited the power of the Hasmonean priest-kings, the Essenes were a group that opposed and were perhaps even oppressed by that power. Some think that an Essene we know of as the "Teacher of Righteousness" actually served in the temple until the Hasmoneans forced him out of service, eventually causing him to retreat to a desert location known as Qumran. It is here that the Dead Sea Scrolls were found in the late 1940s. At Qumran, the Teacher of Righteousness and his followers kept a standard of purity similar to that required of priests on duty in the Jerusalem temple.

The Dead Sea Scrolls have an apocalyptic flavor. This means they see Israel's struggles as an invisible battle between spiritual forces in the heavens, a battle that will end with the final judgment of the world. A book quoted in the New Testament, 1 Enoch, was probably considered Scripture by the Essenes, as were other books of a somewhat apocalyptic bent.

A number of interesting parallels exist between the Essenes and the earliest Christians. For example, the New Testament sometimes has an apocalyptic bent similar to that found in the Dead Sea literature. The book of Revelation is a symbolic portrayal of heavenly conflict with similarities to other apocalyptic works found at Qumran. The Gospel of John speaks of Jesus in terms of light (John 1:5; 8:12), and Paul called believers "sons of light" (1 Thess. 5:5)—exactly the kind of language we find in the Dead Sea Scrolls. The picture of the early church in Acts shows a group holding their possessions in common, much as they did at Qumran. Among the known Jewish literature of the period, Paul's language of divine predestination, his view of human sinfulness, and the cosmic scope of salvation all find their closest parallels in the Dead Sea Scrolls.

At this point, however, most scholars do not see any direct relationship between the Scrolls and the early Christians. Rather, the greatest contribution of the Dead Sea literature is the way it helps us better understand the world behind the New Testament. For example, the Scrolls have added greatly to our understanding of what many Jews were expecting the messiah to be. They pictured a political leader who would restore Israel's kingdom and then rule with righteousness and faithfulness to the covenant.

The Pharisees

To us, the Pharisees are probably the best-known group of Jews from the time of Christ, not least because the early Christians seem to have had more conflicts with them than with any other Jewish group. Popularly, they are often associated with *legalism*—a tendency to keep rules just because one likes rules, not because a rule serves any purpose. The English word *Pharisaic* illustrates this fact, since it is used of someone who is self-righteous or hypocritical. This reflects an unfortunate tendency throughout the last two thousand years to equate this view of the Pharisees with Jews in general, sometimes contributing to anti-Semitism (or, more accurately, anti-Judaism), hatred of Jews.

Yet, this typical view of the Pharisees reflects a great deal of misunderstanding of what they were about. Pharisees made up only a small minority of Jewish individuals (about six thousand) at the time of Christ. And their concern for keeping the Law was based solidly on the four pillars of Judaism we discussed in chapter 7. The Old Testament clearly teaches that Israel was to observe the covenant found in the Jewish Law. But how could Jews be sure they were keeping the covenant? If they truly wanted to serve God, they would no doubt be careful to do everything He wished.

Therefore, when one of the Ten Commandments said not to work on Saturday, the Jewish Sabbath, the Pharisees wanted to know just how much effort would constitute "work"? They wanted to make it clear so that the commandment could be kept properly. For example, how much walking could I do on Saturday until I had "worked"? What about an emergency situation that required me to "work" to save someone's life? Could I "work" if it would save someone's life? The Pharisees wanted to spell out exactly what it would take to keep the covenant. The number of rules they came up with is not a proof of their legalism. After all, we have more traffic laws than all their laws put together.

Understanding the way the four pillars worked in the minds of many Jews helps explain their fervor in keeping the Law. The covenant was not just a matter of giving God His due. Israel was promised blessing in their land if they would keep their end of the agreement. Many Pharisees no doubt kept the Law vigorously—and encouraged others to do the same—because they believed that God in return would be faithful and free Israel from the control of the Romans. While not all scholars agree that the Pharisees had such revolutionary aims, the literature clearly indicates that some Pharisees took leading roles during uprisings against the Romans. As the spiritual heirs of the Maccabean fighters mentioned in the last chapter, it would be no surprise if their zeal for the Law followed similar lines.

Revolutionaries

The conflict between Jews and Romans came to a head in A.D. 66, when the Jews revolted against Roman rule. While distinct groups such as the Zealots or the Sicarii came into existence around that time, the drive to revolution often cut across Israel's other divisions. For example, we know of both Pharisees and Essenes who participated in uprisings. Interestingly enough, one of Jesus' disciples is called "Simon the Zealot" in Luke 6:15. It is indeed possible that some of Jesus' followers came to Him under the expectation that He would be the one to restore Israel's kingdom (cf. Acts 1:6).

The revolutionary attempt to oust the Romans, the Jewish War, resulted in the destruction of Jerusalem and the temple in A.D. 70. These events drastically transformed Judaism and detached Christianity even further from its Jewish roots. With the temple gone, the Sadducees disappeared from the scene, as did the Essenes, whom the Romans tracked down and obliterated. Only the Pharisees survived in Palestine. Many think their heirs formed the core of the rabbinic Judaism with which we are familiar today.

The People of the Land

Most of the Jews in Palestine at the time of Christ did not belong to any of the major parties. They were simply eking out an existence. A large percentage of them worked at farming the land, thus earning the designation "the people of the land" (the *'am ha'arets*). They were not Pharisees, Sadducees, Essenes, or Revolutionaries. They were just common, ordinary people trying to make it from day to day.

Nevertheless, they were Jews, and this designation alone said something about what they were like—at least in the eyes of the non-Jews of the time. As we have already observed, there were certain practices that set the Jewish people apart from other nations: circumcision; dietary restrictions; observing the Sabbath; and most significantly, adherence to monotheism.

While many Palestinian Jews spoke some Greek, the majority spoke Aramaic, a language that evolved out of Hebrew, the main language of the Old Testament. Aramaic is the language Jesus spoke to the people of the countryside. Undoubtedly, this "silent majority" was not indifferent to the temple or the political situation. A fair number of them probably made regular trips to Jerusalem each year for one of the many festivals. No doubt many also resented having to pay taxes to the Romans. But most were not involved in any particular political or ideological movement. They were doing what so many of us do today—getting through one day at a time, putting one sandal in front of the other.

> "Among themselves [the Jews] they are inflexibly honest and ever ready to show compassion, though they regard the rest of mankind with all the hatred of enemies. They sit apart at meals, they sleep apart, and though, as a nation, they are singularly prone to lust, they abstain from intercourse with foreign women. Among themselves nothing is unlawful. Circumcision was adopted by them as a mark of difference from other men. Those who come over to their religion adopt the practice, and have this lesson first instilled into them—to despise all gods, to disown their country, and set parents, children, and brethren at nothing."
>
> —Tacitus (Roman historian)
> Histories 5.5

Greek-Speaking or "Hellenistic" Jews

Interestingly, more Jews lived outside Palestine than inside at the time of Christ. The word *Diaspora* refers to the dispersion of Jews to all parts of the known world in the centuries preceding the birth of Jesus. Most of these Jews spoke *Greek* and may not have known any Aramaic, let alone Hebrew. Greek had become the "business language," the *lingua franca* of the ancient world. Just as English speakers can communicate effectively in much of the world today, a Greek-speaker could make it in the ancient Mediterranean. We call Greek-speaking Jews Hellenistic Jews, because *Hellenistic* means *Greek*. Since the Hebrew Scriptures were translated into Greek in the third century before Christ (the 200s B.C.), the Bible was available to these Jews in their first language.

Some Diaspora Jews probably did not keep Jewish traditions as scrupulously as many Palestinian Jews. Nevertheless, as noted earlier in this chapter, the Roman historian Tacitus described the Jews in Rome as following the same basic practices as those in Palestine. These included circumcision, Sabbath observance, and dietary laws. Even the most "enlightened" Jews, those who were most influenced by Greek culture and philosophy, showed allegiance to the Jewish temple in Jerusalem.

Not all Greek-speaking Jews lived outside Palestine. Members of the "upper crust" in Jerusalem, the center of Judaism, demonstrated their sophistication by a basic proficiency in Greek. About 40 percent of the tombstones available in Palestine as a whole were written in Greek. The Greek-speaking elite in Jerusalem may have looked down their noses at the poorer, Aramaic-speaking crowds. On the other hand, Aramaic-speaking Jews probably were somewhat suspicious about the "purity" of the Greek speakers. Perhaps some Aramaic speakers saw themselves as more faithful to God than the "tainted" Greek speakers.

These kinds of tensions between Greek- and Aramaic-speaking Jews would show up in early Christianity as well. Acts 6 mentions a conflict among early Christians in which Aramaic-speaking Christians failed to provide for Greek-speaking widows while feeding well their own Aramaic-speaking widows. Further, it is possible that some Greek-speaking Christians broke with the Jewish law more radically than Aramaic-speaking Christians did. Indeed, Acts indicates that it was the Greek-speaking Christians more than any other group that first brought Christianity to non-Jews. Understanding the makeup of Jewish groups at the time of Christ enhances our understanding of the dynamics of the early church.

Samaritan Jews

In the previous chapter, we briefly mentioned the Samaritans. Samaritans lived in Samaria, the region between Judea (where Jerusalem was located) and Galilee, where Jesus grew up and carried out most of His ministry. The northern kingdom had occupied this region during the period of the kings. After the Assyrians destroyed the northern kingdom, the remaining Jews intermingled with the other ethnic groups that came to live there. In the minds of many Jews, this mixed ethnicity made Samaritans a "tainted" race. Jesus' Parable of the Good Samaritan was particularly shocking because it took a stereotypical bad guy (a Samaritan) and made him the hero of the story. Some Samaritans live in Palestine today. They are the only Jewish group that still offers sacrifices.

Questions for Study and Discussion

1. Name nine or ten different groups of Jews discussed in this chapter. Describe each group in a sentence or two.
2. What did priests do in Israel at the time of Christ? What did a high priest do?
3. To which of the groups mentioned in this chapter did most Jews belong at the time of Christ? To which group did most Jews living in Palestine belong?

4. In terms of the first century, which Jewish group was most conservative in its approach to the Jewish Law? Which group followed a great number of oral traditions about how to keep the Law? Which group kept the highest standard of purity?
5. What kind of a messiah or king were these groups expecting to come?
6. To which group does Christianity seem most similar? In what way?

The Life and Teachings of Jesus

An Overview

The keynote of Jesus' preaching was the kingdom of God or the rule of God that was coming to the earth.

Framing the Story of Jesus

The New Testament gives us four different presentations of Jesus' earthly mission. Each gospel records slightly different events and sayings, sometimes in a different order. Since biographies in the ancient world were primarily concerned with capturing the character of a person, they arranged events and paraphrased words so that the person's character came through loud and clear. In a similar way, each gospel has framed the story of Jesus to bring out the particular emphases and themes that would speak most powerfully to its intended audience.

At a Glance

- John the Baptist baptized people to symbolize the forgiveness of their sins in preparation for God's coming judgment.
- Jesus' early ministry was extremely positive and optimistic, including healings, exorcisms, teaching, and miracles.
- Jesus preached about the coming reign of God, with judgment for the wicked and salvation for the righteous.
- Jesus appointed twelve men as His key followers or disciples.
- Jesus' crucifixion paid the price for the wrongdoing of God's people.
- God raised Jesus from the dead.

History is the backdrop of the Gospels. Since the portraits of Matthew, Mark, and Luke in particular are much the same, it's helpful to get the big picture of Jesus' earthly mission before we go on to look at each gospel in detail. This chapter presents an overview of Jesus' life and teachings, relying mostly on Mark, but dabbling in Matthew and Luke as well. John's portrait is significantly different from those of the other gospels, so we will wait until later to look at it.

The Events of Jesus' Mission

A story has three basic elements: what takes place (events), where those things take place (settings), and those involved in what takes place (characters). In Mark, for example, Jesus' earthly ministry takes place between two events: it starts when He is baptized by John the Baptist and essentially ends when He is crucified (although Mark certainly indicates that Jesus rose from the dead).

These two events tell us who Jesus is and explain the significance of His ministry. John the Baptist's mission was to prepare the way for the coming king and for God's coming judgment. John urged people to repent and turn from their sins in order to escape God's judgment. By dipping people in the waters of the river Jordan—baptizing them—he symbolized the washing away of their sins and their turning toward God. In other words, John the Baptist urged his fellow Jews to renew their commitment to the Jewish covenant in preparation for God's coming judgment and the renewal of His people. Jesus was also baptized, which at the very least shows that He agreed with John's message.

According to the Gospels, Jesus was the king or Messiah for whom John was preparing the Jewish people. Ironically, the gospel of Mark most powerfully affirms that Jesus is the Messiah at the most unlikely moment of the story—His crucifixion. Jesus' death frees His people from their sins and thus from God's judgment. He takes the punishment for their wrongdoing so that they will not have to pay the price themselves. For Mark, this act captures Jesus' kingship more meaningfully than anything else He did on earth.

Some incredibly important events in the Christian story occurred before and after these two pivotal events of baptism and crucifixion. We learn more details of these events in the other gospels. The resurrection, for example, is an extremely important event in the New Testament. Jesus rising from the dead signals Christ's victory over death and God's approval of Jesus' entire mission on earth. For many New Testament authors, the resurrection is even more significant than Jesus' death. Matthew, Luke, and John present several occasions in which Jesus' followers see Him alive after His death.

Matthew and Luke also present the story of Jesus' miraculous birth—the virgin birth. They tell how a young woman named Mary gave birth to Jesus, even though she never had sex with a man. Rather, the Holy Spirit—God's Spirit—supernaturally brought about her pregnancy.

Another event in Mark divides Jesus' earthly mission into two parts, although Matthew and Luke do not present the story in quite the same way. In Mark, the first half of the gospel presents Jesus' public ministry in overwhelmingly positive and optimistic terms. He has a wide following and is busy helping and healing, announcing the coming reign of God.

Then, in the middle of Mark, Jesus reveals His identity as Messiah to His closest followers. One of the leaders, Peter, acknowledges or confesses for the first time that Jesus is the Messiah. From this point on, Mark portrays Jesus as focused on His upcoming death, and Jesus interacts mostly with His twelve main followers. It is in this part of the gospel that Jesus discusses the coming judgment. Peter's confession of Jesus as Messiah, or Christ, is thus an important turning point in the story of Jesus as Mark presents it.[1]

We should probably mention one other event before we move on—the transfiguration of Jesus, in which three of Jesus' disciples see Him transformed into a heavenly form (Mark 9:2–10). Moses (representing the Old Testament Law), Elijah (representing the Old Testament Prophets), and Jesus turn spectacularly white. God affirms from heaven that Jesus is the Son of God, just as He had at Jesus' baptism (Mark 1:11). It's as if Peter, James, and John are allowed to see Jesus' true identity as He momentarily takes on a heavenly appearance. This event takes place just after Peter confesses that Jesus is the Christ—perhaps demonstrating a little of what this means.

The Kinds of Things Jesus Did

In the first part of Mark, Jesus engages in several activities that indicate the reign of God has begun. For example, Jesus heals the sick and casts out demons. Jesus' exorcisms—when He made evil spirits to leave people's bodies—indicate that God is "cleaning house" in the earthly realm, where Satan and his evil spirits had taken over. Every demon Jesus casts out demonstrates that God is in fact king and that the kingdom of God is on its way; in some respects, it was already here.

Ancient Family Values

People in the ancient world defined themselves and others by three factors: gender, family, and race. They evaluated themselves and others based on the honor or shame they brought on their group or tribe.

Ancient families (husbands and wives, parents and children) did not typically share the intimacy that is considered ideal today. Men worked in public to bring honor to the family; women directed the home. Sons were valued and brought legitimacy to their mothers; daughters were mostly considered a potential source of shame.

Jesus' ministry focused on the physical needs of the Jewish people as well as on their spiritual needs. In fact, they would have had difficulty separating the two. The gospel of Luke in particular emphasizes Jesus' ministry to the poor and needy. Jesus also performed miraculous deeds that showed God's approval of Him. He walked on water (Mark 6:47–52), for example, and turned a few fish into a meal for several thousand people on more than one occasion (Mark 6:30–44; 8:1–10).

Jesus also did a significant amount of teaching, even appointing twelve disciples. A *disciple* was a follower or a learner who, like an apprentice, followed a carpenter or a blacksmith around in order to learn those trades. Jesus taught many disciples in the countryside of Galilee, where much of His ministry took place, but He also picked out twelve special disciples from the crowds that followed Him.

It is extremely significant that Jesus chose twelve disciples, for this was the number of the tribes of Israel. It highlights the fact that at least part of the good news Jesus preached was the restoration of Israel. What is more significant is that He did not include himself among those twelve. In other words, He saw himself in another category. Jesus saw himself as the king, not as one of the subjects. It is no coincidence that He was crucified with a sign, "King of the Jews," above his head.

The keynote of Jesus' preaching was the kingdom of God or the rule of God that was coming to the earth. Jesus' power over evil spirits was an important sign that to some extent God's rule had already arrived. This reign of God meant "good news" to the people of Israel, particularly those who were like "lost sheep" that had strayed from the flock (Luke 15:1–7). According to the Gospels, Jesus did not target those who were trying to keep the Jewish covenant, like the Pharisees. Rather, He proclaimed good news to those who were spiritually off track—tax collectors, prostitutes, and sinners (Matt. 21:31–32). He also aimed at those who were simply in need—like the poor, widows, and orphans (Luke 4:18–19).

Jesus' primary method of teaching was by telling stories called parables. While we often think that such stories make Jesus' message clearer, the gospel of Mark indicates that Jesus himself told these stories to confuse those whose hearts were not in the right place (Mark 4:11–12). One of Jesus' parables, sometimes known as the parable of the prodigal son, captures the different ways Jesus' audiences reacted to His message (Luke 15:11–32).

Those who had strayed from faithfulness to God were like a son who had disgraced and shamed his father, treating him like he was dead. Astonishingly, the father (God) gave the son another chance when he repented of what he had done. Even more shocking is that the son who had been faithful all along rejected his father in the end. Those who heard this parable would have known what Jesus was saying: God was taking back the sinners of Israel and forgiving them. The "righteous" of Israel, on the other hand—like the Pharisees who had tried to keep the covenant—were now rejecting God and would face His judgment.

It's interesting that in the gospels of Matthew, Mark, and Luke, Jesus teaches little about the need to believe in Him, although at times He hints at the importance of His role in the coming of the kingdom. Instead, the gospel of John and the rest of the New Testament highlight the importance of faith in Christ in order to be saved from God's wrath. In Matthew, Mark, and Luke, Jesus proclaims the good news of God's reign without highlighting His own role in that kingdom. The rest of the New Testament, on the other hand, proclaims Jesus as the one through whom God's reign comes about.

In the Gospels, Jesus also participates in debates. Throughout His ministry, He got into controversies with various religious leaders. Such events were honor challenges, like chess matches, to determine the most worthy teacher and leader. Jesus won every such challenge. In the pages of the Gospels, Jesus encounters scribes, Pharisees, Sadducees, and other Jewish leaders who pose difficult questions. In every case, the Gospels present Him as the supreme teacher, one who speaks with unchallenged authority.

Settings of the Story

Timing

The Gospels give us slightly different impressions regarding the time frame during which Jesus' ministry took place. For example, if all we had were Matthew, Mark, and Luke, we would have the impression that Jesus' mission took place largely over the course of one year, although they do not specifically say how long Jesus' ministry lasted. The gospel of John, on the other hand, clearly presents Jesus' ministry as lasting two to three years.

Lay of the Land

According to Matthew and Luke, Jesus was born in the village of Bethlehem, just southwest of Jerusalem, the capital city of the Jews. Both of these cities were located in the region of Judea, which was the size of an average American county. The large sea to the west of Palestine is the

Mediterranean Sea. It spans the distance from Israel to Greece, Italy, and finally to Spain. The North African coast follows its southern coastline. To the east of Jerusalem is the Jordan River, which runs from the Sea of Galilee in the north into the Dead Sea in the south.

John the Baptist baptized the Jews of the countryside and Jesus himself in the Jordan River. However, Jesus grew up in Nazareth, in the region to the north of Judea known as Galilee. The events recorded in Matthew, Mark, and Luke for the most part take place here. Jesus may actually have had a home at one time in the small village of Capernaum on the north shores of the Sea of Galilee (Mark 2:1). It was near this place, apparently, that Jesus performed most of His miracles (Matt. 11:20–21).

Samaria is the region between Galilee and Judea. Some Jews seem to have avoided this region, although according to John, Jesus traveled through it. John 4 presents a shocking conversation between Jesus and a disreputable Samaritan woman. The well-known parable of the good Samaritan (Luke 10) also shows how open Jesus was toward Samaritan Jews.

Also according to the gospel of John, Jesus spent much more time in Judea and Jerusalem than the other

> ### How Ancients Viewed the World
>
> - Many Jews believed in several different heavens (layers of heaven with God himself in the highest heaven).
> - Many ancients believed the earth and its people were inferior to the heavens and spiritual beings that inhabited them.
> - The ancients had a strong sense of fate. The Stoics believed the best way to happiness was to accept your fate.
> - There were a variety of views on the afterlife: resurrection of all; resurrection of only the good; impersonal existence; or no afterlife at all.

gospels record. In Matthew, Mark, and Luke, we only see Jesus in Jerusalem at the end of His earthly ministry. It was during this time that He encountered conflicts with the religious rulers, created a disturbance in the temple, and was finally arrested and crucified. He seemed to stay just outside the city in a little village called Bethany. As recorded in John, however, Jesus made regular trips to Jerusalem from Galilee to observe the various Jewish festivals. John's presentation thus gives us the impression that a significant part of Jesus' earthly mission took place in the city of Jerusalem.

Keep the events, characters, and settings mentioned in this chapter in mind as you go through the individual gospels. Note how each gospel presents a slightly different emphasis than Mark, which we have used as the starting point for this overview. What you may find is that some of the other gospels also used Mark's presentation as the starting point for framing their own portraits of Jesus and His mission.

Questions for Study and Discussion

1. What are the main settings of Jesus' ministry? How do the settings differ slightly in the gospel of John?
2. What are the key events of Jesus' earthly life and ministry? Which ones are most important for the salvation of humanity? Why?
3. Who are the main characters in the gospel story? In what ways do these individuals provide good examples for us to imitate? In what ways should we avoid their example?

Jesus, the Son of David

The Gospel of Matthew

The gospel of Matthew presents Jesus as a teacher of
God's wisdom, but also as God's wisdom itself.

The Character of Jesus in Matthew

The main point of ancient biography was to capture the character of a person, and the gospel of Matthew gives us several insights into who Jesus was. The primary identifying feature is that Jesus is the Jewish Messiah, the King of the Jews. The gospel begins with the genealogy or family tree of Jesus, tracing His father's line back through David and the kings of Judah to Abraham. By beginning his gospel in this way, Matthew wanted his audience to know for sure that Jesus was the son of David.

At a Glance

Matthew presents Jesus:

- As the Jewish Messiah, the Son of David.
- As a new Moses, the authoritative interpreter of the Law for God's people.

Matthew emphasizes the continuity between Jesus and the Hebrew Scriptures by portraying events in Jesus' life:

- As the fulfillment of various Old Testament Scriptures.
- By showing that his earthly mission was focused on the Jews.
- By implying that the Jewish Law continues to be authoritative for Israel when it is understood appropriately.

But Jesus was not just an ordinary king to Matthew. Like King David's son, Solomon, who was known for his wisdom, Jesus, the son of David, was also the supreme teacher of God's wisdom. In fact, merely to call Him a teacher or a rabbi did not capture how significant Matthew believed Jesus to be. Throughout the gospel, Matthew portrays Jesus as the greatest teacher of God's wisdom that ever walked the earth—even greater than Moses. In fact, some scholars would say that the gospel of Matthew presents Jesus not just as a teacher of God's wisdom, but as God's wisdom itself.

Jesus, the Son of David

The gospel of Matthew begins with a genealogy; its main point is that Jesus is the son of David, the expected king of Israel, the Messiah. Matthew was eager to trace Jesus' lineage back to Abraham, the ultimate starting point for the Jewish race. But even more important, Matthew divided the list of names in such a way that each part pointed to David, the ideal king of Israel. Matthew's arrangement of Jesus' genealogy emphatically shouts: "Jesus is King of the Jews; Jesus is King of the Jews; Jesus is King of the Jews!"

Matthew's unique gospel brings out Jesus' kingship elsewhere. When Jesus is born, for example, wise men (interpreters of the stars) recognize that a king of incredible importance has been born. They travel to Bethlehem and bow before the world's new king (Matt. 2:11). On the other hand, Herod the Great, who was ruler of Judea at that time, treats Jesus as a rival king and attempts to have Him killed. In either case, both recognize that Jesus is a king.

What Is a Gospel?

The word *gospel* generally refers to good news of an extraordinary sort. The first meaning of gospel for the New Testament is the good news that Jesus brought to Israel—the restoration of God's people and the reestablishment of God as their king. The second meaning is the good news that God accomplished salvation through Jesus. As a literary genre, gospel is a type of literature that aims to present the good news of Jesus Christ.

With the exception of Luke, the gospels of the New Testament resemble ancient biography more than any other ancient genre. Ancient biography focused on the character of an individual, who was assumed to fit a certain type.

Jesus, a New Moses

Although the gospel of Matthew does not explicitly compare Jesus to Moses, a Jewish audience would have seen Jesus as a leader like Moses. For example, Matthew's birth account reminds us of the story of Moses in the Old Testament. Just as Moses lived in Egypt and later led Israel out of that land, so Jesus lived in Egypt for a time as an infant and then was led out by God (Matt. 2:13–22). Just as the child Moses escaped the hand of an evil ruler who killed the children of Israel, so Jesus escapes Bethlehem as the evil ruler Herod the Great puts the children of that city to death. The gospel of Luke includes none of these elements in its presentation of Jesus' birth. The gospel of Matthew probably includes them because Matthew wished to make known that Jesus was a new Moses, the one through whom God was making a new covenant with His people.

One of the most striking features of Matthew is the way it presents Jesus as the supreme teacher of the Law. Just as God gave the Old Testament Law to Moses on Mount Sinai, Jesus also delivers the heart of His message on a mountain. In the Sermon on the Mount (Matt. 5–7), Jesus gives authoritative interpretations of the Jewish Law, at times correcting the way other religious leaders interpreted it (e.g., Matt. 5:43–48).

Of all the gospels, Matthew includes Jesus' strongest rebukes of religious leaders like the Pharisees (e.g., Matt. 23). Some scholars have suggested that the gospel was written in the years after the destruction of Jerusalem (A.D. 70), when the Pharisees were the dominant force in Judaism. According to this hypothesis, the Christian writer of Matthew wished to show his fellow Jews that Jesus' interpretation of the Law was more authoritative than the interpretations of the Pharisees. As Matthew 7:28–29 says, "When Jesus had finished saying these things, the crowds were amazed at his teaching, because he taught as one who had authority, and not as their teachers of the law."

You can even divide Matthew into five sections, similar to the Jewish Law, with a major block of teaching by Jesus in each part. Each section ends with exactly the same words: "And it came about when Jesus finished . . ." (7:28;

11:1; 13:53; 19:1; 26:1, author's translation). Some scholars suggest that Matthew arranged Jesus' ministry into five blocks of teaching and miracles because the Jewish Law is made up of the five books of Genesis, Exodus, Leviticus, Numbers, and Deuteronomy. In other words, as the Jews thought Moses had written the five books of the Law, Matthew presented Jesus' teaching in five blocks to show that Jesus was an authoritative teacher like Moses, presenting God's law to His people.

The Continuity of Jesus with the Hebrew Scriptures

Jesus, the Fulfillment of Scripture

Another feature of Matthew is the way it presents events in the life of Jesus as the fulfillment of Old Testament Scripture. For example, after Herod the Great finds out that Jesus has been born, he tries to kill Him by having all the children in Bethlehem under two years of age killed. Matthew's conclusion is that this event fulfilled the words of the Old Testament prophet Jeremiah: "A voice is heard in Ramah, weeping and great mourning, Rachel weeping for her children and refusing to be comforted, because they are no more" (Matt. 2:18).

Time after time, in the birth story and in other places in this gospel, Matthew points out events in Jesus' life and ministry that fulfill various things the prophets of the Old Testament had foretold. Even in His teachings, Jesus tells the crowds that He has not come to abolish the Jewish Law and the Prophets—the Old Testament. Instead, Jesus says that He has come to fulfill them (Matt. 5:17).

What's important to realize, however, is that what Matthew meant by "fulfill" is not what you might think at first. He was using Jewish methods for extracting meaning out of the Old Testament—methods that did not read Scripture so much for its original meaning, but for what its words might mean if applied to what was going on in Matthew's day. As was perfectly acceptable at the time, Matthew read the Old Testament spiritually rather than in terms of what it actually meant when it was originally written.

For example, if you turn to Jeremiah 31:15 (the passage Matthew says is fulfilled when Herod kills the infants of Bethlehem), you will see that it is not a prediction that some day in the future a king will kill babies. It actually refers to the fact that most of Israel at that time had been destroyed by the nation of Assyria. God went on to tell the prophet Jeremiah that this group of people "will return from the land of the enemy" (Jer. 31:16). The "children" Jeremiah was talking about, therefore, were grown people. Unlike the children of Bethlehem, God promised that these would return. This event in the life of Jesus thus fulfills the Old Testament in that it gives a fuller meaning to Jeremiah's words. It is not a straightforward prediction that came true. This was Matthew's standard way of interpreting the Old Testament.

> **The Sermon on the Mount**
>
> The Sermon on the Mount (Matt. 5–7) encapsulates Jesus' teaching on how to live on earth while waiting for the kingdom. One of the best known sections of the sermon is the Beatitudes—a set of blessings Jesus proclaims on individuals who normally would not receive honor on earth.
>
> In the sermon, Jesus emphasizes that His teaching fulfills the Jewish Law and that God rewards the person who orients himself or herself around heavenly rather than earthly reward. Other key parts of the sermon include the Lord's Prayer (6:9–13), the Golden Rule (7:12), and the admonition to "love your enemies" (5:44).

The Jewish Law Is Still Valid

Another important feature of Matthew is the way in which it affirms the ongoing validity of the Jewish Law. Jesus tells the crowds that He did not come to abolish the Law or the Prophets. Further, He tells them that anyone who disobeys the least commandment in the Law is in the wrong (Matt. 5:19).

In fact, Jesus even tells the crowds to do the things that the Pharisees were telling them to do (Matt. 23:3) and affirms the Pharisees' attention to detail in keeping the Law (23:23). His critique of them is not because of the energy they expend in keeping the minute details of the Law, but because they miss its most important points—like mercy and justice (23:23).

Matthew probably wrote to Jewish Christians, not Gentile Christians. The rest of the New Testament makes it clear that few Jews abandoned their observance of the Jewish Law in the early days of Christianity. Some Jewish Christians even refused to eat with Gentile Christians for fear they would become ceremonially unclean (see Gal. 2:11–12).

Matthew is a Jewish gospel, and it emphasizes that Jesus' earthly mission was directed toward the Jews, not the Gentiles. Whereas Luke highlights Jesus' interaction with non-Jews, Matthew emphasizes that Jews were the focus of Jesus' ministry while He was on earth. When Jesus commissions His disciples in Matthew 10:6, He tells them not to preach to the Gentiles or the Samaritans. His earthly ministry focuses on the lost sheep of Israel. It is only after He has risen from the dead that He commands His followers to "go and make disciples of all nations" (Matt. 28:19).

The Who's and When's of Matthew

The gospel of Matthew is technically anonymous. Although we do not know of a time when Christians thought the author was anyone other than the tax collector Matthew (mentioned in 9:9), the book itself never names him as author. The titles of the New Testament books were not part of the original documents. They were added more than a hundred years after the books first appeared. As with many questions we have about the Bible, we will not know for certain who wrote the gospel of Matthew while we are on this earth.

The earliest mention that Matthew wrote something about Jesus appears around the year A.D. 140 in the writings of a Christian named Papias. He told us that "Matthew arranged the sayings in the Aramaic language, and everyone translated them as well as he could."[1] There are some significant differences between the writing to which this comment refers and the gospel of Matthew as we now have it. First of all, Papias suggests that Matthew wrote in a language called Aramaic.[2] However, the first gospel in our New Testament is written in Greek. Some of this Greek does seem to be a translation from Aramaic, particularly some of Jesus' sayings. However, most of our gospel of Matthew was originally composed in Greek.

Another possible difference between our gospel of Matthew and the writing Papias referred to is that Papias said it contained the sayings of Jesus. The gospel of Matthew contains much more than just quotations of Jesus, which appear in red print in many Bibles. What Papias mentioned sounds a little like some of the collections of sayings we have found from the same time period. For example, the gospel of Thomas, which is not in our Bible, is basically a collection of sayings attributed to Jesus, although many of them may not be genuine. The Dead Sea Scrolls also contain fragments of documents that are collections of verses on a single theme.

What these differences mean is that while there may be some relationship between what Papias said Matthew wrote and what the book of Matthew in our New Testament actually says, the differences probably outweigh the similarities. Some have suggested that one of the main sources behind the gospel of Matthew in our New Testament is the apostle Matthew's own collection of sayings. But we cannot know for sure.

> **Being a Follower of Christ**
> - A disciple is someone who follows a teacher in order to learn from and model that teacher.
> - Jesus' disciples learn to "fish" for people for God's kingdom.
> - To be a disciple requires absolute allegiance to Jesus and the cause of God's kingdom.
> - The Sermon on the Mount teaches Jesus' followers how to live.
> - Matthew's mission speech (Matt. 10) tells disciples how to preach the gospel to Israel.
> - Matthew ends with the Great Commission (Matt. 28:18–20), the command to make disciples for Jesus from all nations.

What we can do, however, is form some general impressions of what kind of person put together the gospel of Matthew and what kind of audience he had in mind. We have already made some educated guesses along these lines. We can feel fairly confident that the author was a Jew who was fluent in Greek and who wrote to Greek-speaking Jews. Not only is Matthew written in fairly fluent Greek, but this gospel is the most Jewish of the four in our New Testament.

For example, Matthew consistently uses the phrase "kingdom of heaven" (e.g., Matt. 4:17), whereas Mark and Luke use the phrase "kingdom of God"

(Mark 1:14). It was common for Jews like the scribes and Pharisees to show reverence for God by not saying His name directly but by using indirect ways to refer to Him. They might refer to the place where God lives or to His glory instead of stating His name.

Using "kingdom of heaven" instead of "kingdom of God" is just one hint indicating the author of the gospel of Matthew was a reverent Jew, perhaps even a converted scribe whose job was to copy the Law and other documents. While the author of the gospel of Mark explained Jewish practices (Mark 7:3–4), Matthew evidently did not need to, for his audience was Jewish (Matt. 15:1–3). Matthew's method of interpreting the Old Testament also reminds us of the methods used in the Dead Sea Scrolls and by the later rabbis—very Jewish ways of arguing from Scripture. These are just a few indications that the author and audience of the first gospel were Jews.

Questions for Study and Discussion

1. How do the events that Matthew presents and the way this gospel arranges the story of Jesus' ministry work together to emphasize certain aspects of Jesus' character?
2. Do you think that Jewish Christians today are still obligated to keep the Jewish Law? How would you fit the claim that Jesus did not abolish the Law (Matt. 5:17) with Paul's claim that Jesus did abolish the Law (Eph. 2:15)?
3. Would it change your faith in the Bible if you learned that the disciple of Jesus named Matthew did not actually write the gospel of Matthew?

Jesus, the Suffering Messiah

The Gospel of Mark

Mark shockingly proclaims that Jesus is
king because He dies!

The gospel of Mark, like the gospel of Matthew, presents Jesus as a king. But while Matthew presents Jesus as the kind of king we would expect—someone who rules and leads—Mark shockingly proclaims that Jesus is king because He dies! For Mark, Jesus' kingship becomes most evident when the Romans put Him to death—because Jesus died for the sins of His people (Mark 10:45). This unexpected twist is just one example of the way Mark presents the gospel as something that only those with true faith will understand. To everyone else, the meaning of the gospel is hidden.

At a Glance

- Mark presents Jesus as the Messiah, Son of David, and Son of God, but emphasizes that Jesus is king most meaningfully at His death.
- Mark highlights the secrecy with which Jesus tried to conduct His mission, forbidding those who knew His identity to tell others.
- Mark portrays the disciples more negatively than the other gospels.
- Mark was probably written around the time of the destruction of Jerusalem (A.D. 70).
- Mark's original audience was probably non-Jewish.

The "Messianic Secret"

A noticeable trait of Mark's gospel is Jesus' consistent effort to keep His identity and activities a secret. For example, He commands those He has healed not to tell anyone who healed them. In Mark 1:43–45, Jesus tells a man healed of leprosy, "Don't tell this to anyone. But go, show yourself to the priest and offer the sacrifices that Moses commanded for your cleansing." Interestingly, none of those Jesus healed obey Him, and soon He finds the crowds around Him so great that He cannot enter a town openly without being mobbed (Mark 1:45).[1]

Yet the hidden feel to Mark's gospel goes well beyond this attempt at secrecy. In Mark, Jesus also keeps His identity as the Messiah very secret. From the very beginning of the gospel, for example, the demons recognize that Jesus is the Holy One of God—a title that may imply that Jesus is a heavenly being as well as an earthly king. But Jesus commands the demons to be silent about His identity, a command they have no choice but to keep.[2]

Two other times Mark's gospel gives us hints that Jesus is not of this earth. One is when He is transfigured and becomes dazzling white (Mark 9:2–10), as if His heavenly identity is finally coming out into the open. As with the demons, the disciples who see this event are commanded not to tell anyone what they have seen until after Jesus rises from the dead (v. 9).

Jesus also hints at His heavenly origin when He stumps the religious leaders on the nature of the Messiah. Jesus points out that King David called the Messiah "Lord." If that is the case, Jesus asks them, how then could the Messiah be David's son? Jesus may imply here that the Messiah is much more than human—He is a heavenly being that existed before David and has come down to earth. Yet in all these cases where Mark hints that Jesus is not an ordinary human being, an air of secrecy prevails.

Matthew, who may have based his gospel presentation on Mark, incorporated many of these elements into his gospel as well. But they are not nearly as noticeable in Matthew. The clandestine feel of Mark, on the other hand, permeates his entire gospel.

Whereas Matthew and Luke mention one sign that Jesus provides for the Jewish people (the sign of the prophet Jonah), Mark quotes Jesus emphatically stating that "no sign will be given to this generation" (Mark 8:12 NRSV)—no exceptions are mentioned. Clearly, Jesus' purpose in using parables is so that those who stand against Him will not understand His message (Mark 4:10–13). Mark does not tell us of Jesus' spectacular birth, as Matthew and Luke do. Even more surprisingly, Mark ends without the news getting out that Jesus is no longer dead.[3] While a young man tells the women who visit Jesus' tomb that He is alive again, "They said nothing to anyone, because they were afraid" (Mark 16:8).

Perhaps the most significant example of Jesus commanding secrecy occurs near the end of His earthly life when Peter finally acknowledges that Jesus is the Messiah, the Christ. Jesus accepts this designation, but then warns His disciples not to tell anyone (Mark 8:30). Because Jesus consistently commands this silence about His identity in Mark, some scholars have called this the "messianic secret."

> **Religious Thinking at the Time of Christ**
>
> - No clear dividing line existed between the "religious" and the "political."
> - The Greeks and Romans worshiped many gods.
> - Mystery religions were prevalent and offered secret knowledge and rituals exclusively to members.
> - The ancients believed a personal force was behind everything that happened.
> - Some Roman emperors demanded to be worshiped.

The hidden, secretive feel to Mark seems too consistent to be a coincidence. The other gospels tell the same events without the same degree of secrecy. There is a message in the way Mark presents these things. A scholar named William Wrede suggested that Mark invented Jesus' claim to be Messiah. Wrede believed that no one actually thought of Jesus as Messiah while He was on earth, so Mark made up the idea that Jesus had kept it a secret.[4]

However, there is good reason to believe not only that Jesus' disciples thought of Him as the Messiah while He was on earth, but that Jesus also viewed himself in these terms. When Jesus appointed twelve disciples, He implied that the nation of Israel was being restored, for there were twelve tribes in Israel. But Jesus did not include himself among the twelve, implying that He placed himself in a different category. The most likely role He would have had in mind was that of king over Israel.[5] The way He entered Jerusalem resembled the procession of a king. Jesus was also crucified with the sign "King of the Jews" hanging above His head. Thus, there is good historical evidence that both Jesus and His followers understood His role in messianic terms.

The Messiah Must Die

On the other hand, the popular Jewish idea of what a Messiah would look like and the reality of what Jesus did look like, were quite different. No Jew expected the royal Messiah to die. Messiahs did not lose—that would prove they were false messiahs. No, the true Messiah would win when He came. He would drive out the Romans from the land of Israel and reestablish the kingdom as it used to be.

However, Mark teaches that Jesus' kingship was demonstrated most emphatically when He died for the sins of His people. When the Roman soldier at the cross sees how Jesus dies, he exclaims: "Truly this man was God's Son" (Mark 15:39, author's translation). After Peter acknowledges that Jesus is the Messiah, Jesus immediately begins to tell the disciples about His coming death (Mark 8:31). In other words, Jesus' death defines what it means to be the Messiah in the gospel of Mark.

Jesus tells His disciples two more times on the way to Jerusalem that He is going to die (Mark 9:31; 10:32–34). Interestingly, in each of these times

---

The Synoptic Question: How Do Matthew, Mark, and Luke Fit Together?

Matthew, Mark, and Luke are called the Synoptic Gospels because their portraits of Jesus are so similar to one another. The synoptic "problem" is that the content, wording, and order of the events they narrate are so similar. The most likely answer to the question is that Matthew and Luke both drew from Mark when creating their gospels.

If Mark is the main source for Matthew and Luke, many think there must have been a second source consisting mostly of Jesus' sayings. Scholars call this second source "Q" from the German word for "source."

---

that Jesus predicts His coming death, the disciples misunderstand His kingship. The very first time Jesus speaks of His death, Peter rebukes Him for what He is saying. After all, the Messiah cannot lose! But Jesus rebukes Peter: "Get away from me, Satan!"

Mark has framed this episode in such a way as to show that while Peter correctly believes Jesus to be the coming king, he misunderstands what being a king is all about. Mark wanted his audience to know that the hallmark of the Messiah was His death for sins, not His military victory—at least in this phase of Jesus' mission. While Mark teaches that Jesus will return as the Son of Man to judge the world in power (Mark 13:26; 14:62), that was not the order of the day while Jesus was on earth.

After Jesus predicts His death again in Mark 9:31, the disciples similarly demonstrate a lack of understanding about Jesus' kingship. This time they argue over who will be the greatest in the new Israel. After the final incident in which Jesus announces His coming death, James and John ask Him if they can have places of authority in the coming political kingdom. The culmination of Jesus' response is His statement that He came to give His life "as a ransom for many" (Mark 10:45). He came to pay the penalty for the sins of God's people.

In Mark's presentation of Jesus, therefore, the heart of Jesus' identity as Messiah comes with His death on the cross for the sins of God's people. This claim radically contradicted the traditional Jewish views of what a messiah would do. Thus, it made sense for Jesus to be somewhat ambiguous and secretive about who He was. To proclaim himself as Messiah certainly would have created a different set of expectations. For most Jews, the claim to be a messiah was a call to arms, not a signal of self-sacrifice.

The Failure of the Disciples

It is important to connect the so-called "messianic secret" of Mark with the failure of Jesus' disciples to understand Him as Messiah. Historically, it was perhaps not so much that they lacked faith in Jesus as that they had the wrong expectations of Him. They seemed prepared to go into battle with a political messiah, but they were caught completely off guard by a suffering messiah. From Mark's perspective, on the other hand, they misunderstood who Jesus was from the very beginning.

Mark's presentation of the disciples is the harshest of all the gospels. As we have already mentioned, each time Jesus announces His coming death, one or more of the disciples display a blatant lack of understanding. First, Peter rebukes Jesus, earning him the response, "Get away from me, Satan!" Next, the disciples argue over who is the greatest among them. Finally, James and John want positions of high honor in the coming kingdom. When the moment of truth comes, they all scatter. Peter denies that he even knows Jesus; and Judas betrays Him, turning Him over to the religious leaders.

But these examples of the disciples' lack of understanding and faith are not the first recorded in Mark. For example, although both Matthew and Luke record the parable of the seeds (Matt. 13; Luke 8), neither of them indicate that Jesus was shocked at the disciples' lack of understanding. In Matthew, when the disciples ask Jesus what the parable means, Jesus says, "Blessed are your eyes because they see, and your ears, because they hear" (13:16).

But Jesus' reaction is much different in Mark: "Don't you understand this parable? How then will you understand any parable?" (4:13). Jesus is shocked because the disciples do not understand a parable whose meaning can only be understood by those who have faith. The implication is startling—could it be true that the disciples do not have faith? Only Mark records this reaction on Jesus' part.

In three boat scenes, the disciples also demonstrate a lack of faith (Mark 4:40; 6:51–52; and 8:17–18). In each case, Mark's presentation is harsher on the disciples than Matthew's or Luke's. In the first instance, for example, Mark's Jesus asks the disciples, "Do you still have no faith?" (Mark 4:40). Matthew's presentation of Jesus points out that they have little faith, rather than no faith at all (Matt. 14:31). Luke's presentation of Jesus just asks them where their faith is (Luke 8:25). The Jesus presented in Mark on the other hand, speaks bluntly of a complete absence of faith.

Mark 6:52 boldly states that the hearts of the disciples were hardened, unreceptive to Him, and that this was the reason they did not believe Jesus could walk on water. Matthew does not draw this conclusion—in fact, Peter tries to walk out to Jesus (Matt. 14:28–31).

Finally, one of Mark's harshest conversations between Jesus and the disciples occurs after He has miraculously fed a great crowd for a second time. Jesus asks the disciples once again if their hearts are still hardened, if they have eyes but cannot see, ears but cannot hear (Mark 8:17–18). While Mark's Jesus ends this scene by asking the question again—"Do you still not understand?"—Matthew ends this story by saying the disciples finally did understand what He was saying (Matt. 16:12).

Mark's gospel thus is more critical of the disciples and their lack of faith than the other gospels. A number of different explanations can be offered. Some think that Mark's gospel reflects the actual regrets of the early disciples and their own sense of failure. Others think Mark's presentation is meant to inspire its audience to succeed where the original disciples failed. Whatever the explanation, the theme of the disciples' failure to understand contributes to the hidden feel of Mark's gospel.

> **The Gospels and Judgment Day**
>
> - In all three Synoptic Gospels, Jesus predicts God's judgment of Israel and the destruction of Jerusalem.
> - Matthew and Mark teach that one day, Jesus will return with angels to judge the world.
> - These two images—judgment day and the destruction of Jerusalem—are often mixed, particularly in Matthew and Mark.
> - According to Luke, there are both good and bad destinations in the afterlife.
> - In all four gospels, Jesus teaches that the dead will one day become alive again, especially the ones God will reward. Luke and John also teach a resurrection that will follow judgment.

The Who's and When's of Mark

As with the gospel of Matthew, the earliest reference to the gospel of Mark comes from the first half of the second century in the writings of the early Christian Papias.[6] In his works, Papias indicated that someone named Mark wrote down stories about the ministry of Jesus, stories he had heard from the apostle Peter. However, Papias noted that Mark did not write down these events in the order in which they happened. Further, he indicated that Peter "adapted his teaching to the situation," which may mean that he told these stories in different ways to serve different audiences.

While Papias claimed to have received his information from a follower of Jesus named John, we are not sure how much of his information came from John and how much was his own thinking. Perhaps he was trying to defend the gospel of Mark against those who thought it was disorganized or out of synch with the gospel of John, which may have been the favorite where Papias lived. Mark's gospel does indeed jump from one event to another without much continuity. It is the shortest gospel of the four and includes the least amount of teaching. It tells us nothing of Jesus before John the Baptist and does not record any of Jesus' resurrection appearances. One could understand why Papias saw Mark as a somewhat random collection of short stories about Jesus.

From the oldest evidence we have available, the church has believed that the author of this gospel was John Mark, the same Mark who in Acts traveled briefly with Paul and who also seems to have been a traveling companion of Peter. This tradition about Mark traces all the way back to a man who had actually known Jesus, a man named John. Since the gospel is technically anonymous, however, we should probably be careful not to superimpose our idea of its authorship into its words.

As with Matthew, a few things about the situation in which the gospel was written can be gleaned from clues scattered here and there in Mark. For example, when some Pharisees ask Jesus why His disciples do not wash their hands before they eat, Mark explains that "the Pharisees and all the Jews do not eat unless they give their hands a ceremonial washing, holding to the tradition of the elders. When they come from the marketplace they do not eat unless they wash. And they observe many other traditions . . ." (Mark 7:3–4). While Matthew also recorded this event, he did not feel the need to explain Jewish practice. After all, Matthew's gospel was written to Jews who would know such things. Mark's explanation, therefore, probably means that his gospel was written to non-Jews or Gentiles.

There is another parenthetical comment in Mark that might clue us in on when the gospel was written. In Mark 13 Jesus responds to a question from His disciples concerning when God will destroy the Jerusalem temple in judgment, an event that took place in A.D. 70. Jesus warns of something He calls the "abomination that causes desolation." Whatever this horrible thing was, it would be placed somewhere it should not be (Mark 13:14). At this point in Jesus' speech, the author of Mark interrupts with a warning: "Let the reader understand." The author may have wanted those who heard the gospel to realize that the events about which Jesus spoke were in the process of taking place.

Many of the events in Mark 13 did take place in the years surrounding the Jewish War (A.D. 66–73). Roman soldiers sacrificed to some of their gods within the confines of the Jewish temple, desecrating it. Jerusalem and the temple were destroyed. An old tradition holds that the Christians of Jerusalem fled the city just before it was destroyed (Mark 13:14–18). Indeed, Luke's version is worded in such a way that one can visualize the Roman armies surrounding the city of Jerusalem (Luke 21:20–24). While we cannot be absolutely certain, it seems quite possible that Mark was written some time in the early part of the Jewish War, A.D. 66–70.

Questions for Study and Discussion

1. In what way was Jesus' death on a cross a victory for God's people?
2. Why do you think Jesus would want to keep His identity as Messiah a secret from the crowds?

The Beginnings of Jesus' Mission

The Gospel of Luke

Luke and Acts claim that God has brought salvation
to the whole world through Jesus.

The Certainty of Things

Luke and Acts are two parts of the same work. Acts begins where the gospel of Luke leaves off. Both books have the same author, audience, themes, and general perspective. While Luke presents the things Jesus "began to do and to teach until the day he was taken up to heaven" (Acts 1:1–2), Acts presents the things Jesus continued to do through His Spirit-empowered disciples. For this reason, scholars often refer to them both as a single work: Luke-Acts.

> **At a Glance**
> - The gospel of Luke is the first of a two-volume history written to demonstrate the certainty of Christianity.
> - Luke teaches that the salvation Jesus brings is for all peoples, and that God always planned to bring salvation in this way.
> - Luke emphasizes Jesus' ministry to the poor, to women, and to the oppressed.
> - Luke highlights the role of prayer and the Holy Spirit in Jesus' ministry.
> - Luke was probably written several years after the Romans destroyed Jerusalem.

Many believe that these books fit best in the genre of ancient historical writing. They may even be classified as general history, a special kind of history that traces the origins of a race or people. Others think that Luke by itself still comes closest in genre to ancient biography.

Luke actually gives us a general sense of its purpose: "It seemed good also to me to write an orderly account for you . . . so that you may know the certainty of the things you have been taught" (Luke 1:3–4). In a way, Luke and Acts together are a defense of Christianity. What exactly do they defend? They defend the claim that as part of His plan, God has now brought salvation to the whole world through Jesus.

For Israel, this salvation seems to include its restoration as a nation, with deliverance from its political enemies (Luke 1:68–75; Acts 1:6). It also means bringing back into the fold those in Israel who have not been keeping the covenant, like prostitutes and or tax collectors (e.g., Luke 15). God also gives full place to society's downtrodden, like the poor, women, and widows (Luke 8:3; Acts 6:1–6). Finally, God restores those who are physically impaired, like the blind and the lame (Luke 14:13; Acts 3:1–10), as well as those who spiritually are under the control of Satan. All these aspects of salvation are God's doing, leaving a strong warning to anyone who might oppose Jesus' followers: "If it is from God, you will not be able to stop these men; you will only find yourselves fighting against God" (Acts 5:39).

Salvation for the Whole World

In Luke's account, after Jesus is born, His parents bring Him to the temple to present Him to the Lord. While they are there, a man named Simeon blesses the baby Jesus and joyfully expresses what has come to be known as Simeon's song. This hymn reflects several key themes in Luke-Acts. It emphasizes that Jesus brings salvation to the whole world. For Israel, this salvation seems to mean an escape from its political enemies (e.g., Luke 1:71). After Jesus rises from the dead, His disciples ask if He will now restore the kingdom to Israel. Interestingly, His answer is not that the disciples have misunderstood His mission; rather His answer is more like a "not yet" (Acts 1:6–7).

This salvation is unifying. For Israel, it means bringing back into the fold many who have been like lost sheep. In the well-known parable of the prodigal son in Luke 15, Jesus compares the tax collectors, prostitutes, and other notorious sinners of his day to a son who abandons and shames his father, treating him as if he were dead. When this son returns to his father and begs forgiveness, the father welcomes him back. So God was now recklessly welcoming back into Israel those who had lost their way.

However, an older brother finds God's forgiveness extremely unfair, since he has stayed and worked faithfully for the father his whole life. This brother represents the Pharisees and those in Israel who had actually tried to keep the covenant. Ironically, they also ended up shaming their heavenly Father by rejecting His plan and desires. By the end of Jesus' mission, many of those outside the kingdom had come back in, while many that were trying to keep the Law lost out.

Simeon's song affirms that salvation is universal; it is for everyone. Jesus is a "light for revelation to the Gentiles." The gospel of Luke does not give us the impression that Jesus focused exclusively on Israel during His earthly mission. Luke does not tell the story of Jesus calling a foreign woman a dog and His hesitating to heal her daughter because she was not an Israelite (Matt. 15:21–28; Mark 7:24–30). On the contrary, in addition to the mission of the twelve disciples to Israel, Luke includes a mission of seventy-two individuals, a number that symbolized all the nations of the world.[1] Luke includes positive material about Samaritans (Luke 10:25–37) and shows Jesus trying to minister to Samaritans (9:51–56; 17:11–19), unlike the impression we get in Matthew 10:5. Also unlike Matthew, Luke presents Jesus' genealogy all the way back to Adam, the father of all people (Luke 3:23–38). Matthew starts with Abraham, the father of the Jewish race (Matt. 1:1–17).

In keeping with the universal focus of Luke, the message of Acts verifies that the gospel is for everyone. The key verse of Acts says that the disciples will be witnesses to Jesus' resurrection all over the world (Acts 1:8). While Jewish Christians continued to keep the Jewish Law to a great degree (e.g.,

Acts 21:24), Acts makes it clear that Gentile Christians were in no way inferior to them. God had put no distinction between the two because He had given the Holy Spirit to both equally (Acts 15:9).

A final aspect of Simeon's song that reflects Luke's perspective is the belief that God had planned this salvation from the very beginning. Luke has a strong sense that God is in control of the world and that the events that happen are all a part of His plan. In the sermons of Acts especially, the disciples make it clear that Jesus' death was not a victory for His earthly opponents. Rather, God himself was bringing about what He had promised in the Old Testament.

> ### Stories of Jesus' Birth
>
> Matthew and Luke are the two gospels that present the story of Jesus' birth. Both gospels agree that Jesus was born to Mary before she had sex with any man (the virgin birth) and that Jesus was born in Bethlehem.
>
> There are differences in the way each writer tells the story of Jesus' birth. Matthew presents it from the standpoint of His royalty and portrays Him as a new Moses. Luke presents Jesus' birth in a way that identifies Him with the lowly and the downtrodden.

Some have suggested that Luke paints a more human picture of Jesus than some of the other gospels. For example, several times Luke calls Jesus a prophet (e.g., Luke 7:16; Acts 7:37) and even describes him as a "man accredited by God to you by miracles, wonders, and signs" (Acts 2:22). Interestingly, while Luke's gospel tells us that Jesus was born of Mary while she was still a virgin (Luke 1:34), Luke gives us little indication that Jesus had existed before His birth. Acts claims that Jesus became Lord and Messiah most meaningfully after He rose from the dead (Acts 2:36; 13:33). This aspect of Luke reminds us why the church believes that Jesus is not only fully God, but fully man as well.

Good News for the Poor and the Oppressed

Luke's presentation of Jesus' ministry begins in His hometown of Nazareth. A sermon in Jesus' home synagogue sets the tone for the rest of His ministry, as if it were a kind of inaugural address. Picking up the scroll of Isaiah, Jesus reads this Scripture:

"The Spirit of the Lord is upon me, for he has anointed me to preach Good News to the poor. He has sent me to proclaim that captives will be released, that the blind will see, that the downtrodden will be freed from their oppressors, and that the time of the Lord's favor has come" (Luke 4:18–19 NLT, quoting Isa. 61:1–2).

Jesus' ministry to the poor and those on the edges of society is one of the main emphases of Luke-Acts. When John the Baptist sends his disciples to Jesus to confirm that He is the Messiah, Jesus proves so by pointing out these same things: He is giving sight to the blind, preaching good news to the poor, and raising the dead (Luke 7:18–23). Jesus' salvation brings a wholeness to those who are physically, spiritually, and socially broken.

There are significant differences between what it meant to be poor in the ancient world and what it means today. Basically, poverty in an agrarian society like ancient Israel was not so much about a lack of money as about being knocked off track from one's inherited place in society. If you lost the land on which your ancestors had lived for generations, if you had to sell yourself into slavery to pay debts, if you were dependent on others for the basic resources of living—this was being poor. Being poor was not necessarily about losing money, since the exchange of goods (trade) was more typical of buying and selling than the exchange of coins.

Since poverty involved a lack of goods, many thought of rich people as thieves or the descendants of thieves. After all, the rich were the ones who received these goods from those who lost them. Today we don't usually connect one person's prosperity with another's loss; however, the ancient world had a sense of "limited good." In a world with only so many apples to go around, the only way to get more was to take someone else's apples.

In general the New Testament has almost nothing positive to say about money and the rich, but Luke's presentation of Jesus is especially negative toward the rich. While Matthew's version of the Beatitudes says, "Blessed are the poor in spirit"—those who have an attitude of dependence on God (Matt. 5:3)—Luke states bluntly, "Blessed are you who are poor" (Luke 6:20). And in Luke, Jesus goes on to say, "Woe to you who are rich" (Luke 6:24). It is Luke that tells the parable of a rich man and a poor beggar named Lazarus (Luke 16:19–31). In this story the rich man dies and wakes up in a place of fiery torment, while God greatly rewards Lazarus in paradise. When Acts describes the earliest Christians, it says, "There were no needy persons among them. For from time to time those who owned lands or houses sold them, brought the money from the sales and put it at the apostles' feet, and it was distributed to anyone as he had need" (Acts 4:34–35). In other words, they were the exact opposite of the rich, who took land and houses from others, making them poor.

In some of the passages we have just mentioned, Luke mentions the physically impaired, such as the blind or the lame, along with the poor. He associated both kinds of individuals in his mind. Luke joins the other gospels in presenting Jesus as a healer of such people. As in the other gospels, Jesus also casts out demons. In Acts, the early Christians continue Jesus' ministry along these same lines. Through the power of the Holy Spirit, they also heal the impaired and cast out demons.

We have already mentioned how Jesus welcomes the disenfranchised of Israel back into the fold in Luke. Luke also has an emphasis on those that ancient Jewish society often neglected, people like Samaritans and women. Women are so noticeably present in Luke's gospel that some scholars have wondered if the author of Luke-Acts was actually a woman.

Luke is the only gospel, for example, that mentions the women who support Jesus' ministry from their own means, including a woman who manages the household of Herod Antipas (Luke 8:1–3). Acts also mentions women of high status, like Lydia, a seller of expensive purple cloth (Acts 16:14) and the prominent women of Berea (Acts 17:12). Luke tells us about Jesus' stay in the home of two women, Mary and Martha (Luke 10:38–42); and Luke's presentation of Jesus' birth is oriented around His mother, Mary.

The Samaritans were another Jewish group on the edge of society in the first century. In Luke, Jesus is seen rebuking James and John for wanting to pray down fire on a Samaritan village (Luke 9:54). Luke gives us the impression that many of the seventy-two disciples Jesus sends out actually go to the villages of Samaria. And Luke is the only gospel that gives us the parable of the good Samaritan. All these aspects of Luke's presentation emphasize that the salvation Jesus brings is truly for all.

The Power of Prayer and the Holy Spirit

A final feature of Luke-Acts is the emphasis on prayer and the power of the Holy Spirit in the lives of Jesus and the apostles. For example, Luke is the only gospel that tells us Jesus is praying when the Holy Spirit descends on Him at the Jordan River (Luke 3:21). While the other gospels record this event, they do not mention the prayer. The same is true of Jesus' transfiguration; only Luke mentions that Jesus goes up the mountain to pray and is transformed while He is praying (Luke 9:28–29).

Luke also includes unique teaching on prayer that is missing from the other gospels. Luke is the only gospel to tell the parable of the persistent widow, the story of a widow who keeps bothering a judge until he finally provides her with justice (Luke 18:1–8). In the same way, Luke says God will answer the continuing Israelite prayer for justice. And only Luke tells the parable of the Pharisee and the tax collector (18:9–14). The Pharisee prays boastfully in order to be seen and heard by others; the tax collector is truly repentant and does not even lift his eyes.[2]

> ### Money and Power in the Ancient World
>
> - The Romans were the ultimate political power in the Mediterranean world.
> - They ruled Palestine by way of "client kings" or Roman governors.
> - The Sanhedrin also had a great deal of authority over Jerusalem and its surrounding region.
> - Society functioned on the basis of informal patron-client relationships: the "haves" took care of the "have nots" in return for the prestige the "haves" received.
> - Most individuals preferred to trade goods rather than exchange coins or money for them.
> - Ancients operated under the idea of limited good—if one person had more, then someone else must have less.

In Acts especially, the Holy Spirit is the power behind everything the apostles do. But the Holy Spirit similarly empowers Jesus to do miracles in Luke (Acts 10:38). As in the other gospels, Jesus' ministry really does not start until after the Spirit descends on Him at His baptism (Matt. 3:16; Mark 1:10; Luke 3:22). But Luke is the one that points out He was "full of the Holy Spirit" (Luke 4:1) and "in the power of the Spirit" (4:14) as a result. These glimpses of the Holy Spirit in Luke will take main stage in Acts.

The Who's and When's of Luke-Acts

As with Matthew and Mark, the gospel of Luke is technically anonymous. However, Christianity has never associated this gospel with any other author but Luke, a physician who sometimes accompanied Paul (cf. Col. 4:14; 2 Tim. 4:11). Certain passages from Acts give the impression that its author traveled with Paul (e.g., Acts 16:10; 20:6), and Luke's name must rank high on the list of possibilities. Nonetheless, various scholars have also suggested that at these points of the story the author of Luke-Acts was relying on someone else's travel diary or even that Acts is a novel not meant to be taken historically.

Both Luke and Acts are addressed to someone named Theophilus. This name is so uncommon in the ancient world that some have suggested it does not refer to a real person. The name Theophilus means "lover of God," which could suggest that Luke was writing to all who love God. However, the way the author of Luke-Acts refers to Theophilus is also similar to the way ancient authors dedicated their writings to the patron who sponsored and funded their work. If Theophilus was a real person, therefore, he was probably the one who funded the writing of Luke-Acts.

Jesus and the Downtrodden

More than any other gospel, Luke focuses on the good news Jesus' mission brought to the disenfranchised and downtrodden of Israel:

- Jesus offered good news to the poor and oppressed of society.
- Jesus welcomed women and Samaritans into the restored kingdom of Israel.
- Jesus cast out demons and healed the sick, making the benefactors whole members of Israel.

The church has traditionally believed that Luke was a Gentile; in fact, the only non-Jewish writer in the New Testament (cf. Col. 4:11–14). If the author was not Luke, it could have been a Greek-speaking Jew. Luke-Acts is striking in its implications that Jewish Christians must continue to keep the Jewish Law (cf. Luke 1:6; Acts 13:39; 21:21–24), as well as the central role it gives to the Jerusalem temple. The intended audience was probably a mixture of both Jews and Gentiles, although the focus on Gentiles in the gospel and Acts might suggest that it was primarily Gentile. Also noticeable in Luke is the use of the term *Savior* (e.g., Luke 2:11). Greeks and Romans, rather than Jews, tended to use this Greek term.

We can say with great probability that Luke-Acts was written after the destruction of the Jerusalem temple in A.D. 70. Some have argued that the author wrote Acts (and therefore Luke) in about A.D. 62 because Acts ends in Rome without telling us the outcome of Paul's trial before Nero. If Luke wrote Acts so much later, the argument goes, why did he stop so abruptly? But while we are curious about the outcome of Paul's trial, Luke's audience likely knew such information already.

The strongest evidence that Luke-Acts was written after the destruction of the temple comes from a comparison of the way Luke presents Jesus' prediction of Jerusalem's destruction to Matthew's and Mark's predictions. For example, Mark warns: "When you see the desolating sacrilege set up where it ought not to be (let the reader understand), then those in Judea must flee to the mountains" (Mark 13:14 NRSV). Perhaps written during the Jewish War of A.D. 66–73, this statement is somewhat cryptic.

Luke's version of this prophecy, however, is worded vividly: "When you see Jerusalem surrounded by armies, then know that its desolation has come near" (Luke 21:20 NRSV). Given that Luke probably drew from Mark, it is difficult to explain why Luke is so clear and Mark so vague, unless Luke wrote after the events had taken place. He took an indistinct prophecy and gave it the depth of hindsight (cf. the similar drama of Luke 19:43–44).

Questions for Study and Discussion

1. What kind of person would you classify as a Samaritan today—someone you would find the hardest to love as your neighbor? Someone of a different race? A homosexual? A serial killer? Reread the parable of the good Samaritan with this type of person in mind.

2. Some Christians oppose the idea of helping today's poor, even though our poor are often in far more dire straits than even the poor of the first century. What do you think Jesus would say about the attitude of modern churches toward our society's marginal people?

3. How does Luke's presentation of Jesus in relation to Samaritans and Gentiles compare to Matthew's? Can you explain the difference in orientation on the basis of author and audience?

Stories Jesus Told

The Parables

The kingdom of God is about God ruling on earth—in the hearts of His people today, in the person of His Christ tomorrow.

Ears to Hear

The primary method Jesus used to teach the crowds in the countryside was storytelling. He taught in *parables*, a word that can also mean *riddles*. An older definition of a parable is "an earthly story with a heavenly meaning"—in other words, a story told in terms of everyday life in order to teach something about God, heaven, or something of a spiritual nature. Some have even taken Jesus' use of stories as a model for how to preach. The assumption is that Jesus taught in stories so that the crowds could better understand His message.

At a Glance

- A parable is much more like a riddle than a teaching tool used to make the message clearer.

- At least in part, Jesus taught in parables to screen the understanding of His audience.

- Some of Jesus' parables relate to the varying reactions to His message. Some who were on the outskirts of Israel were reclaimed; others who had kept the Law now found themselves out of God's favor.

- Several parables, notably in Matthew, deal with the judgment of all, especially followers of Jesus who are unworthy.

- Several parables in Luke deal with topics like prayer and money.

We can imagine that this comprises one aspect of Jesus' storytelling, but Matthew, Mark, and Luke highlight a much different reason for Jesus to speak in parables.[1] They present Jesus' parable of the seeds as the key to understanding all of His parables (Matt. 13:3–9; Mark 4:3–8; Luke 8:5–8). In this story, Jesus tells how a farmer's seed lands on four different kinds of soil. Some seed falls on the path and is eaten by birds. Some falls on rocky ground and is scorched by the sun. Some falls among thorns and is choked. Only a portion of the seed falls on soil good enough for the seed to grow and produce a harvest.

This parable illustrates the fact that not everyone will accept Jesus' message about the kingdom of God. In fact, only those who "have ears to hear" will even understand it. Jesus goes on to tell His disciples why He speaks in parables: "You are permitted to understand the secret about the Kingdom of God. But I am using these stories to conceal everything about it from outsiders, so that the Scriptures might be fulfilled: 'They see what I do, but they don't perceive its meaning. They hear my words, but they don't understand'" (Mark 4:11–12 NLT).

Matthew, Mark, and Luke make the astonishing claim that Jesus spoke in parables, not to make His message clearer—at least not to most of His audience. He spoke in riddles to obscure His message to those whose hearts were not truly oriented to the kingdom. No wonder Jesus is astonished that His own disciples do not understand the parable of the seeds. "How then will you understand any parable?" he asks them (Mark 4:13). In keeping with the hidden feel of Mark's presentation, he notes that Jesus "did not say anything to them [the crowds] without using a parable" (Mark 4:34).

The Kingdom of God

Jesus' parables teach about many different topics. Several of Matthew's parables deal with God's judgment of humanity. A number of the parables found in Luke are about issues such as prayer and money. Still others tell what the kingdom of God is like.

Mark 1:15 tells us that Jesus' primary message to Israel was about the kingdom of God. Scholars have debated for years what Jesus meant by this phrase. Was He talking about something still to come in the future, or did the kingdom of God begin while Jesus was on earth? Was Jesus referring to a spiritual kingdom among Christians here on earth now, or did He mean a kingdom in heaven that awaits us when we die? Still others think Jesus referred to the political restoration of Israel or the kingdom He would set up after He returned to earth in apocalyptic glory.

What makes the issue so complicated is that almost every one of these positions can find support from one passage or another in the Gospels. While Jesus looked forward to God's kingdom in many respects, in other respects He saw himself as inaugurating the kingdom on earth. Perhaps the Lord's Prayer captures it best when it says in reference to God, "your kingdom come, your will be done on earth as it is in heaven" (Matt. 6:10). The kingdom of God is about God ruling on earth—today in the hearts of His people; tomorrow in the person of His Christ.

One of the parables that best captures this understanding of the kingdom is the parable of the mustard seed (Matt. 13:31–32; Mark 4:30–32; Luke 13:18–19). In this parable, Jesus compares the kingdom of God to a mustard seed, one of the smallest of seeds. While the mustard seed starts out small, it grows to be a disproportionately large plant. So, Jesus implies that the kingdom of God starts small, but in the end will manifest itself throughout the entire world.

Parables of Israel

It is easy for Bible readers today to lose sight of the fact that Jesus was a Jew and that He directed His message to ancient Israel. This audience stands behind a number of stories often taken out of context by modern readers.

In the short parable of the two sons (Matt. 21:28–32), Jesus compares those in His audience to two sons whose father tells them to go work in his vineyard. One son says he will, but does not. The other, who initially says he will not work, changes his mind.

The Parables of Jesus

Parable about Parables
The parable of the seeds (Matt. 13:3–9; Mark 4:3–8; Luke 8:5–8)

Parables of the Kingdom
The parable of the mustard seed (Matt. 13:31–32; Mark 4:30–32; Luke 13:18–19)

The parable of the yeast (Matt. 13:33; Luke 13:20–21)

The parable of the growing seed (Mark 4:26–29)

The parable of the treasure (Matt. 13:44)

The parable of the pearl (Matt. 13:45–46)

Parables of Israel
The parable of the lost sheep (Matt. 18:12–14; Luke 15:3–7)

The parable of the lost coin (Luke 15:8–10)

The parable of the lost son (Luke 15:11–32)

The parable of the unforgiving servant (Matt. 18:21–35)

The parable of the day laborers (Matt. 20:1–16)

The parable of the two sons (Matt. 21:28–32)

The parable of the tenants (Matt. 21:33–46; Mark 12:1–12; Luke 20:9–19)

The parable of the wedding banquet and the great banquet (Matt. 22:1–14; Luke 14:15–24)

Parables of Judgment
The parable of the weeds (Matt. 13:24–30)

The parable of the net (Matt. 13:47–51)

The parable of the ten virgins (Matt. 25:1–13)

The parable of the talents or ten minas (Matt. 25:14–30; Luke 19:11–27)

The parable of the sheep and the goats (Matt. 25:31–46)

Parables of Kingdom Values
The parable of the good Samaritan (Luke 10:25–37)

The parable of the persistent widow (Luke 18:1–8)

The parable of the rich fool (Luke 12:13–21)

The parable of the Pharisee and the tax collector (Luke 18:9–14)

The parable of the shrewd manager (Luke 16:1–13)

The parable of the rich man and Lazarus (Luke 16:19–31)

These two sons were like those in Israel who heard Jesus' message. The tax collectors and prostitutes were like those who said they would not keep Israel's covenant with Yahweh. But then they accepted Jesus' message and repented. While they initially said they would not work in God's vineyard, they did in the end. On the other hand, the chief priests, elders, and Pharisees who were questioning Jesus were like those who said they would work but then did not. While such individuals had previously made an effort to keep the Jewish covenant, they rejected what God was doing through Jesus.

Several variations of this basic message can be found in other parables. In the parable of the lost (prodigal) son (Luke 15:11–32), for example, the one son prematurely asks for his inheritance, treating his father as if he were dead.[2] Then he turns his back on Israel and his home, living it up in a foreign land. But after he reaches rock bottom and returns to his father, he is wholeheartedly welcomed back.

Meanwhile, an elder brother who has remained faithful his whole life resents the almost shameful forgiveness his father shows toward his younger brother. This brother, like the son who said he would work but did not, ends up shaming his father when he refuses to join in the celebration over the lost son's return. Like the Pharisees who had tried to remain faithful to God's covenant, the elder brother loses out in the end because he does not honor his father's wishes.

In the parable of the day laborers (Matt. 20:1–16), a landowner agrees to pay workers a denarius to work for a day. At various times during the day, the landowner hires more workers, each time promising the same wage. At the end of the day, those who have worked all day grumble because they receive the same pay as those who have only worked for an hour. So God welcomes the sinners of Israel back into His covenant alongside those like the Pharisees who never stopped keeping the Law.

Two very similar parables about a banquet occur in Matthew and Luke: the parable of the wedding banquet (Matt. 22:1–14) and the parable of the great banquet (Luke 14:15–24). In both parables, a certain person throws a banquet. In both stories, those who were initially invited do not come. In both cases, less likely individuals are given an invitation. In keeping with Luke's emphasis on the poor and downtrodden of Israel, "the poor, the crippled, the blind and the lame" are invited (Luke 14:21). In keeping with Matthew's understanding of the church as a mixture of both true and false followers of Jesus, the servants of the king bring both good and bad individuals to the banquet

(Matt. 22:10). Those who are not properly "dressed" are cast out into the darkness (Matt. 22:11–13). Once again, those initially invited were probably those in Israel who were trying to keep the Jewish Law, God's covenant with Israel. Since they refused God's invitation through Jesus, however, God turned instead to less likely guests like the disenfranchised of Israel.

The parable of the tenants (Matt. 21:33–46; Mark 12:1–12; Luke 20:9–19) makes a good transition to the next group of parables. In this parable, a landowner goes away for some time and leaves his land in the hands of some farmers. When the landowner sends for some of the crop, his servants meet opposition and even death. Finally, the landowner sends his own son, hoping they will listen to him. Instead, they kill him because he is the heir.

The landowner's anger is understandable under such circumstances, and the Gospels liken such a situation to the way in which the Jewish religious authorities rejected and then killed Jesus, God's Son. As such, God would judge Israel for its rejection of Jesus, a judgment that came most significantly in A.D. 70 when the Romans destroyed Jerusalem and its temple.

Parables of Judgment

Jesus' parables of judgment both echo the message Jesus took over from John the Baptist and spell out the fate of those who reject His message. Matthew in particular has a number of parables about the final judgment of the whole world, not just the judgment of Israel. Most of these parables are oriented around the time between Christ's resurrection and His final return.

In the parable of the weeds (Matt. 13:24–30; 36–43), a farmer finds that both good seed and weeds are growing together in his field, much as servants of the king (in the parable of the wedding feast) had invited both good and bad to the feast. The farmer instructs his servants to wait until the harvest, at which time God's angels will "weed out" the kingdom of heaven and throw the unworthy into hell. The implication would seem to be that the church includes both genuine and false followers of Jesus. On the day of judgment, God will show who are truly His and who are not.

The parable of the sheep and the goats (Matt. 25:31–46) has the same basic message, although the focus is more on the whole world than the church. On the day of judgment, God will separate the sheep from the goats, largely on the basis of how each has treated those who are downtrodden in life—those without food, water, and clothing.

Two other parables focus on readiness for Christ's return and on what we are doing in the meantime. The parable of the ten virgins (Matt. 25:1–13) contrasts two groups of bridesmaids: those who keep enough oil in their lamps in order to see the bridegroom when he arrives, and those who do not. This parable again relates best to Jesus' followers. While all followers of Jesus appear to await His coming, some evidently will be rejected when He comes.

The parable of the talents or ten minas (Matt. 25:14–30; Luke 19:11–27) tells about a king that goes on a trip, leaving three of his servants with varying amounts of money. The first two servants use the king's money to make more money for him. The third is so scared of the king that he buries it (Matthew) or hides it in a cloth (Luke). The king is very angry with the servant who has done nothing with the money he gave him. So the king decides to give the money in his charge to the servant who gained the most interest for his master. The implication is that God expects His servants to have made gains for His kingdom (perhaps converts) by the time He returns.

Parables of Kingdom Values

A final category of Jesus' parables deals with various aspects of living. Whom am I supposed to love in this world? How should I pray? What should my attitude be toward wealth and poverty? The gospel of Luke especially presents us with parables on such topics.

The parable of the good Samaritan in Luke 10 (vs. 25–37) deals with the question of whom we are to love and how. In context, Jesus notes that the whole of the Jewish Law can be summarized as: Love God and love your neighbor. This statement leads to the question, "Who is my neighbor?" Jesus answers with this parable.

A traveler was mugged on his way from Jerusalem to the village of Jericho. As he lay there, both a priest and a Levite (someone of priestly descent) passed by but did nothing to help the traveler. Finally, a Samaritan helped the man and took him to a place of shelter.

Since many Jews at this time looked down on Samaritans as half-breeds and did not include them in Israel, Jesus' answer would seem to be: "Everyone is your neighbor, including those you despise. You are to love everyone."

In keeping with Luke's interest in prayer, it is not surprising that he gives us some parables on how to pray. In the parable of the Pharisee and the tax collector (Luke 18:9–14), we learn that one needs to pray with a humble attitude in order to be heard. A tax collector who prays with an attitude of dependence on God finds favor, while a Pharisee who boasts about how he has kept the Law finds God's rejection.

In the parable of the persistent widow (Luke 18:1–8), Luke teaches that persistence in prayer pays off, like a widow who bugged a judge so much that he finally gave her justice. It is possible that this parable also originally had political connotations.

Other parables fit in with Luke's focus on the poor and his correspondingly negative attitude toward money and wealth. In the parable of the rich fool (Luke 12:13–21), Jesus tells of a foolhardy man who makes a lot of plans to use his wealth and then dies before he can carry them out. Jesus encourages us to live in submission to what He has planned for our lives rather than what we might plan.

In the parable of the rich man and Lazarus (Luke 16:19–31), Luke contrasts a beggar with a rich man. While the rich man enjoyed his time on earth, he finds himself in reversed circumstances after death. The implication is that those who enjoy their money in this life (while allowing the poor to continue in abject need) will suffer in the afterlife.

Finally, one of the parables most difficult to understand is also about money: the parable of the shrewd manager (Luke 16:1–13). In this parable, a manager has misused his master's possessions. As he faces the loss of his master's patronage, he shrewdly does favors for the people who owe his master money—he reduces their debt. The rich man then salutes his manager for his cleverness. Jesus concludes that his followers should also "use your worldly resources to benefit others and make friends" (Luke 16:9 NLT).

While to us Jesus may seem to applaud this servant for his dishonesty and stealing, the parable probably reflects Luke's sense that money in and of itself is morally negative and that the appropriate thing to do with money is to give it away. In fact, the key to the parable may be Luke's implication that the rich will be judged by how they use their wealth (Luke 16:11). To pass the test, you must give the resources in your control to those who are in need.

Questions for Study and Discussion

1. Do you think that Jesus' parables made His message clearer or more difficult to understand? To whom did they make His message clearer and to whom did they make it harder to understand? Why would Jesus want to make His message hard for some individuals to understand?

2. If the kingdom of God was about God's rule returning to the earth, is the kingdom already here? If so, in what way? Is the kingdom still to come? If so, in what way? Is the kingdom both here and yet to come? If so, in what ways?

3. What can we learn of Israel's restoration from Jesus' message? Was its restoration fulfilled in 1948 when Israel became a nation again? Did God reject Israel as a nation forever because of its failure to accept Jesus and the early Christians? Can you find a spiritual meaning in Jesus' message to Israel?

4. Many Christians believe that God's sense of justice demands that someone must pay the penalty for every human wrongdoing, as well as pay back every debt. Can you find this picture of God in these parables? Does God ever just forgive without demanding someone pay a debt or incur a punishment? In the parables, do some individuals have more for God to forgive than others—is the amount of God's grace equal toward all individuals?

Jesus, the Way

The Gospel of John

John wants us to know that when we are looking at Jesus,
we are seeing nothing less than God's presence among us.

The gospel of John differs strikingly from Matthew, Mark, and Luke. For example, it has no parables, no exorcisms, no commands of silence concerning Jesus' identity, and little mention of the kingdom of God—all things that are featured prominently in the other gospels. Many of the stories in John do not appear in Matthew, Mark, and Luke. In fact, even when John does present events that appear in the others, he usually tells them in a substantially different way. For this reason, some early Christians considered John to be a "spiritual" gospel. It was more a picture of Jesus' spiritual significance

At a Glance

- The gospel of John does not record any exorcisms, parables, nor any commands of silence concerning Jesus' identity. And it differs in many other ways from the Synoptic Gospels.
- The purpose of John is to lead its audience to faith in who Jesus is and what He has done. It emphasizes that believing only in Jesus is what frees you from condemnation.
- John presents Jesus as one who came down from heaven, God's Word in human form.
- John is filled with "I am" statements that point out Jesus' spiritual significance.
- John, the son of Zebedee, is the traditional author, although a certain "John the elder" has some claim as well. The gospel is technically anonymous.

than a presentation of how He would have appeared to those who first saw and heard Him.

Differences between John and the Other Gospels

We have already mentioned some of the ways John differs from Matthew, Mark, and Luke. For example, while Mark 4:34 says that Jesus "did not say anything to them without using a parable," Jesus tells no parables in John. While the casting out of demons portrayed in Matthew, Mark, and Luke signals the fact that the kingdom of God is arriving on earth (e.g., Luke 11:20), Jesus performs no exorcisms in John and scarcely mentions the kingdom of God. On the other hand, the other gospels indicate that the kingdom of God is the essence of what Jesus preached (Matt. 4:23; Mark 1:14–15; Luke 4:43).

Another difference between John and the other gospels is how open Jesus is about His identity. In Matthew, Mark, and Luke, Jesus commands the demons and His disciples to be silent about the fact that He is the Messiah (e.g., Mark 1:34; 8:30). In John, Jesus not only proclaims openly that He is the Messiah, He publicly claims to be from heaven, someone who existed in heaven before He was born (e.g., John 8:23–24, 58; 10:22–39). Matthew, Mark, and Luke give only the barest hints that Jesus is a heavenly being. And while in Mark Jesus flatly states that He will give no signs to the people of that day (Mark 8:12), the gospel of John is filled with the signs Jesus provides. In fact, John states that "Jesus did many other miraculous signs in the presence of his disciples, which are not recorded in this book" (John 20:30).

Jesus appears much less human in John than He does in the other gospels. John presents little of Jesus' human struggles and tends to avoid anything that might make Jesus appear weak or less than superhuman in any way. In Luke, for example, Jesus sweats drops of blood under the pressure of His coming death (Luke 22:44). In Mark, He asks God if it is possible for Him to avoid death (Mark 14:35–36)—He would rather not "drink the cup" that has been given to Him. But in John, Jesus says He will not ask to escape His coming death (John 12:27; 18:11). When they come to arrest Him, the soldiers fall to the ground at the power of Jesus' presence (John 18:6).

In the other gospels, the words Jesus says on the cross differ distinctly from what is recorded in John. Matthew and Mark record Jesus crying out in anguish: "My God, my God, why have you abandoned me?" (Matt. 27:46; Mark 15:34, author's translation). In John, however, Jesus victoriously says, "It is finished" (John 19:30), and then hands over His spirit to God. More than any of the other gospels, John emphasizes that Jesus is in control of everything that is going on during His trial and crucifixion.

What do we make of these differences? Even if we believe John's presentation can fit together with that of Matthew, Mark, and Luke in some way historically, John still has a much different feel to it than the others. Some have completely rejected the gospel of John as unhistorical for this reason. Others try to account for the differences by supposing that John simply did not want to paint the same picture of Jesus all over again, but instead wanted to record events omitted from the other gospels. Indeed, the church has long believed that the gospel of John was written last and perhaps even long after the other gospels had appeared. Whichever position one takes, John gives us a picture of Christ the way Christians eventually came to see Him—a presentation of Jesus in hindsight as He really was, even if some did not fully recognize Him at the time.

Why John Was Written

The gospel of John helpfully states why it was written. Although Jesus provided countless signs that showed who He truly was, the ones in John were "written that you may believe that Jesus is the Christ, the Son of God, and that by believing you may have life in his name" (John 20:31). There are only small hints in Matthew, Mark, and Luke that believing in Jesus himself is important for escaping God's coming judgment. The focus is rather on God's coming rule of the earth and on obtaining His forgiveness through repentance for our wrongdoings. Christ is someone to be imitated (Matt. 10:38) and His death pays the price for sins (Mark 10:45), but the other gospels do not clearly state that one must believe in Jesus to be saved from judgment.

John, however, like the rest of the New Testament, teaches repeatedly that one must believe or have faith in Jesus in order to escape eternal death. Perhaps the verse best known to present this theme in the entire New Testament is John 3:16. Jesus came from heaven to earth. Whoever believes in His true identity will live forever; anyone who does not will perish. Jesus tells the crowds these things numerous times. After He miraculously feeds five thousand people, they ask Him what God wants them to do. Jesus replies, "This is what God wants you to do: Believe in the one he has sent" (John 6:29 NLT). At another point Jesus compares himself to manna—food that fell from heaven to feed the Israelites

> "For God so loved the world that he gave his one and only Son, that whoever believes in him shall not perish but have eternal life."
>
> —John 3:16

when they were wandering in the desert. He calls himself the bread of life and encourages the crowds to "feed" on Him so that they can live forever: "I tell you the truth, he who believes has everlasting life" (John 6:47). This theme of faith in Jesus is thus one of the distinctive features of the gospel of John. One of Jesus' many "I am" statements sums it up well: "I am the way and the truth and the life. No one comes to the Father except through me" (John 14:6).

More than any of the gospels, John connects the truth about Jesus' identity with His miraculous signs. The first part of John's gospel presents seven of these signs that in one way or another reveal His true identity. This divine power provides the single most convincing indication that He is who He says He is in John. While Jesus also performs miracles in Matthew, Mark, and Luke, these gospels do not say that His miracles are signs. In the other gospels, a sign is something like a miracle on demand, such as when Jesus' opponents ask Him to give them a sign to prove that He is the Messiah. He flatly refuses to give them any such signs.

The gospel of John, however, was written to a group of Christians in the late first century—its presentation is geared more to its audience than to Jesus' original situation. The author wanted his audience to know with certainty that Jesus' deeds showed who He truly was, regardless of whether His first audiences understood them to be signs. Thus, while Jesus himself may have avoided calling His miracles signs, the gospel of John in hindsight recognizes His powerful deeds for what they really were—indications and signs that Jesus was divine.

Jesus is God's Word for the World

Matthew and Luke both begin their gospels with the story of Jesus' birth, as was appropriate for ancient biographies. Mark's introduction noticeably lacks a birth story. John's introduction is even more striking. While John does start at the beginning, the beginning for John is not Jesus' birth. John starts before the creation of the world.

"In the beginning," he says in the first sentence, "was the Word" (John 1:1). This Word was with God, John explains; in fact, it was a divine Word. John goes on to say that God made everything through this Word. It was thus a Word that brought life, a creative Word. God's Word brought light out of darkness, and His Word can also bring hope to humanity (John 1:3–5). In John 1:14 we find out what this Word of God to humanity was and is: "the Word became flesh and made his dwelling among us." This Word, John makes clear, was Jesus.

One of the distinctive features of John's gospel is the claim that Jesus came from heaven. While there are hints in the Synoptics that Jesus has a heavenly identity (e.g., the transfiguration), John is the only gospel that explicitly teaches that God sent Jesus to earth from heaven. In what is sometimes called Jesus' "high priestly prayer" (where He prays for all those who would later believe in Him), Jesus prays to God, "Now, Father, bring me into the glory we shared before the world began" (John 17:5 NLT). In John 6:38, Jesus says, "I have come down from heaven . . . to do the will of him who sent me." In John 8:23, He says to the Pharisees, "You are from below; I am from above."

Telling His opponents that Abraham looked forward to the day He would come is perhaps the most startling thing that Jesus says in John. His opponents scoff at the boldness of such a claim, pointing out that He is not even fifty years old. The New International Version brings out part of the meaning of Jesus' response well: "I tell you the truth, before Abraham was even born, I Am!" (John 8:58). "I Am" is the name God used to introduce himself to Moses at the burning bush in Exodus 3:14. Jesus' opponents recognize by His statement that He is claiming to be divine.

To return to the opening of the gospel of John, we can see that it also indicates Jesus came down from heaven. What you may not realize, however, is what John meant by calling Jesus the Word—the *Logos* in Greek. *Logos* is a Greek word that had been around for a long while before the gospel of John was written. It was a way for Jews to refer to the fact that God's commands, His "word," always came to pass. For example, "God said, 'Let there be light,' and there was light" (Gen. 1:3 NLT). Isaiah 55:11 says this of God's word: "I send it out, and it always produces fruit. It will accomplish all I want it to" (NLT).

Some Jews around the time of Christ viewed these verses through the glasses of a philosophy known as Stoicism. The Stoics believed that the world had a certain order, an order that they also called the *Logos* or *word*. For them, the Logos gave order and purpose to the world. Therefore, when John says the Word became human, it probably implies that Jesus embodies God's purpose for the world.

Further, when John says that the human Word "made his dwelling among us" (John 1:14), it uses a term that basically means "to set up a tent" among us—like the tent where God met the Israelites while they were traveling in the desert. John wishes us to know, therefore, that when we are looking at Jesus, we are seeing nothing less than God's presence among us. Jesus' opponents in John understand these claims and repeatedly pick up stones in order to kill Him. "You, a mere man," they say, "claim to be God" (John 10:33). The gospel of John is unique in presenting Jesus in such high, exalted language.

The idea that Jesus was—and still is—God in human form is one of the most important teachings of Christianity. The central part of the most important Christian creed states that in order to save us, Jesus "came down from heaven and was incarnate by the Holy Spirit from the Virgin Mary, and was made man."[1] The word *incarnation* means Jesus was put *in-flesh*. This Christian teaching comes primarily from the gospel of John (see also Phil. 2:6–7).

Pictures of Who Jesus Is

Chapter 15 of this text discusses some of the unique features of John's story of Jesus' ministry. We should at least mention some of them in this overview of John. In particular, John presents a number of events that define Jesus' spiritual significance, usually "I am" statements in which Jesus tells the audience who He is.

In most cases, these "I am" statements relate to a particular situation Jesus confronts at the time. Before Jesus raises Lazarus from the dead, for example, He tells Lazarus's sister, "I am the resurrection and the life. He who believes in me will live, even though he dies" (John 11:25). Not long after Jesus has miraculously fed well over five thousand people from five loaves of bread and two fish, He tells a crowd, "I am the bread of life. He who comes to me will never go hungry" (6:35). John provides a number of these pictures of Jesus' true identity, such as John the Baptist's statement that Jesus is the Lamb of God (1:29) or Jesus' description of himself as the good shepherd (10:11). The next chapter will discuss these in more detail.

The Who's and When's of John

One of the unique features of the gospel of John is its references to the "disciple whom Jesus loved." This disciple is first mentioned in John 13 after Jesus has arrived in Jerusalem for the last time (John 13:23). He then appears occasionally throughout the rest of the gospel. Interestingly, though, the gospel never tells us his name. John 21:24 tells us that he "is the disciple who testifies to these things and who wrote them down. We know that his testimony is true." But nowhere does the gospel tell us who he was.

Since the late A.D. 100s, the church has more often than not believed that this disciple was John the son of Zebedee, one of the core disciples in the other three gospels (e.g. Mark 9:2). The reasons are easy enough to see. The beloved disciple was present at the last dinner Jesus had with His disciples, so it seems likely he was one of the twelve core followers of Jesus (Matt. 10:1–5; Mark 3:13–19; Luke 6:12–16; Acts 1:13). Indeed, the disciples closest to Jesus are Peter and the sons of Zebedee (James and John). These are the ones who seem closest to Jesus both at the transfiguration (Mark 9:2) and in the garden of Gethsemane (Mark 14:33). A title like the "beloved disciple" surely would apply most appropriately to one of these three.

Of these three it cannot be Peter, since the gospel distinguishes Peter from the beloved disciple on every occasion when the beloved disciple is mentioned. It is unlikely that it would be James, the son of Zebedee, since Herod Agrippa I killed him in the early A.D. 40s. No one argues that the gospel was written this early. John thus seems the most likely candidate among the core group of disciples mentioned in Matthew, Mark, and Luke. Interestingly, while the gospel of John mentions Peter, Andrew, Nathaniel, Philip, Thomas, and Judas Iscariot by name, it does not explicitly mention John. Some think such an omission would be appropriate if John were the actual author.

The idea that John the son of Zebedee was the author is not without its complications, however. For one thing, although the disciple Jesus loved is the ultimate source of the gospel's information, he was not likely the person that wrote down the gospel exactly as we now have it. Would this disciple have written of himself, "We know that his testimony is true" (John 21:24)? The story is never in any place told in the first person: "I saw these things" or "We went to Jerusalem." In fact, John 21:2 uses the third person when stating that the sons of Zebedee (including John) were by the Sea of Galilee. The author does not say, "I was there by the Sea of Galilee," let alone that one of these sons of Zebedee was the beloved disciple. In other words, the present form of the gospel of John most likely comes from the people who were associated with that person, rather than from the disciple himself.[2]

One of the strongest arguments against John being the author comes from Mark 10:35–40, in which James and John ask Jesus for high positions of honor in the kingdom of God. Jesus asks them if they can "drink from the cup" He is about to drink—in other words, whether they are prepared to die for their faith. After they claim that they are prepared, Jesus indicates that they would indeed drink from that cup of martyrdom. As we just mentioned, Herod Agrippa I put James to death in the early 40s. The gospel of Mark leads us to believe that John was martyred as well. In fact, many think Mark hints that John was already dead by the late A.D. 60s when Mark was probably written. If the author of the fourth gospel was not martyred, as church tradition has long held, then John was not likely its author.

> "Peter turned and saw that the disciple whom Jesus loved was following them . . . When Peter saw him, he asked, 'Lord, what about him?' Jesus answered, 'If I want him to remain alive until I return, what is that to you? You must follow me.' Because of this, the rumor spread among the brothers that this disciple would not die."
>
> —John 21:20–23

At this point we should probably mention that some early Christians were aware of another John whose life and ministry may have paralleled that of John the son of Zebedee—a man called John the elder. The church father Papias, writing about A.D. 140, mentioned him as a second-level disciple—not one of the twelve, but a disciple nonetheless.[3] Dionysius of Alexandria recognized early on (A.D. 200s) that the style, language, and thought of the gospel of John is strikingly different from that of the book of Revelation. The church historian Eusebius, writing in the early 300s, suggested accordingly that John the elder must have written one of these two books and John the son of Zebedee, the other.[4] In this light it is extremely interesting to see that some of the books associated with the gospel of John (namely, 2 and 3 John) were both written by someone who called himself "the elder." Some take this fact to indicate that John the elder stands behind the fourth gospel rather than John the son of Zebedee.

If John the elder was the man behind the gospel, he was probably from Judea, which would explain why he is not mentioned until Jesus arrives in Jerusalem for the last time. It would also explain why the gospel of John highlights Jesus' visits to Jerusalem more than the other gospels. This man was known to the high priest (John 18:15) and was present at the crucifixion (19:35). Whoever the author was, tradition holds that he eventually made his way to Ephesus in Asia Minor. In this context, perhaps in the last decade of the first century, the community of this beloved disciple edited and passed on to the church this magnificent gospel that is the favorite of so many.

Questions for Study and Discussion

1. In what way does Jesus provide us with the meaning and purpose of the universe?

2. Jesus never explicitly tells His followers to have faith in Him in the other gospels, yet this idea is central to Jesus' message in John. How would you explain this difference?

3. John is the only gospel to clearly tell its audience that Jesus existed before He came to earth. What is the significance of Jesus' preexistence? In what state did He preexist?

4. Who do you think wrote the gospel of John?

The Story of Jesus in John

Of all the gospels, John paints the most exalted portrait
of Christ, equating Him most clearly with God.

The previous chapter explained how strikingly different the gospel of John is from the other gospels and highlighted some of its special features. The purpose of this chapter is to highlight some of the stories unique to John and to see his unique perspective on events his gospel has in common with Matthew, Mark, and Luke. We've already seen that John begins with the incarnation, the fact that Jesus is God's word in human form (John 1:1–18). Many divide up the rest of the gospel into two main parts, with John 21 as a kind of epilogue or wrap-up of the book. We will focus on these two main parts in this chapter.

At a Glance

- In John, Jesus' earthly ministry takes place over a period of two to three years and includes a number of trips to Jerusalem.
- The gospel of John has two basic parts. The first presents Jesus' public ministry, while the second focuses on His disciples.
- John includes seven signs that demonstrate Jesus' messianic identity.
- John places great significance on the festivals Jesus attends, aligning their Old Testament symbolism with Jesus himself.
- John links several statements of Jesus' spiritual identity ("I am" statements) to the situations in which He finds himself.
- In contrast to the Synoptics, John writes of Jesus giving long speeches to His disciples (almost philosophical discourses).

The "Book of Signs" (1:19—12:50)

Seven Signs

Many scholars believe that one of the sources the author of John used to write this gospel was an account of seven signs that Jesus had performed. The first two signs in John's gospel are numbered: (1) Jesus turns water into wine in a little village called Cana in Galilee (John 2:11), and (2) Jesus heals the son of a royal official (4:54). Accordingly, some suggest that this "signs source" recorded seven signs in order to prove that Jesus was the Messiah. Whether or not we accept this theory, these seven signs help us get acquainted with some of the stories in John.

Several of these signs are unique to the gospel of John. For example, the changing of water into wine appears nowhere else in the New Testament. Also, while the other gospels record Jesus healing the blind and the lame, the particular healings mentioned in John are found only in John. Even the stunning sign that climaxes this section of John's gospel, the raising of Lazarus from the dead, is unique to John. If these stories originate from a separate source, it surely had a missionary purpose and was meant to convince the doubtful that Jesus truly was the Messiah.

The Seven Signs in John

1. Turning water into wine (John 2:1–11)
2. Healing the royal official's son (4:43–54)
3. Healing the lame man at the pool (5:1–15)
4. Feeding the five thousand (6:1–15)
5. Walking on water (6:16–24)
6. Healing the blind man (9:1–12)
7. Raising Lazarus from the dead (11:38–44)

Several of these signs connect with Jesus' "I am" statements. It's after He feeds the five thousand, for example, that Jesus says, "I am the bread of life" (John 6:35). The gospel of John thus powerfully uses the signs Jesus performs to teach who Jesus is. The literal event teaches us about Jesus' symbolic identity.

It is probably no coincidence that Jesus says, "I am the light of the world" (John 8:12), and then heals a blind man in the next chapter (9:1–12). Both illustrate a greater truth, namely, that Jesus brings understanding while the Jewish leaders perpetuate blindness. In the following chapter of John, Jesus goes on to say, "I am the good shepherd" (10:11), contrasting himself with the Pharisees as thieves and robbers (10:7–11). Jesus' statement "I am the resurrection and the life," (John 11:25) also fits this pattern, since He says it just before raising Lazarus from the dead.

We mentioned the most startling "I am" statement of all in the last chapter—when Jesus says that He existed before Abraham: "Before Abraham was born, I am!" (8:58). The way He words this statement implies that He is divine, since God names himself "I Am" when He appears to Moses at the burning bush (Ex. 3:14).[1] Thus, of all the gospels, John paints the most exalted portrait of Christ.

Jesus, the Way to Life

Another unique feature of Jesus' public ministry as expressed in the gospel of John is seen in His frequent trips to Jerusalem. If all we had were Matthew, Mark, and Luke, we might think that Jesus' public ministry was limited mostly to Galilee and took place within the space of about a year. In those gospels, Jesus only visits Jerusalem at the very end of His ministry. But in John, Jesus regularly attends the festivals in Jerusalem, as well as such feasts as Passover, Tabernacles, and even the Feast of Dedication (Hanukkah). Jesus attends three Passovers in John, and since Passover comes only once a year, the gospel of John implies that Jesus' earthly ministry lasted two to three years.

The gospel of John may use Jesus' attendance at these festivals, along with the things He says, to underscore Jesus' spiritual significance in relation to the practices of Old Testament Judaism. For example, in John 1:19—6:71 John seems to present us with events and teaching that show us Jesus as the only way to eternal life. As Jesus later says in John 14:6, "I am the way and the truth and the life. No one comes to the Father except through me."

One of the ways John presents this truth is through the idea that Jesus is the Lamb of God. At the first Passover Jesus attends, He overturns the tables of those who exchange money and sell animals for sacrifices, proclaiming that He will destroy the temple and raise it up again in three days

(John 2:19). What He means is that His sacrifice as the Lamb of God replaces the need for an earthly temple with its animal sacrifices and blood (cf. 2:21; 4:23). He is now the way to God.

Many scholars believe that John has powerfully arranged and presented the events of Jesus' life to bring out this message. Of all the gospels, John uniquely teaches that Jesus is the Lamb of God. Only in this gospel does John the Baptist proclaim, "Look! There is the Lamb of God who takes away the sin of the world!" (John 1:29 NLT). To emphasize this point, John's gospel alone seems to time Jesus' death just as the Passover lambs are being slaughtered, a fact that powerfully parallels His designation as the Lamb of God.

Further, while Matthew, Mark, and Luke indicate that Jesus threw the money changers out of the temple in the last week of His life, John places this event right after Jesus turns water into wine at Cana, in the first year of Jesus' ministry. John probably thought of this wine as a symbol of Jesus' blood. It may have made sense to him to place the temple incident—which showed that Jesus' body would replace the temple—right next to it. Here we have both the body and blood of Jesus, a symbolic reference to the Eucharist or Christian Communion. John probably wanted his audience to know that Jesus' body and blood have taken the place of the Jewish sacrificial system as the way to life.

John seems to allude to the Christian celebration of Communion several times in his gospel. As we just mentioned, both the miracle at Cana and Jesus' actions in the temple have overtones of this celebration of Jesus' death as a sacrifice for sins. The feeding of the five thousand may also carry these overtones. After feeding the crowds, Jesus tells them that He is the bread of life and explains what He means: "Unless you eat the flesh of the Son of Man and drink his blood, you cannot have eternal life within you" (John 6:53 NLT). This comment was very difficult for the crowds to accept, and many of His disciples stopped following Him at that point (6:66). At the very least, John was saying that salvation from God's condemnation comes only through Jesus' death.

Another image that Jesus uses to explain what He means by the designation "bread of life" comes from Israel's distant past. During the time that the Israelites wandered in the desert, God sent down food called manna to keep them alive. Jesus compares himself to that same manna, saying He provides spiritual food that gives life (John 6:31–33).

This statement reminds us of something Jesus tells a Samaritan woman in John 4, another incident unique to John. Jesus meets a Samaritan woman at a well and asks her for a drink. In the course of their conversation, Jesus reveals not only that He knows everything about her, but also that He is the giver of living water: "Whoever drinks the water I give him will never thirst" (John 4:14). Both as living water and as the bread of life, Jesus gives eternal life to those who feed on Him.

John 3 gives us some of the clearest teaching on how to receive eternal life. This chapter tells of Nicodemus. He comes to Jesus secretly, believing Him to be a great teacher with answers to his questions. Jesus gets right to the point: unless a person is "born again," he or she cannot be a part of the kingdom of God (John 3:3). What Jesus means is that one must receive the Holy Spirit in order to be a part of God's kingdom, a teaching John shares with most of the New Testament.

> ### Some of the
> ### "I am" Statements of Jesus
>
> "I am the bread of life" and "I am the living bread" (John 6:35, 51)
>
> "I am the light of the world" (8:12)
>
> "Before Abraham was born, I am!" (8:58)
>
> "I am the good shepherd" (10:11, 14)
>
> "I am the resurrection and the life" (11:25)
>
> "I am the way and the truth and the life" (14:6)
>
> "I am the true vine" (15:1)

Jesus also alludes to the importance of Christian baptism in this chapter: one must be born of water as well as of the Spirit (3:5). John's most important verses appear in the middle of Jesus' conversation with Nicodemus: "For God so loved the world that he gave his one and only Son, that whoever believes in him shall not perish but have eternal life. For God did not send his Son into the world to condemn the world, but to save the world through him" (3:16–17). These verses emphasize the theme that in so many different ways appears throughout the first six chapters of John: Jesus is the only way to eternal life.

Jesus and Jewish Opposition

After Jesus' radical statement about the need to feed on His body and drink His blood, He loses many followers. John 7–12 details the steadily increasing opposition to Jesus. In these chapters, the theme turns to Jesus as the good shepherd, an image that contrasts to the Jewish leaders who help perpetuate blindness. It is probably no coincidence that in this section Jesus heals a blind man; attends Hanukkah, the Feast of Lights (John 10); and attends the Jewish Feast of Tabernacles, a festival also involving lights and water. Jesus proclaims on that occasion that He is a provider of living water (John 7:37–38), echoing the same image He used with the Samaritan woman (John 4).

Here we see again John's penchant for revealing Jesus as the replacement of the Old Testament festivals. We indicated this earlier in the image of Jesus as the Lamb of God, thus replacing the temple and Passover. These passages thus imply that He is the true symbolic replacement of Tabernacles and Hanukkah as well. John also pictures Jesus replacing Sabbath observance. In contrast to the Jewish observance of the Sabbath, for example, Jesus is always working like God His Father (5:17).

Jesus and the Jewish Festivals

Sabbath—Like God, Jesus is always working; even on the Sabbath (John 5:17).

Passover—Jesus is the Lamb of God; His body replaces the temple (1:29; 2:21).

Tabernacles—Jesus is God "tabernacling" with humanity (1:14); He provides living water (7:37–38) and is the light of the world (9:5).

Dedication (Hanukkah)—Jesus is the light of the world (9:5) and the new temple (2:21).

The climax of the first half of John comes in John 12 with the Jews' rejection of Jesus' message. The gospel of John is distinct in having Jesus refer to His enemies as "the Jews." This feature is striking because, after all, Jesus and His loyal followers were also Jews. Because of this wording, the gospel of John has unfortunately played into the hands of anti-Semitism, even though the gospel probably was not racist in its original context. However, many scholars have suggested that the members of the community the author was writing to had, like the blind man of John 9, been cast out of the synagogues of Ephesus because of their faith in Christ (cf. 9:22, 34).

The "Book of Glory" (13:1—20:31)

Scholars have often called the second half of John the "Book of Glory" because of the way it presents Jesus' death and resurrection as His achievement of glory (e.g., John 13:31–32). Whereas the events highlighted in the first half of John are conducted in public, these last chapters focus on Jesus' teaching to His disciples. In fact, five consecutive chapters (John 13–17) all describe events that take place at the last dinner Jesus has with the disciples who have remained with Him. Jesus demonstrates His love to the very end, noticeably when He washes their feet, another event recorded only in John (13:2–12).

Jesus makes a long speech to His disciples in this part of John. Some of the main themes are Jesus' oneness with God, His imminent departure from earth, and His promise to send a helper back from heaven—the Holy Spirit. The Holy Spirit, Jesus says, will lead the disciples to understand things like what constitutes truth (John 14:17, 26), sin, and right living (16:8–9). Here we have some of the clearest references in the New Testament to the Holy Spirit as a person.

In John 17, John presents what is sometimes called Jesus' high priestly prayer; included in that prayer are those of us who would believe many years later. Jesus' main thrust is that we would be one, just as Jesus was one with God. This message may have had special meaning for John's original audience, since some of its members had probably left the church at some point (see 1 John 2:19).

John's presentation of Jesus' death is extremely victorious in tone. Jesus tells Judas when to leave to betray Him (John 13:27). John does not record

Jesus' anguish in the garden of Gethsemane (cf. 12:27; 18:1–2). The soldiers who arrest Jesus fall all over themselves at the mere mention of His name (18:6). John makes it very clear that Jesus is in complete control of His trial and crucifixion. Jesus tells Pilate that the only reason he has any authority over Him is because it is God's will (19:11). On the cross, He gives instruction to the beloved disciple to watch over is mother (19:26–27). He then appears to die by an act of will after He fulfills a final prophecy by saying, "It is finished" (19:30).

The gospel of John ends with a number of resurrection appearances that the other gospels do not record. The best known of these is Jesus' appearance to "doubting Thomas," a disciple who doubts whether Jesus has really risen from the dead. Skeptically, he says he will not believe until he touches the scars from Jesus' crucifixion. Only when Jesus suddenly appears and offers Thomas that opportunity does Thomas believe, calling Jesus "my Lord and my God" (John 20:28). Jesus' concluding statement to Thomas aptly fits John's purpose in this gospel: "Blessed are those who have not seen and yet have believed" (20:29).

Epilogue (John 21)

John 21 comes almost as a surprise—the last two verses of John 20 sound somewhat like an ending in their own right. For this reason, some have suggested that John 21 was added after the gospel had already been completed. In any case, this chapter presents us with an interesting encounter between the resurrected Jesus and Peter.

The main players in this encounter are Jesus, Peter, and the beloved disciple. Jesus asks Peter three times if he loves Him, perhaps echoing Peter's three denials after Jesus had been arrested. Peter responds each time that he does, after which Jesus commands him to take care of the church. Jesus then prophesies that Peter will die by crucifixion.

Peter, interested in the fate of the beloved disciple, asks what his end will be. Jesus refuses to answer, but allows for the possibility that he might live until the second coming. The editor of John then implies that many in his day believed John would live until Christ's return. This editor then tells us that this beloved disciple was the basis for the gospel—a gospel whose testimony is true.

What Do We Do with John?

For some Christians, the symbolic meanings many scholars find in John are exciting and give life to the text beyond what they might have imagined. For many others, however, the suggestion that John presents a spiritual message more than a blow-by-blow historical presentation is highly suspect. If God inspired John to speak truth in this way, of course, then God surely was not in error—nor is John. It just requires us to read this gospel with the right expectations. Whether you see it as highly symbolic or as a straightforward historical account, John remains one of the most meaningful books in the New Testament.

Questions for Study and Discussion

1. What are some of the "I am" statements in John and what do they tell us about the character of Jesus?
2. What do you think the "seven signs" signify at the beginning of John?
3. Do you think John was deliberately comparing Jesus to Jewish festivals and the Sabbath?
4. What would you make of the claim that John gives us more of a symbolic than historical portrait of Jesus?

section three

Acts

16

Luke's Sequel

Acts

Acts is the sequel to Luke, picking up
the story right where it left off.

"Acts of the Holy Spirit"

Acts, the fifth book in the New Testament, begins with a reference to a previous book the author had written to the same person. It begins, "Dear Theophilus: In my first book I told you about everything Jesus began to do and teach" (Acts 1:1 NLT). The mention of the name Theophilus tells us that this previous book is none other than the gospel of Luke. Acts is thus the sequel to Luke, picking up the story right where it left off. Although our Bibles separate these two books by putting the gospel of John in between, they

---

At a Glance

- Acts is the sequel of Luke, written by the same author.
- Acts emphasizes the same themes as the gospel of Luke, such as the significance of women and concern for the poor and downtrodden.
- Even more than Luke, Acts emphasizes that the gospel is for all people. It points out that Christians are not troublemakers or seditious individuals and highlights the importance of prayer and the Holy Spirit.
- The genre of Acts is probably history. In ancient times, this allowed for more creativity on the part of an author than modern histories do.
- Acts, like Luke, is technically anonymous and was likely written after A.D. 70.

really should be read together. They originally worked together toward a common purpose.

The gospel of Luke, the author tells us, was about all the things that Jesus began to do and teach. The implication is that Jesus continues to do and teach in Acts as well. But in Acts, Jesus works through the Holy Spirit. The Holy Spirit brings Jesus' continued presence to His disciples. Therefore, some have suggested that rather than call the book the "Acts of the Apostles," a more accurate name for the book would be the "Acts of the Holy Spirit."

Special Emphases of Acts

Since Luke and Acts are really a single work in two volumes, it is no surprise to find that they share the same basic themes. If the gospel of Luke brings out the universal implications of Jesus' mission more than the other gospels, the book of Acts shows even more emphatically that the gospel is for everyone. Acts shares Luke's concern for the poor and oppressed, and also highlights the role of women in the spread of the gospel. Acts emphasizes even more the importance of prayer in the life of the early Christians and the centrality of the Holy Spirit. Finally, Acts demonstrates the unified and peace-loving nature of Jesus and His followers, indicating that the opponents of Christianity were those who stirred up trouble rather than the Christians themselves.

The Gospel Is for the Whole World

Acts may start in Jerusalem, but it ends with the gospel being preached in Rome. In the interim the word spreads not only throughout Palestine, but also throughout Greece and what we now call Turkey. The book summarizes this expansion in the very first chapter: "You will receive power when the Holy Spirit comes on you; and you will be my witnesses in Jerusalem, and in all Judea and Samaria, and to the ends of the earth" (Acts 1:8). The next chapter of this text gives further details about how the good news spreads to all these different places, starting with the incredible growth that takes place among the Jews in Jerusalem and ending with the spread of the gospel throughout the Mediterranean.

More important than the geography of this expansion is the way Christianity goes from being exclusively Jewish, to a movement that includes people from countless other races and cultures. The gospel of Luke more than any other gospel pictures the interaction and concern of Jesus for people of all races. Even when Jesus is born, a man named Simeon foretells that Jesus will be "a light for revelation to the Gentiles and for glory to your people Israel" (Luke 2:32). The book of Acts shows the fulfillment of his prediction.

Acts' presentation leaves no doubt about the possibility for non-Jews to escape God's wrath. For example, it is Peter—the most significant disciple for Luke—who first brings the gospel to the Gentiles (Acts 10). Acts shows the Holy Spirit filling these Gentiles before they had even been baptized (10:44); by "converting" them himself, God leaves no room for debate. James, Jesus' brother and apparently the leader of the Jerusalem church, agrees that they can become Christians without converting to Judaism first (15:13–21). Finally, more than half of Acts narrates Paul's mission to the Gentiles and clearly indicates that God is the one who commands him to go to them (e.g., 22:21). So Acts not only tells us that the gospel is for everyone, but it also shows us this truth on almost every page.

However, Acts differs from Luke in one very important respect with regard to the gospel—it defines the "good news" more precisely than the gospel of Luke does. The gospel that Jesus preaches in Luke is good news for the poor, the oppressed, the blind, and the downtrodden in general (e.g., Luke 4:18–19). Of course, the gospel is good news to these individuals in Acts as well. But after God raises Jesus from the dead, the resurrection becomes the central feature of Christian good news, the most important element in the gospel in Acts. Acts thus gives us the "rest of the story." It shows us that it is through Jesus' victorious resurrection that all of the promises of the gospel can actually come true.

Good News for Women, the Poor, and the Oppressed

As the gospel of Luke features the role of women in Jesus' ministry and His concern for the poor more prominently than the other gospels, Acts also features these things as important elements in the ministry of the early church.

From the very birth of the church on the day of Pentecost, Acts makes it clear that both men and women receive the Holy Spirit equally and thus both receive revelations from God to proclaim to the church (Acts 2:17–18; cf. 21:9). Acts mentions numerous women of status in the early church, many of whom open their homes for the worship of the early Christians.

For example, Peter goes to the house of a woman named Mary after an angel frees him from prison. Christians were evidently accustomed to gathering there to pray (Acts 12:12). Both the men and the women of the church at Philippi seem to meet in the house of a wealthy Christian woman named Lydia (16:15, 40). And Acts typically mentions a wife named Priscilla first when it speaks of a husband-wife team who ministered with Paul (18:18–19, 26). This woman evidently played an important role in teaching a man named Apollos the basics of the Christian faith (18:26). Apollos would go on to become an important Christian preacher at the famous city of Corinth. In short, the book of Acts not only wants us to see that both men and women can be saved, it also shows us that women played an important role in early Christian ministry (cf. 8:12; 17:4, 12, 34).

Acts also continues Luke's concern for the poor and downtrodden. Acts 4:32–35 notes of the earliest Christians that "no one claimed that any of his possessions was his own, but they shared everything they had . . . There

---

The Basic Christian Message

The sermons of Acts provide a clear and consistent picture of the earliest Christian preaching:

- God is in control of history and His plan is revealed in the Old Testament.
- This plan involves Jesus of Nazareth, whom God raised from the dead, an event the apostles witnessed.
- God exalted Jesus to His right hand and sent the Holy Spirit, signifying the beginning of a period of renewal.
- The appropriate human response to the message is repentance and baptism, after which one receives the Holy Spirit.
- Miraculous power and unity will follow.

---

were no needy persons among them. For from time to time those who owned lands or houses sold them, brought the money from the sales and put it at the apostles' feet, and it was distributed to anyone as he had need." Acts indicates that the early church distributed food to widows (6:1) and sent help to one another in times of famine (11:27–30).

Jesus' ministry of healing also continues in Acts. In fact, Acts seems to want us to notice a similarity between Jesus' healing ministry and that of early Christians like Peter and Paul. As Jesus healed a crippled man (Luke 5:25), so do Peter (Acts 3:7) and Paul (14:10). As Jesus raised the dead (Luke 7:15), so do Peter (Acts 9:40) and Paul (20:12). These events demonstrate that the early Christians preached the same gospel that Jesus preached and shared the power of the same Spirit of God.

The Centrality of Prayer and the Holy Spirit

Just as Luke highlights the role of prayer in Jesus' earthly ministry, Acts also features prayer as the key to obtaining power and direction from God. The believers of Acts seem to pray constantly (e.g., Acts 1:14; 2:42), especially when a special need arises. For example, the early Christians pray when they are facing strong opposition. When the Jewish ruling council, the Sanhedrin, opposes them, they pray (4:23–31). When Stephen is being stoned to death, he prays (7:59). When Peter is in prison facing execution, Christians pray (12:5, 12), just as Paul and Silas do when they are imprisoned at Philippi (16:25). In many instances, God miraculously delivers the person for whom they pray.

In Acts, the Holy Spirit often comes during prayer. After they pray about the opposition of the Sanhedrin, the apostles get a "refill" of the Holy Spirit to give them the power to be bold in the face of attack (Acts 4:31). The apostles Peter and John lay hands on believers in Samaria who have been baptized so that they will receive the Holy Spirit (8:15–17). Although Acts 6:6 does not specifically mention the Holy Spirit, we can imagine that the apostles lay hands on these seven men so that they will be filled with the power necessary to minister appropriately.

The Holy Spirit is truly the power behind everything good that happens in the book of Acts. In fact, receiving the Holy Spirit is the key ingredient in becoming a Christian in Acts. When some Samaritans are baptized and yet have not received the Spirit, the apostles come to them to help them receive the Spirit, so that they can become Christians fully. God ends all debate over whether Gentiles can be Christians by sending them the Holy Spirit and thus fully "converting" them. In fact, Acts 15:9 shows that it is the Holy Spirit that cleanses people of their sins after they repent and turn to God.

The main result of having the Holy Spirit is power (cf. Acts 1:8). This power shows up sometimes as boldness to proclaim the gospel (e.g., 4:31). On three occasions, believers speak in tongues, languages they have never learned (e.g., 2:4; 10:46; 19:6), when they receive the Holy Spirit. At other times the Holy Spirit enables the apostles to perform miracles (e.g., Acts 3) or provides them with direction. He reveals the future to early Christians through prophets (e.g., 21:11) and tells them what to do when they need direction (e.g., 16:7).

Christians Are Not Troublemakers

Even more than Luke, Acts is careful to show the unity of the early church. Acts portrays the conflict that sometimes accompanies early Christianity as something that comes from those who oppose it rather than as a result of Christians themselves. Acts 28:22 indicates the reputation the author of Acts was up against: "The only thing we know about these Christians is that they are denounced everywhere" (NLT). It appears that Acts is carefully presented in such a way as to show that Christians are orderly and peace-loving individuals.

The early chapters of Acts give us a church that is "one in heart and mind" (Acts 4:32). They "were together and had everything in common" (2:44); they regularly share in "breaking of bread . . . and prayer" (2:42). When problems and conflicts arise, they resolve them in an orderly manner with clearly drawn lines of authority. The apostles and James, for example, give the final ruling on matters of controversy (e.g., 6:1–6; 15:6–35). The church then submits to the decisions that those in authority make under the direction of the Holy Spirit (e.g., 6:5; 15:31).

From what we know of church conflicts from Paul's writings, we can see that Acts is putting the church's best foot forward. For example, Acts does not mention an important argument between Peter and Paul at a city called Antioch (Gal. 2:11–14). Even Barnabas, a traveling companion of Paul, sided against Paul on that occasion regarding the issue of whether Jewish and Gentile Christians should eat together. Interestingly, Acts only tells us that Paul and Barnabas argued over whether Barnabas's cousin should travel with them (Acts 15:36–41). Acts may omit this other argument because it reflects one of the most precarious moments in the early church, jeopardizing not only the unity of the church but its mission to the world as well. As a result, the next phase of Paul's ministry seems to have taken place without the clear blessing of the leaders of the Christian movement.

On the other hand, Acts wants us to see the fundamental continuity and unity between the missions of Peter and Paul. We have already mentioned how Acts shows Peter and Paul both doing the same kinds of things that Jesus himself did while on earth. Yet Acts also hints at the fact that many Jewish Christians had misgivings about Paul's mission: "Our Jewish Christians here at Jerusalem have been told that you are teaching all the Jews living in the Gentile world to turn their backs on the laws of Moses" (Acts 21:21 NLT). Acts wants its audience to know that these claims are untrue — Paul still observes the Jewish Law. Acts has thus given us a somewhat "Gentile-friendly" picture of Peter and a "Jew-friendly" picture of Paul.

Similarly, Acts provides us with a fairly simplistic picture of the opposition Christians faced around the world. Acts regularly blames Jewish opposition to Christianity as the culprit for the riots and controversy that sometimes followed the early Christians. Local authorities, on the other hand, regularly affirm the innocence of Christians or they consider the charges against them as irrelevant in a legal setting.

Just as someone going for a job interview puts his or her best foot forward, so Acts emphasizes the peaceful nature of Christianity and downplays events that might have confirmed the reputation Christians seem to have had as troublemakers. In the process, Acts presents us with a somewhat idealistic picture of the early church. In reality, the early church had most of the same struggles that churches have today.

The Genre of Acts

A quick look through Acts suggests almost immediately that it is a history of the early church, although some scholars creatively have suggested that it is a novel. However, the opening of Luke makes it clear that the author of Luke-Acts wants us to think of these two works as a record of things that actually happened, rather than as a fictional portrayal of Jesus and the early Christians (Luke 1:1–4). Many think that Acts fits best into an ancient genre called general history, a kind of history writing that presented the history of a nation or people from its origins down to contemporary times. Luke and Acts would fit this pattern since they present the origins of the people known as "Christians" from their "birth" on the day of Pentecost to the time near the deaths of the first apostles.

The question for us as readers is how ancient history writing might have differed from modern history writing. In other words, should I expect from Acts the same things I would expect of a modern history book, or are there some differences? When we compare the ending of Luke and the beginning of Acts, we may catch a glimpse of one such difference.

If all we had were the ending of the gospel of Luke, we would probably conclude that Jesus not only rose from the dead on Easter Sunday, but also made all His appearances to the disciples and ascended to heaven on that same day—all in and around the city of Jerusalem. Luke 24:13 says that Jesus appears to two men on their way to the village of Emmaus "that same day" that He rose from the dead. That same evening Jesus has supper with them and reveals himself to them (Luke 24:29–31). Once they realize Jesus is alive, they return "within the hour" to Jerusalem (24:33 NLT). While they are telling the disciples what happened, Jesus appears to the disciples as well (24:36). After He finishes explaining things to them, He takes them out near the village of Bethany and is taken up to heaven (24:50–51). The gospel of Luke gives us the impression that Jesus rose, appeared, and ascended all on Easter Sunday.

Thus, you might be surprised to turn to Acts 1:3 and read that Jesus was with His disciples in Jerusalem for forty days—or turn to Matthew or Luke where Jesus never appears to His disciples in Jerusalem at all but in Galilee instead (Matt. 28:7, 16; Mark 16:7). At this point, a skeptic might cry foul! But to accuse Luke of error is to misunderstand the genre in which he was writing. Since Luke and Acts both have the same author and the same audience, it seems highly unlikely that Luke was just hoping Theophilus would miss the apparent difference in timing. The genres of ancient biography and history writing allowed for some artistry in presentation.

> "I have found it difficult to remember the precise words used in the speeches that I listened to myself and my various inform-ants have experienced the same difficulty. My method, therefore, has been to make the speaker say what, in my opinion, was called for by each occasion, while keep-ing as closely as possible to the general sense of the words that were actually used."
>
> —Thucydides, Greek historian, The Peloponnesian War 1.22

This conclusion may apply to the sermons of Acts as well. In Acts 20:9, Paul preaches so long that a young man dozes and falls out of a third-story window, yet you could read any one of the sermons of Acts in less than five minutes. At the very least, the sermons of Acts are shortened versions of what was actually said. Further, one of the most respected ancient historians tells us that he sometimes composed speeches when he did not have access to eyewitnesses. While you will have to decide whether you think Luke has composed any of the sermons in Acts, Thucydides makes it clear that doing so was acceptable within the ancient genre of history writing.

The Who's, When's, and Why's of Acts

Chapter 12 of this text has already discussed some of the general background of Luke (and thus, of Acts), since they both have the same author and audience in mind. Acts, like Luke, is technically anonymous, although the only name tradition has ever suggested for the author is that of Luke, the physician, occasionally a traveling companion of the apostle Paul. Chapter 12 also presented the basic argument that Luke and Acts were written after the destruction of the temple in Jerusalem in A.D. 70. The primary evidence is the clarity with which Luke portrays the destruction of the temple by the Romans in Luke 21:20—Matthew and Mark's picture is much more ambiguous (Matt. 24:15; Mark 13:14). The fact that Luke probably used Mark as a reference also makes a date after A.D. 70 likely.

Like the gospel of Luke, Acts is a tool of the gospel message. Like Luke, it reassures Theophilus that the things he has been taught are true (cf. Luke 1:4). The main truth is the resurrection of Jesus, the central message of the sermons in Acts. In the process, Luke confirms that Christians are honorable and that Christianity is a movement whose bad reputation is completely undeserved. While both he and his audience already knew the dark chapter that soon followed in Rome—the deaths of Peter and Paul at the hands of Nero, along with many other Christians—he ends the story on an appropriately high note. Just as Jesus predicted that the gospel would go everywhere, Acts ends with the gospel reaching Rome, the end of the civilized world. The time of the Gentiles was in full season (Luke 21:24). Christians were waiting for a day when the Jews too would accept Christ, and God would restore the kingdom of Israel (Acts 1:6).

Questions for Study and Discussion

1. What themes does Acts most noticeably share with the gospel of Luke?
2. How does the content of the "good news" change after Jesus has risen from the dead?
3. How close to a documentary do you think Acts is? How much freedom do you think Acts takes in its presentation? At what point, if any, would such creative license negate the authority or inspiration of Acts?

Jerusalem, Judea, and Samaria

The Story of the Church in Acts Part 1

The message and miracles of the apostles had two
basic results: expansion and persecution.

The Overall Plot

Acts 1:8 is this book's key verse. Jesus tells His disciples, "You will receive power when the Holy Spirit comes on you; and you will be my witnesses in Jerusalem, and in all Judea and Samaria, and to the ends of the earth." This verse gives us an outline of the story in Acts. The first seven chapters are set in and around Jerusalem. Chapters 8 through 12 take place in the broader area of Palestine; that is, in the regions of Judea and Samaria. The last sixteen chapters present the ministry of Paul

At a Glance

- The story of Acts has three parts: the spread of Christianity in Jerusalem (Acts 1–7), throughout the regions of Judea and Samaria (Acts 8–12), and throughout the broader Mediterranean world (Acts 13–28).
- The main character is the Holy Spirit, who brings the power behind everything good that happens in the story.
- The day of Pentecost is the birthday of the church and Christianity.
- Peter's ministry to the Jews dominates the first part of the story in Jerusalem (Acts 1–7), while Paul's ministry to the Gentiles dominates the last part (Acts 14–28).
- The church at the Council of Jerusalem (Acts 15) recognizes that Gentiles can be Christians without first becoming Jews.
- Acts ends with Paul in Rome where he awaits trial before the emperor, Nero.

as the gospel reaches the "ends of the earth." In that day and for all intents and purposes, this meant Rome.

The main character in the story of Acts is the Holy Spirit, who stands behind everything good that happens in the story. If the gospel of Luke is about the things Jesus began to do and teach (Acts 1:1), then Acts shows us what the Spirit of Jesus continues to do in the church through His followers (e.g., 16:7). Whenever the Spirit comes, the followers of Jesus receive power. This power not only gives them boldness to proclaim Jesus' resurrection, but it also enables them to perform miracles and sometimes speak in languages they have never learned.

Besides the Holy Spirit, Peter and Paul are the next two most prominent characters in the story. Peter's ministry to the Jews dominates the first part of the story in Jerusalem (Acts 1–7), while Paul's ministry to the Gentiles dominates the last part, as the gospel reaches the ends of the earth (Acts 14–28). We might almost think of the first half of Acts as the "Peter half" and the second as the "Paul half." Since Luke viewed the period of history in which he lived as the "age of the Gentiles" (Luke 21:24), it is no coincidence that the story of Acts shows a gradual shift of Christianity from Jews to Gentiles. While Acts begins in Jerusalem with Jewish Christians, it ends in Rome with Paul turning decisively to the Gentiles (Acts 28:28).

In Jerusalem

Both the gospel of Luke and the book of Acts demonstrate a greater interest in Jerusalem and its temple than Matthew and Mark do. In the gospel of Luke, this interest shows up primarily in the events surrounding Jesus' birth and after He rises from the dead. In Acts, Jerusalem features as the center of Christianity, the place where the highest authority of the church resides. It is in Jerusalem that Acts depicts the birth of the church on the day of Pentecost, the Jewish festival on which the Jews celebrated the first fruits of the grain harvest. From that day on, the disciples are called apostles, individuals who have been sent on a mission as ambassadors, in this case for God. At least in theory, Jerusalem remains the center of the church throughout the book of Acts. Even while the church is under persecution, the apostles remain there (Acts 8:1). When the church makes important decisions in Acts, it makes them in Jerusalem (Acts 15). Even Paul returns to Jerusalem near the end of his ministry and near the end of the story of Acts (Acts 21).

In Jerusalem, the temple plays an important role in the lives of the early Christians. Acts 2:46 mentions that they meet daily in the temple courts, and it is while they are there to pray that Peter and John heal a lame man (3:1). What is a little surprising is the implication that they also continue to participate to some extent in the temple's sacrificial system. For example, Acts depicts Paul near the end of his ministry offering a sacrifice at the temple — paying for certain Christian men to finish a vow they had made (21:24–27). The book of Hebrews implies that all earthly sacrifices are now inappropriate, since Christ's death definitively accomplished everything they symbolized (e.g., Heb. 7:12; 9:9–10; 10:1). Either Luke and Hebrews have slightly different theologies, or we conclude that it was a long process for the early Christians to figure out all the implications of Christ's death — a process we can witness as we read through the pages of the New Testament.

The first seven chapters of Acts begin with the ascension of Jesus and end with the stoning of Stephen, the first Christian martyr. In the meantime, the Holy Spirit comes, the church is born, the gospel is preached, miracles and judgment take place, and the Christians face their first conflicts and opposition. This period of beginnings probably covers about the first three to five years after Jesus' resurrection (ca. A.D. 30–33).

Since according to Acts a person cannot really be considered a Christian until he or she has received the Holy Spirit, there are technically no Christians until the day of Pentecost, which for Acts is the birthday of the church and Christianity.[1] Not even the original disciples were technically Christians until that day. After forty days of teaching, Jesus tells the disciples to wait in Jerusalem until the Holy Spirit comes and fills them with power

(Acts 1:8). While the disciples are waiting, they decide to name a replacement for Judas, the disciple who betrayed Jesus into the hands of the Jewish authorities. To do this, they cast lots, which was something like throwing dice; when the lot fell on Matthias, they trusted that God had chosen him to replace Judas (Acts 1:15–26).

Once the Spirit comes, a typical chain reaction occurs. The Holy Spirit emboldens the apostles to proclaim the message of Jesus' resurrection (e.g., Acts 2:14; 4:31). On the day of Pentecost, He miraculously enables the disciples to speak in languages they have never learned so that the crowds can understand the good news (2:4). The Spirit also brings the power to perform miracles. One example of this takes place when Peter and John heal a crippled man (Acts 3). Beyond boldness and miraculous power, the Spirit also brings unity to the church (4:32).

The message and miracles of the apostles elicit two basic responses. On the one hand, the church experiences phenomenal growth as, first, three thousand received the message (Acts 2:41), then five thousand (4:4), then "more and more people believed and were brought to the Lord—crowds of both men and women" (5:14 NLT). Acts mentions not only Pharisees who came to believe (15:5), but also a large number of priests (6:7). By the end of the book, people everywhere have heard about Christianity (28:22).

On the other hand, the Jewish leaders who put Christ to death have a different reaction to the message—they become increasingly hostile to the early Christians. After Peter and John heal a lame man, these religious leaders bring them in and interrogate them. They bring the apostles in a second time when they do not stop preaching. The climax of their opposition in these

---

Baptism with the Holy Spirit

"Baptism with the Holy Spirit" refers to the inner cleansing of one's sins that takes place when a person becomes a Christian. Along with repentance and baptism, Acts depicts baptism of the Holy Spirit as an essential element in becoming a Christian.

In Acts, receiving the Spirit results in power, which translates into preaching the gospel boldly, performing miraculous deeds, and maintaining the astounding unity of the early church. The demonstration of this power often leads not only to Christianity's expansion, but to strong opposition by its enemies.

chapters takes place when they put Stephen to death, the first Christian to die because of his commitment to Christ (Acts 7:60).

In the meantime, the church experiences its first inner conflicts as well. In Acts 5, we hear a story about a couple named Ananias and Sapphira. While the early Christians were not required to sell all their possessions, Acts tells us that many did sell their houses and land in order to take care of the needy among them (Acts 4:34). Barnabas, for example, sells a field and gives the money from the sale to the apostles (4:36–37). Ananias, on the other hand, lies to Peter about how much he had made on the sale of his land. For his attempt to gain honor from this falsehood, the Holy Spirit causes him and his wife to die (5:1–11).

In Acts 6 we read about a very significant conflict in the early church, one that involved the social division between Jews that spoke Aramaic, the language of Palestine, and Jews that spoke Greek, the language of the broader world. Evidently, those who distributed food to the widows of the community were showing favoritism to the Aramaic-speaking widows (Acts 6:1). The significance of this event is that it probably indicates a bigger problem, namely, that the church was not ministering effectively to the non-Aramaic-speaking Jews of Jerusalem.

The appointment of seven Greek-speaking men in Acts 6:3–6 prepares us for the second part of Acts, in which the gospel spreads beyond Jerusalem to the broader regions of Judea and Samaria. Philip, one of the seven, is a key player in that expansion. The story of Acts 6 also introduces us to Stephen, who is one of the seven. The first part of Acts' story ends in chapter 7 with his death. Stephen is so zealous—and perhaps so much more controversial in his preaching than the apostles—that the Sanhedrin has him stoned.

Throughout Judea and Samaria

Acts 8–12 are transitional chapters in some ways. To a great degree they prepare us for the last section of Acts, in which Paul carries the gospel throughout the Mediterranean world. However, we should not think of them as unimportant chapters—quite the opposite is true. Stephen's death pushes the gospel out of Jerusalem and the focus of the mission turns increasingly to Greek speakers, a process that we see expand throughout the rest of Acts. These transitional chapters (Acts 8–12) include some significant events. The gospel first comes to the Gentiles when Peter preaches to a centurion named Cornelius (Acts 10). Paul has a vision of the risen Jesus and joins the Christian movement (Acts 9). The church at Antioch in Syria is founded and begins to flourish. It is from this city that Paul will launch all the missionary journeys recorded in Acts. These chapters cover a space of approximately ten to fourteen years (A.D. 33–46?), some of the most crucial years in the development of Christianity.

The Ministry of Philip

In Acts 8, Philip the evangelist, one of seven men appointed to take care of the Greek-speaking community, takes the gospel to the region of Samaria, initiating its spread beyond Palestine. Interestingly, the converts he baptizes do not receive the Holy Spirit, and Peter and John have to come up from Jerusalem. One of those who hears Philip in Samaria is a man named Simon, "the wise man."[2] According to tradition, Philip starts a chain of events that eventually brings the gospel to Ethiopia. God leads him to an Ethiopian eunuch, someone who manages a king's affairs.

Saul (Paul) Becomes a Christian

Acts 9 presents us with the story of how one of the most important figures in the history of Christianity came to join the Christian movement.[3] Most people know him by his Roman name, Paul, but Acts begins his story with his Jewish name, Saul. This use of names in Acts subtly tells a story in and of itself. By starting with Paul's Jewish name, Acts highlights the fact that Paul was a Jew—in fact, a very militant Pharisee who persecuted Christians before he had a life-changing encounter with Jesus. Acts then uses the shift in names from Saul to Paul to illustrate the shift in Paul's mission from Jew to Gentile. His Roman name also hints that he was a person of some status in the Roman world, since he was both a Roman citizen and a Hellenistic Jew.

Acts tells us that he came from one of the largest cities in the ancient world, Tarsus, which was located in the southeast corner of what is now modern-day Turkey (Acts 9:11). But Acts also tells us that he was raised in Jerusalem and received his education "at the feet of" a famous and highly respected Pharisee named Gamaliel (22:3). An important earlier reference to Gamaliel is found in Acts 5.

We should not think of this event as Paul's "conversion" to Christianity, as if he changed from one religion to another. For Paul, Christianity was nothing other than true Judaism. What does happen on this occasion, however, is a call to the truth. Jesus appears to Paul while he travels to Damascus in order to persecute Christians. Paul was convinced that he was serving God by putting a stop to this group. On the way, Jesus gives him a wake-up call, validating that the Christians are correct about what God is doing in history. Not only does God tell Paul to

> **Key Events of Acts 1–7**
>
> Jesus ascends to heaven (Acts 1:9).
> The disciples replace Judas with Matthias (Acts 1:26).
> The church is born as the Holy Spirit comes on the day of Pentecost (Acts 2).
> Peter and John heal a lame man at the temple (Acts 3).
> The disciples face opposition from the Sanhedrin (Acts 4).
> God judges Ananias and Sapphira for lying to the Holy Spirit (Acts 5).
> The Jerusalem Christians have a conflict over the feeding of Greek-speaking widows. They appoint seven men for this task (Acts 6).
> Stephen becomes the first Christian martyr (Acts 7).

preach the good news of Christ's resurrection, but Acts 22:21 and 26:17–18 also depict this experience as a call to go to the Gentiles. God leads Paul to a man named Ananias. He is then baptized and receives the Holy Spirit.

The Ministry of Peter and the Opposition of Herod

Acts 9 through 12 focuses on the ministry of Peter in Judea and Samaria. Peter heals a bedridden man, Aeneas, and raises a woman, Dorcas, from the dead. In one of the most significant events in the book of Acts, Peter brings the gospel to Cornelius, the first Gentile to become a Christian in Acts (Acts 10).

While Peter is preaching, God sends the Holy Spirit to Cornelius and the Gentiles with him, demonstrating that Gentiles can be Christians just like Jews.

The book of Acts makes it clear that the possibility of salvation for non-Jews is anything but a foregone conclusion, even after Christ rises from the dead. Not only does Peter himself resist this idea at first, but Acts 11 also relates how the Jewish Christians in Jerusalem question Peter when he returns. They even object to the fact that Peter had entered a Gentile's home. However, when they hear about the vision God had given Peter and what the Holy Spirit had done, they accept this unexpected turn as the way God has chosen to deal with the world.

In Acts 12, we hear about the exploits of Herod Agrippa I, the grandson of the Herod who put the babies to death (Matt. 2). He was also a nephew of Herod Antipas, the one who beheaded John the Baptist (Matt. 14). Herod Agrippa I puts the apostle James to death and tries to do the same to Peter. However, as an answer to prayer, God miraculously delivers Peter from prison. Herod meets his end when the angel of the Lord causes worms to eat him. Because Herod had accepted worship from his people, God causes him to die.

Key Events of Acts 8–12

Philip takes the gospel to Samaria and the broader area of Palestine (Acts 8).

Saul (Paul) joins the Christian movement (Acts 9).

Peter ministers outside Jerusalem (9:32–43); takes the gospel to the Gentiles (Acts 10).

The church at Antioch in Syria begins to thrive (Acts 11:19–30).

Herod Agrippa I beheads James the apostle (Acts 12:2). When Herod tries to kill Peter, God delivers him (Acts 12:3–19).

The angel of the Lord kills Herod (Acts 12:20–23).

Questions for Study and Discussion

1. How would you describe the Holy Spirit in Acts?
2. Why do you think Luke focuses on Jerusalem to such a degree in his presentation?
3. How did the martyrdom of Stephen help the spread of the gospel?
4. Do you agree with the claim that Paul would not have interpreted his encounter with Christ as a call or conversion to a new religion?

To the Ends of the Earth

The Story of the Church in Acts Part 2

The last sixteen chapters of the book of Acts (13–28)
cover the missionary activities of Paul throughout
the Mediterranean world.

Paul's missionary activity is usually thought to include three missionary journeys, although Acts itself does not number them. In fact, Acts seems to combine what we call his second and third journeys. Nevertheless, we will refer to three journeys for convenience.

Paul's First Missionary Journey (Acts 13:1—14:28)

All three missionary journeys in Acts begin at Antioch in Syria, the northernmost part of Palestine. This city had an immense impact on the history of the church. Although Acts portrays Jerusalem as the center of early Christianity, the church at Antioch is the one Christians today might find most appealing. For example, the Christians here did not let racial boundaries get in the way of their fellowship with one another— Jew and Gentile intermingled and ate together (Acts 11:20; Gal. 2:12). According to Acts, this church both submitted to those in authority above them (e.g., Acts 15:2) and freely gave to their fellow churches when they were in need (e.g., 11:29–30). Most notable of all, of course, is this city's role in sending out missionaries like Paul to spread the good news of salvation from God's coming wrath. Somehow it seems appropriate that the followers of Jesus were first called Christians in the city of Antioch (11:26). Acts indicates that the more usual term at the time was "followers of the Way."

The first missionary journey took place in the years A.D. 46–48, covering the island of Cyprus and the southeast part of Asia Minor or modern-day Turkey. "Saul," Barnabas, and Barnabas's cousin John Mark start out from Antioch in Syria on the mission, but only "Paul" and Barnabas finish it. After arriving on the mainland of Asia Minor, Mark goes back home.

Why did he leave them in the middle of their missionary journey? Acts gives us the impression of a lack of commitment on Mark's part (cf. Acts 15:37–38). Perhaps Mark was just tired of the woes of travel. Perhaps he and Paul just did not get along.

However, Acts and Galatians give us hints that there was more to it than just Mark's weariness and lack of commitment. The later argument between Paul and Barnabas over Mark probably had a lot to do with the way Paul was relating to Gentiles in his ministry (cf. Gal. 2:13). It is probably no coincidence that Acts begins to call Paul by his Roman name at this point in the story—he increasingly focuses on the Gentiles. Nor is it a coincidence that it is shortly after Paul, Barnabas, and John Mark depart from Cyprus—Barnabas's homeland—that Mark leaves them and returns to Jerusalem. What started out as a mission to Jews—perhaps with Mark's cousin Barnabas in charge—had become a mission primarily to Gentiles under the direction of Paul (13:13)!

A number of interesting things happen on this journey in Acts. Paul strikes a sorcerer blind on the island of Cyprus. In the village of Lystra, the villagers not only acclaim Paul and Barnabas as gods—they also end up stoning Paul! Acts gives us a small peek at the way some early churches were organized when it mentions that Paul and Barnabas appointed elders in each church to oversee them (Acts 14:23). The implication seems to be that a group of individuals, probably older men in each particular congregation, directed these churches.

The Jerusalem Council (Acts 15:1–35)

The "Jerusalem Council" described in Acts 15, probably took place in about the year A.D. 49. While Acts does not call this meeting a council, it looks somewhat like the Christian councils of the 300s and 400s — which decided issues like the Trinity and the nature of Christ.

The basic issue under discussion in the Jerusalem Council is whether Gentile men need to be circumcised to escape God's judgment. In other words, could they be Christians without first becoming Jews? Some Jewish Christians who were also Pharisees insisted the Gentiles must become Jews first and fully observe the Jewish Law (Acts 15:5). Paul and Peter argue that God

> ### Key Events of Acts 13–28
> Paul's first missionary journey (Cyprus, Pamphylia, Pisidia, Lycaonia).
> The "Jerusalem Council."
> Paul's second missionary journey (Turkey, Macedonia, Greece, mostly in Corinth).
> Paul's third missionary journey (Turkey, Macedonia, Greece, mostly in Ephesus).
> Paul is arrested in Jerusalem, imprisoned for two years at Caesarea.
> On his way to Rome to appear before Caesar Nero, Paul is shipwrecked. He remains under house arrest in Rome for two years.

accepted them as they were, giving them the Holy Spirit while they were still uncircumcised (15:8, 12). James seems to strike a middle position, one that probably would allow Jewish and Gentile Christians to eat together. His judgment is that the Gentiles can remain uncircumcised, but they are to abstain from four things: meat offered to idols, meat from animals that have been strangled, blood, and sexual immorality (15:20).

Paul's Second (Acts 15:36—18:22) and Third Missionary Journeys (Acts 18:23—21:16)

Paul's second and third missionary journeys in Acts cover roughly the same territory. Both begin in Antioch of Syria (Acts 15:35; 18:23). Both traverse the length of Asia Minor (e.g., 15:41; 18:23). Both involve missions in Greece and Macedonia (e.g., Acts 16–18; 20:1–5). Both involve a trip to Jerusalem at the end of each journey (18:22; 21:17), although the second journey continues on from Jerusalem back to Antioch (18:22).

These two journeys in Acts also feature some of the same traveling companions Paul had taken on the first. However, before the second journey, Paul and Barnabas have an argument about whether Mark is suitable to go with them (Acts 15:36–39). The result is that they each go their separate ways. A man named Silas goes with Paul instead. On their way through Asia Minor, Paul also asks a young man named Timothy to accompany them. Although his mother is Jewish, his father is not, so Paul circumcises Timothy in keeping with the Jewish Law. Interestingly, another person that seems to accompany Paul during parts of these two trips is the author of Acts himself, traditionally a physician named Luke (cf. Col. 4:14).

The main difference between the two journeys is the location where Paul concentrates his missionary efforts. On his second journey, Paul spends about a year and a half in the city of Corinth in Greece (18:11). On his third, he spends about two and a quarter years in the city of Ephesus on the east coast of Asia Minor (19:8, 10). Since the ancients rounded their numbers up, we can say that Paul spent two years in Corinth on his second missionary journey and three years in Ephesus on his third (cf. Acts 20:31).

Christians and Troublemakers in Luke-Acts

Acts tells the story of the first Christians in a way that shows they were not troublemakers, although their opponents often stirred up trouble:

- Luke emphasizes the unity of the early church and downplays conflicts among early Christians.
- Luke depicts the resolution of conflicts that did occur as an extremely orderly and harmonious process.
- Luke points out the innocence of those Christians who were arrested on various occasions.

The second missionary journey (ca. A.D. 50–52) is significant in that Paul leaves the East and crosses over into what is now Europe. After revisiting the churches he and Barnabas had founded on the first missionary journey, he goes northwest across Asia Minor until he comes to Troas, near the site of the famous ancient city of Troy. After Paul has a vision, he crosses into Macedonia, the region just north of Greece. There he follows a famous Roman road called the Egnatian Way, founding churches at the cities of Philippi, Thessalonica, and Berea. He would later write letters to the first two of these cities.

Acts tells us about a number of interesting events in Philippi, a Roman colony whose official language was Latin.[1] There we meet Lydia, a wealthy Jewish woman who sells purple, a very expensive dye (Acts 16:13–15). In Philippi, Paul and Silas are arrested and put in jail. But their chains fall off in a miraculous earthquake at midnight while they are praying and singing hymns (16:25–26). In the end, the jailer and his whole family become Christians (16:33). At Paul's release, we find out for the first time that he and Silas are Roman citizens—and thus that they have been beaten illegally (16:37). Paul insists that the city officials personally escort them out of jail (16:38–39).

In Thessalonica and Berea, Paul establishes a pattern that is found often in Acts. He founds a church and then is forced to leave town because of Jewish opposition to his message (Acts 17:5–9, 13). After he is forced to leave Berea, he moves south to Athens in Greece, leaving Silas and Timothy behind to work further with the church (17:14–15). This famous center of ancient philosophy does not receive Paul's message well, although Acts 17 records a brilliant sermon Paul preaches there in defense of the gospel. Paul moves on again to Corinth, another Roman colony. He spends a year and a half there (18:1).

At Corinth we first meet Priscilla and Aquila, a wife-husband team that plays a prominent role in the spread of Christianity (Acts 18:2). They arrive in Corinth because the emperor Claudius has expelled all Jews from Rome, perhaps over the controversy Christianity is bringing to the Jewish community there. These two individuals appear several times in the New Testament. For example, they accompany Paul to Ephesus (18:18). A church meets in their house there (1 Cor. 16:19), and they convince a man named Apollos that Christians have the correct understanding of the Jewish Scriptures

(Acts 18:24–26). This man goes on to work with the church at Corinth (e.g., 1 Cor. 1:12). At some point, Priscilla and Aquila move back to Rome. Once there, another church meets in their house (Rom. 16:3–5).

Paul became acquainted with Priscilla and Aquila because they were tentmakers like him (Acts 18:3). This gives us a peek into one way Paul shared the good news with people. While he went to the synagogues to speak with Jews, his tent-making spot in the marketplace gave him an opportunity to speak to Gentiles. Whenever he came to a new city, he probably sought out the part of the city where those in the tent-making trade stayed. Given the likelihood that Paul was a person of some means, he may have "lowered" himself somewhat by actually using his hands to make tents (cf. 1 Cor. 4:12; 2 Cor. 11:7)—of course, he originally might have been the one in charge!

The third missionary journey (ca. A.D. 53–58) covers much of the same ground as the second, but with a different focus. According to Acts, Paul spends more time in the city of Ephesus than he does in any other individual city. From there he writes several letters to Corinth—two of which apparently have not survived (1 Cor. 5:9; 2 Cor. 2:3–4)—and perhaps one to Galatia as well. Paul was also imprisoned in Ephesus, although Acts does not tell us about it (1 Cor. 15:32). It is quite possible that he wrote his letters to Philippi and to Philemon while he was under guard.

Acts tells us about other events at Ephesus, however. Paul convinces some followers of John the Baptist who weren't yet Christians that Jesus is the Messiah (Acts 19:1–7). Incredible miracles take place in Ephesus; people are healed just by touching handkerchiefs and aprons that had touched Paul (19:11–12). Acts 19:19 implies that Ephesus experienced a sharp decrease in the use of magic, a common practice among the lower classes of the empire. Acts also indicates that the idol-making trade was affected enough for a silversmith named Demetrius to stir up a riot (19:23–41).

Paul's Arrest and Trip to Rome
(Acts 21:17—28:31)

The book of Acts takes on a tone of foreboding after Paul leaves Ephesus. As he completes the third missionary journey, we increasingly are made to feel that something bad is about to happen and that Paul's ministry is nearing its end. Paul is determined to get to Jerusalem by the Feast of Pentecost (Acts 20:16; cf. Rom. 15:25), so he stays only a day in Troas. He talks so long that a young man named Eutychus falls out of the third-floor window of the room where Paul is speaking. Paul miraculously revives him.

> "Since the Jews constantly made disturbances at the instigation of Chrestus, he [the Roman emperor Claudius] expelled them from Rome."
>
> —Suetonius, *Claudius* 25

Paul bypasses the city of Ephesus so he will not be delayed. Instead, the elders of Ephesus meet him in Miletus, a city to the south. In his farewell speech, he prophesies that he will never see them again (Acts 20:25). Rather, "the Holy Spirit [tells] me in city after city that jail and suffering lie ahead" (20:23 NLT). When Paul reaches Palestine, a prophet named Agabus binds his own hands and feet with Paul's belt, implying that Paul himself would be imprisoned if he went on to Jerusalem (21:11). So it is no surprise that despite Paul's efforts to please the Jewish Christians in Jerusalem, a riot ensues and the Romans arrest him (21:17–36).

The last chapters of Acts cover the four or five years Paul was imprisoned in Palestine, taken to Rome under guard, and put under house arrest in Rome (ca. A.D. 58–63). Roman soldiers rescue Paul from the riot in Jerusalem, and he is kept in the Roman fortress there until after he has appeared before the Sanhedrin (Acts 21:30–33; 22:30—23:11). When informed by Paul's nephew of a plot by the Jews to kill him, the soldiers transport Paul to the coastal city of Caesarea, the headquarters of Roman rule over Judea and Samaria at that time.

Paul spends the next two years or so imprisoned there, first under the Roman governor Felix (who governed between A.D. 52–60) who would have released Paul for a bribe, and then for a short time under Festus (A.D. 60–62). Neither these two nor Herod Agrippa II, the son of Herod Agrippa I, find any fault in Paul after hearing him. Because Festus attempts to have Paul transported back to Jerusalem, however, Paul invokes his right as a Roman citizen to appeal to the emperor and is transported to Rome to stand trial.

Did the Early Church Have Denominations?

Acts does not tell us much about the diversity of the early church, but here are some of the identifiable groups and leaders within the church.

- **Judaizers** believed all Christians should continue to keep the Jewish Law in its entirety.
- **Antinomians** believed the Law was not binding on any Christian.
- Some **Hellenistic Jewish Christians** (Greek speakers) saw a greater need for breaking with the Law than other Jewish Christians did.
- **Paul** believed that keeping the Law would not save anyone, but he continued to observe most of the Law, insisting that its essence remained valid.
- Although **James** agreed that Gentiles could become Christians, he did not think Jews should eat with them, unless the Gentiles kept certain dietary aspects of the Jewish Law.

The trip is not without its perils. The soldiers do not listen to Paul's advice and attempt to continue sailing too late in the year, when the Mediterranean Sea was particularly hazardous to travel. Ships in the ancient world typically wintered at a suitable port. Because they disregard Paul's advice, the ship wrecks, but miraculously all those aboard survive. Ashore, Paul is bitten by a poisonous snake but remains unaffected. The people of the island of Malta think Paul is a god. Three months later, the ship's survivors leave Malta and sail for Rome.

Paul spends two years in Rome, where Acts leaves him in the last chapter (ca. A.D. 61–63). During that time he rents a house where he is able to see any who come to him. Acts ends with a decisive turn away from the Jews and toward the Gentiles (Acts 28:28). Not that Luke thought God had abandoned the Jews, but perhaps he was foreshadowing the Jewish War that would start less than five years later, ending with the destruction of Jerusalem and the temple in A.D. 70.

What happened to Paul next is uncertain. Many scholars suggest that Paul was freed after his first appearance before Nero. This seems consistent with information found in 1 and 2 Timothy and Titus. If this is right, Paul may not have died in the persecution of A.D. 64, but perhaps as late as A.D. 67. Other scholars note Paul's statement to the Ephesians that he would never see them again (Acts 20:25). Many of these suppose that Acts leads right up to the point of Paul's death.

> "Paul . . . a herald both in the East and West, received the noble glory of his faith. After he had taught the whole world righteousness, come to the limit of the West, and witnessed before the rulers, he left the world and was taken up to the holy place."
>
> —1 Clement 5:6–7, ca. A.D. 96

Questions for Study and Discussion

1. Why do you think John Mark left Paul and Barnabas and returned home?
2. Why does Acts end where it does?

Paul's Letters

The Life and Writings of Paul

During the time Paul was a Pharisee,
he thought he kept the Jewish Law blamelessly.

Next to Jesus, the apostle Paul features most prominently in the New Testament. Some have considered him to be Christianity's true founder—even more so than Jesus—although this claim is highly debatable. Paul started out on the margins of Christianity but became the single most important person behind its spread to the Gentile world. Since Gentile Christians soon overshadowed the original Jewish Christians in number and authority, Paul's writings eventually moved from the margins to the mainstream of the Christian movement.

At a Glance

- Paul (Saul) was a Jew from Tarsus who was a Pharisee before he became a Christian.
- Paul's ministry was primarily directed at Gentiles rather than Jews.
- Paul took at least three missionary journeys, during which he ministered primarily to people in urban centers of the Mediterranean.
- Thirteen letters in the New Testament bear his name: Romans, 1 and 2 Corinthians, Galatians, **Ephesians**, Philippians, **Colossians**, **1 and 2 Thessalonians**, **1 and 2 Timothy**, **Titus**, and Philemon.
- Scholars argue about whether the six letters in bold font above are pseudonymous.
- According to tradition, Paul died in Rome around A.D. 64.

Paul Before Christianity

If you had known Paul in his early years, you would not have picked him as a likely candidate to become a Christian, let alone someone who would associate freely with Gentiles. After all, he was one of the most vigorous opponents of Christianity, a person who traveled long distances to arrest Christians (Gal. 1:13; cf. Acts 9). Paul describes himself in his pre-Christian days as: (1) an Israelite from the tribe of Benjamin, (2) a Pharisee who kept the Jewish Law blamelessly, and (3) someone who persecuted Christians (Phil. 3:5–6).

People who lived in the ancient world found their identity in three key factors, all of which had to do with the groups to which they belonged. Basically, you could know a person if you knew his or her (1) gender, (2) geography or race, and (3) genealogy or family background.[1] In this light, the information Paul gives in Philippians 3 is key information about his identity.

First, Paul was a Jew, which was the most important aspect of his geography. No matter where he might be in the world, people would think of him as from the land of Israel. As far as family background, he was from the tribe of Benjamin. He was also a Pharisee, which means he was fully committed to the Jewish Law, as well as to the tradition of the elders' teachings about how to keep the Law.

Interestingly, Paul does not mention in his own writings that he was born in Tarsus, a city in southeast Asia Minor where Greek was the primary language. We have to turn to Acts for this information (9:30). Perhaps he thought that mentioning his birth outside Palestine would have worked against his argument that he was "a real Jew if there ever was one!" (Phil. 3:5 NLT). Paul even seems to have used a different name in his pre-Christian days—the Jewish name, Saul. But as his mission turned more and more toward the Gentiles, he seems to have used his Roman name, Paul (cf. Acts 13:9) more and more.

Paul persecuted the church before he joined it. We can make a good argument that Paul targeted Greek-speaking Christians like Stephen, rather than the main apostles. The Jewish leaders probably saw more potential for trouble from these people than they did from the apostles, whose teaching seems to have been more conservative. Thus, Paul did not seem to go after the Aramaic-speaking Christians of Jerusalem (Acts 8:1), among whom Acts tells us were a number of Pharisee converts (15:5).

Perhaps the most interesting comment Paul makes was that he had been blameless with regard to "righteousness under the law" (Phil. 3:6 NRSV). Some think he struggled heavily with a guilty conscience before he turned to Christianity. But Paul's writings give us little reason to think he felt inadequate about his keeping the Law. The Pharisees believed that one could keep the Law adequately enough to be accepted before God. Paul evidently considered himself to have done so before he turned to Christianity.

Paul also had strong ties to the Hellenistic world. He was a Roman citizen (Acts 16:37)—a privilege very few enjoyed. This is one reason many believe Paul came from a wealthy family. His parents probably owned the tent-making business, rather than actually making the tents. Not only did he learn from the most prominent Pharisee of his day, Gamaliel (Acts 22:3), many scholars now believe Paul had some Greek education as well.

Paul's Early Days as a Christian

Paul seems to have joined the Christian movement somewhere between A.D. 32–36, although it's impossible to date most of the events in his life with absolute certainty. The drastic turning point came while he was traveling to a city called Damascus, approximately one hundred fifty miles north of Jerusalem. He left Jerusalem an ardent opponent of Christians; but when he arrived in Damascus, he was one of them. Along the road, Jesus spoke to him, and Paul's outlook on Christianity changed drastically. After spending some time processing what had happened, he emerged a different person. He was no longer Saul, the persecutor of Christ; he was Paul, the preacher of Christ (Gal. 2:18).

Paul's turnaround was so dramatic that within three years he found himself fleeing Damascus for his own life (2 Cor. 11:32). Suddenly people started pursuing him for the same reason he had pursued others. People in Paul's day generally did not view such significant changes in direction in a positive light, so it was important for Paul to see his new life as his destiny and calling. Accordingly, Paul believed that God had chosen him from birth as the main person to bring the gospel to the Gentiles (Gal. 1:15).

Paul's activities over the next ten years are sketchy, but we know that he briefly met Peter and James after he left Damascus and that he spent some time in his home country (Gal. 1:18–24). Knowing Paul, he probably preached his newly found faith vigorously there in Tarsus. Barnabas, another important early Christian, went to Paul and brought him to Antioch, a city about three hundred miles north of Jerusalem (Acts 11:25–26). This city was to become the center of Greek-speaking Jewish Christianity—indeed, the most important center of Christianity at this time outside Jerusalem.

Paul's Mission and Message

Paul saw himself as the primary person God had chosen to bring the good news of Jesus Christ to the Gentiles. As a Pharisee, Paul was confident that he had kept the Law well enough for God to accept him. But after he saw the risen Christ, he concluded that the power of sin was so extensive in the world that no one could escape God's wrath. A person could only be justified and found innocent in God's sight by trusting in Christ's death and victorious resurrection.

Christians thus are not under the Law. No one is judged by how well he or she keeps it. Nevertheless, the Holy Spirit enables victory over the power of sin and provides the basis of unity for those in the body of Christ.

Paul's Three Journeys

When people speak of Paul's three missionary journeys, they refer to the three trips described in Acts. Paul initiated each of these from Antioch on his mission to spread the gospel. From what Paul says in his letters, we know that Acts gives us the boiled down version of his missionary work. In reality, he moved around a lot more. For example, 2 Corinthians 13:1 implies a visit to Corinth that goes unmentioned in Acts; Romans 15:19 tells us that Paul preached in a place west of Macedonia, well outside the boundaries Acts gives us.

Paul took his first missionary trip (ca. A.D. 46–48) with Barnabas. This trip seems to have covered the island of Cyprus and a limited portion of Asia Minor. The second and third journeys were more expansive and included Greece. According to Acts, Paul spent about two years in Corinth on his second journey and three years in Ephesus on his third. He was then arrested in Jerusalem after his third journey and was eventually taken to Rome.

An inscription—words carved in stone—has helped us immensely to date Paul's mission to Greece. This inscription from the ruins of ancient Corinth names a man also mentioned in Acts 18:12, Gallio, who held office in Corinth around the years A.D. 51–52. This fixed point in history allows us to date Paul's second missionary journey in the early years of the fifties (ca. A.D. 50–52). The first journey thus would have taken place in the last few years of the forties (ca. A.D. 46–48) and the third journey in the mid-fifties (ca. A.D. 53–58).

Most if not all of Paul's letters were written during his second and third journeys. First Thessalonians, for example, was written from Corinth during Paul's second missionary journey—it's probably the first book of the New Testament to have been written. Paul wrote several letters to Corinth from Ephesus during his third journey. He probably wrote Galatians at this time as well, and perhaps even Philippians and Philemon. He wrote 2 Corinthians after he left Ephesus while traveling through Macedonia to the north of Greece. Finally, he wrote Romans from Corinth near the end of the third journey.

Paul probably arrived as a prisoner in Rome around A.D. 61, where he remained under house arrest for the next two years. Tradition holds that Paul wrote his Prison Epistles from this site, although we certainly know of other places where he was imprisoned. Some would say that he was freed after his first trial before Nero and even went on to Spain. Traditionally, the Pastoral Epistles were his last writings, written soon before he died. We cannot know for certain, but Nero probably had him put to death. He may have been among the Christians Nero blamed for the fire of Rome (A.D. 64). Others place his death at Nero's hands a few years later, perhaps A.D. 67.

Paul's Writings

The New Testament does not present Paul's letters in the order in which he actually wrote them. Rather, Paul's writings were arranged roughly from longest to shortest. It is thus no coincidence that Romans is first and Philemon is last. We will follow this conventional order as we discuss each of these letters in subsequent chapters.

Although it is not bad to read Paul's letters in the order in which they appear in our Bibles, reading them in the order in which Paul actually wrote them has greater advantages. It helps us gain a better sense of the context of his teaching and the flow of his ministry. It helps us to keep a balanced understanding of what Paul preached, particularly as he wrote to different audiences. It even allows us to see some changes in his emphases and approach over the course of his mission.

The following chapters allow you to approach Paul's letters in whichever way you prefer. Except for Philemon, the order of the chapters themselves follows the order in which they appear in your Bible. On the other hand, you may wish to read them in the order in which Paul probably wrote them. Following is one suggestion for the order in which Paul wrote his letters, although scholars disagree on where to place some letters.

1 and 2 Thessalonians (ca. A.D. 51)

Most scholars think Paul wrote 1 Thessalonians before any of his other letters in the Bible. Those who believe Paul wrote 2 Thessalonians date it close to the writing of 1 Thessalonians. Both letters deal with significant issues involving Jesus' return to earth. They show us that Paul's earliest preaching focused heavily on Christ's second coming, not on justification by faith, or heaven and hell.

Possibly Philippians, and Philemon (ca. A.D. 52)

Although tradition holds that Paul wrote these letters at the end of his ministry while he was imprisoned in Rome, it is possible that he wrote them while he was imprisoned in Ephesus on his third missionary journey (cf. 1 Cor. 15:32). Those who believe he wrote it from Ephesus note that Ephesus was closer geographically than Rome to Philippi and Colossae, to which he sent the letters of Philippians and Philemon. Note also Paul's optimism and confidence that he would not be put to death (e.g., Phil. 1:25–26).

1 Corinthians (ca. A.D. 53–54)

First Corinthians was probably the second letter Paul sent to Corinth from Ephesus on his third missionary journey (1 Cor. 5:9), but the first one has not survived. The Corinthian church was plagued with disunity, and this letter addresses a number of the issues over which the Corinthians were arguing. We are truly blessed by their problems, though, for this letter is a gold mine of information about what made the earliest Christians tick!

Galatians (ca. A.D. 54–57?)

Scholars disagree about when Paul wrote the letter to the Galatians. Some think it was written to the churches Paul founded on his first missionary journey; thus, it was the first of his letters and was written about A.D. 48–49. Chapter 23 of this text, on the other hand, gives the reasons why most scholars place it later. One argument we should mention here is the way Galatians fits with what Paul says in 2 Corinthians 10–13 and Romans. All three letters reflect an incredible crisis in Paul's ministry over his authority and the legitimacy of his mission to the Gentiles.

2 Corinthians (ca. A.D. 56–57)

Just as Paul wrote a letter to Corinth preceding 1 Corinthians, he wrote another letter between 1 and 2 Corinthians that we do not have today (2 Cor. 2:4–11). However, some think that the last chapters of 2 Corinthians are actually the missing letter. In other words, they think 2 Corinthians is actually two letters in one; chapters 10–13 make up one letter, and chapters 1–9 are another, later letter.

Paul wrote 2 Corinthians after he had left Ephesus for Greece, near the end of his third missionary journey. He thus wrote it while he was on the road, making his rounds through Macedonia, the region north of Greece. Chapters 1–9 are warm and friendly—they reflect the end of a fierce struggle over Paul's authority in the Corinthian church. By the time Paul wrote these chapters, he had reestablished his legitimacy.

In this light, chapters 10–13 are surprising, for Paul suddenly starts to defend his authority again in some of the strongest language he has used in any of his letters. For this reason, some think these chapters reflect the situation before Paul wrote the first nine chapters. Others think the sudden change in tone resulted from new information he had received from the church after writing the first nine chapters. After hearing that some were still resisting his authority, he finishes 2 Corinthians with yet another vigorous defense of his apostleship.

Romans (ca. A.D. 57–58)

Paul wrote Romans from Corinth at the end of his third missionary journey. He wrote this letter just before he left for Jerusalem, where he would be arrested and sent to Rome (cf. Rom. 15:23–33). Because Paul had never visited Rome and because the church there probably had strong connections with the Jerusalem church, Paul wrote Romans as a basic defense of his mission and message to the Gentiles. He sent the letter to prepare the church at Rome for his upcoming visit and to secure their support for a mission to Spain.

Ephesians, Philippians, Colossians, and Philemon (traditionally, ca. A.D. 61–63)

We refer to these four letters as Paul's Prison Epistles, since they all indicate Paul was in prison when he wrote them. Tradition has it that he wrote them from Rome while he was under house arrest (cf. Acts 28:30). However, a good number of scholars think he wrote Philippians and Philemon from Ephesus almost ten years earlier. Further, a significant number of scholars think Colossians and especially Ephesians are pseudonymous; that is, written under the authority of Paul's name but not by Paul himself. Conservative scholars, on the other hand, strongly tend to support Paul as the author of all the writings bearing his name in the New Testament.

Pseudonymity was a common first-century practice that we probably should not equate with forgery. It was an ancient genre that simply does not exist today. One potential solution to some of the difficulties, particularly with regard to Colossians, is to note that Timothy's name also appears on the letter as an author. It is possible that some of the differences in style and thought between Colossians and Paul's other letters result from Timothy taking a more active role than Paul in its authorship.

1 and 2 Timothy and Titus (traditionally, A.D. 64–67)

We call these three letters the Pastoral Epistles because they reflect how Paul mentored and trained Timothy and Titus for ministry. As with Ephesians, a solid majority of scholars believe that these writings are pseudonymous, meant to give Paul a pastoral voice many years after he had passed from the scene. Once again, conservative scholars strongly argue that we are reading the words of Paul himself, suggesting that the differences in style and thought reflect the personal nature of these letters, as well as Paul's maturity at the end of his life.

First Timothy and Titus deal primarily with matters of how to run the church. We find instructions concerning the overseers and deacons of the church (1 Tim. 3:1–13; Titus 1:5–9), as well as guidelines for women, slaves, and worship (1 Tim. 2:1–15; 5:1—6:2; Titus 2:1–15). Second Timothy is a majestic farewell letter reflecting Paul's strong love for Timothy as a Christian son (e.g., 2 Tim. 1:2; 2:1), as well as his confidence in the face of his approaching death. Despite the fact that many had abandoned him (e.g., 2 Tim. 4:9–18), Paul victoriously looked to the completion of his race (2 Tim. 4:7).

Questions for Study and Discussion

1. What were the three key factors in determining identity in ancient times? Using them, how did the pre-Christian Paul identify himself?
2. How adequately did Paul think he kept the Jewish Law according to Philippians 3? How did this compare to the way the Pharisees assessed their own righteousness in general?
3. What is the traditional number of Paul's missionary journeys? Overall, what regions did Paul visit on his journeys?
4. Do Paul's writings appear in the order in which they were written? If not, how have they been arranged? Which letter do most scholars think was written first? Do we have all the letters Paul wrote to these churches? Over which ones is there debate about pseudonymity?

20

Is God Really Faithful?
Paul's Letter to Rome

Romans boldly proclaims the righteousness of God. God did not divorce Israel or break His covenant. Rather, He found a way not only to save Israel, but to save the whole world as well!

Clear and Systematic

Paul's letter to the Romans is both his best-known writing and the one that has had the greatest impact on Christianity. This book played a major role in the lives of a number of important Christian thinkers. While not everyone may recognize the name Augustine, Christianity would be substantially different if he had not converted while reading Romans. Martin Luther, the father of Protestantism, drastically changed the course of Christianity in the 1500s after he came to have a new understanding of the book of Romans.

At a Glance

- Paul wrote Romans in preparation for his visit to Rome, in part as a defense of his mission and message to the Gentiles.
- Paul's basic concern is to show that his message does not contradict God's faithfulness to His covenant with Israel.
- Paul insists that all humans—both Jews and Gentiles—can only be accepted by God on the day of judgment through their trust in Christ.
- Adam, the first human, brought the power of sin into the world. Christ brought the power of the Spirit into the world—potential victory over sin's power over us.
- Paul asserts that God has not abandoned Israel, but that Israel has rejected Him. In the end, however, all Israel will be saved.
- In the last chapters of Romans, Paul emphasizes the need for love, unity, and peace among Christians.

After he left a Bible study on Romans, the heart of John Wesley was "strangely warmed," eventually resulting in a movement we know today as Methodism—a movement whose influence may very well have helped save England from the bloody revolution its French neighbors experienced.

The book of Romans presents Paul's most systematic thinking, although it is far from a philosophy or theology textbook. Christians often read it slightly out of context, taking arguments that had much to do with the relationship between Jew and Gentile and making them into abstract debates over issues like whether a person can earn his or her salvation. Only in recent years have we begun to regain a sense of how the book tied into Paul's ongoing defense of his mission to the Gentiles.

Romans is Paul's clearest and most systematic argument for how God brought salvation to all people, especially in light of God's special relationship with the Jews. Paul wrote this letter near the end of his third missionary journey, just before he departed from the city of Corinth for Jerusalem. He was hoping to travel to Rome in the near future, something he managed to accomplish—even if it turned out to be under Roman guard. We can thus read Romans as a letter to prepare the existing church at Rome for his arrival, a letter that implicitly defended his mission and message to the Gentiles. If the past was any indication, Paul knew he would face opposition after he arrived.

Romans: How God Has Shown His Righteousness

The book of Romans is about the righteousness of God, that God is faithful to His people Israel. He is a merciful God, desiring to save people of all kinds. Paul believed that God had chosen him as an ambassador to the Gentiles. He preached that the only way anyone could escape God's wrath was by trusting in the death and resurrection of Jesus. Gentiles did not need to convert to Judaism or become circumcised. Further, even Jews could become acceptable only through faith or trust in what Christ had done for

them. While Paul affirmed the continuing validity of the Law's essence—
love—he taught that God did not accept either Jew or Gentile on the basis
of the Law.

Many Jewish Christians found Paul and his Gentile mission alarming,
if not infuriating. The heart of Jewish religion was the Law: Genesis, Exodus, Leviticus, Numbers, and Deuteronomy. These books contained God's
covenant with Israel, the solemn arrangement to which Yahweh and Israel
had agreed over a thousand years prior. God's promise was that if Israel
would keep the Law, He would make them prosperous and free from foreign rule.

Many Jewish Christians saw no contradiction between the importance
of Christ's death and the continuing validity of the Jewish Law (e.g., Acts
21:20). They thought that Christ's death provided essential atonement—
the means of getting or keeping one on good terms with God. But they also
believed that keeping God's covenant with Israel, the Law, was essential.
As Acts 13:39 puts it, "Through him [Christ] everyone who believes is justified from everything you could not be justified from by the law of
Moses." The implication is that the Law of Moses did justify or make you
right with God to some extent, just not completely.

Paul's teaching, however, takes the significance of Christ's death one
step further than some of his fellow Jewish Christians take it. For him, the
Jewish Law does not make anyone acceptable to God—not even Jews.
Rather, it is entirely a matter of trusting in what Christ has done for us. This
means Gentiles can become Christians without keeping the Jewish Law,
and Jewish Christians can have full fellowship with Gentiles, even though
such fellowship requires them to violate some of the Law's rules of purity.

These ideas and practices raised all kinds of questions for many of Paul's
fellow Jewish Christians. Was Paul throwing the Jewish Scriptures out the
window, teaching his followers not to observe Genesis, Exodus, Leviticus,
Numbers, and Deuteronomy? Was Paul implying that being a Jew did not
put you on any special terms with God? Whatever happened to God choos-
ing Israel and electing them as His special people (cf. Deut. 7:6; 32:9)?

Paul seems to be saying that God had suddenly thrown out His marriage vows with Israel, divorcing them for another woman, the Gentiles. And how was it fair that after so many years of the Jews keeping the Law, the Gentiles suddenly could be right with God without putting in all that effort? It is easy to see why Paul's opponents might have said, "If you're right, Paul, then God is not righteous. If you're right, God is unfaithful to His promises and to His covenant with Israel."

It is against this backdrop that we should read Romans. Paul was indeed explaining the process by which anyone could get right with God. But He was doing it in the light of the Jew-Gentile issue he had been debating for so long in his ministry.

This book boldly proclaims the righteousness of God. God did not divorce Israel or break His covenant. Rather, He found a way to save Israel and to save the whole world as well! Such a God deserves no blame, and thus Paul's message does not contradict the character of God or His covenant with Israel. Paul's message affirms these things in the strongest of terms.

How Do You Get to Heaven?

Most Christians have found it helpful to summarize the Christian message in a "plan of salvation." Here are some key points to know about Paul's understanding of salvation:

- The Roman Road provides a good overview of why and how to become a Christian (Rom. 3:23; 5:8; 6:23; 10:9).
- Paul's teaching is oriented around Christ's second coming rather than heaven and hell.
- For Paul, sin is more than just the wrong acts an individual might commit; it is a power that rules over earth and flesh.
- For Paul, Christ's death was a sacrifice that satisfied God's anger and justice.
- We appropriate the benefit of Christ's death through faith in His victorious resurrection. We are joined to Christ's death and resurrection through baptism.
- The down payment and guarantee of future salvation is the Holy Spirit within us.

All—Both Jew and Gentile—Have Sinned

In roughly the first three chapters of Romans (1:18—3:20), Paul establishes the first point of his argument: the Law does not put anyone into a right relationship with God. Rather, if God were to judge people based on the Law, no one would escape the day of judgment. So the claim that Paul was undercutting the validity of the Law was mistaken. For Paul, the goodness of the Law was not disputed (e.g., Rom. 3:31; 7:12) and the faithfulness of God was not in question (e.g., 3:3–4). The problem was with humanity—the Jews had not kept the Law perfectly any more than the Gentiles had.

Romans 1:18–32 establishes a point with which none of Paul's Jewish opponents would disagree: God was angry with some of the sinning that was going on out there. In a sense, these verses set a trap for those who disagree with him. He picks out some typical Gentile sins—idolatry and sexual immorality—and then talks about how those who practice and affirm such things are worthy of death (1:32).

He triggers the trap in Romans 2. Merely to agree that such things are bad does not let you off the hook as far as judgment is concerned: "For it is not merely knowing the law that brings God's approval. Those who obey the law will be declared right in God's sight" (2:13 NLT). Paul's point is that simply being a Jew does not help one escape judgment any more than being a Gentile automatically means you will not escape. The bottom line is that only someone who keeps the Law is considered innocent, regardless of race.

In Romans, Paul arrives at his conclusion. Because no one keeps the Jewish Law perfectly, everyone—both Jew and Gentile—stand under God's wrath. "There is no one righteous, not even one" (3:10). Whether one is Jewish or Gentile, "all have sinned" (3:23). Therefore, God is not unrighteous to find us guilty. As one translation vividly puts it, He "will win his case in court" (3:4 NLT). Thus, the advantage of being a Jew does not lie in acceptability before God but in the privilege the Jews have of receiving God's Word directly.

Faith in Christ—God's Solution

Since no one kept the Jewish Law well enough to escape God's wrath, God found another way to show His commitment to Israel and the world. Jesus was so faithful to God that He was willing to die on a cross (cf. Phil. 2:8); the consequence was that His blood became a sacrificial offering for sins (Rom. 3:25). Through the atonement provided by Christ's death, God passes over the sins of anyone who has faith (3:25). Thus, God not only has proved that He is righteous, but He has provided a way for us to be found innocent on the day of judgment as well (3:26).

The middle chapters of Romans discuss the dynamics of how faith in what Christ did makes salvation from God's wrath possible. Romans 4 discusses how Abraham was considered acceptable to God because of the way he trusted God, not because he was circumcised (cf. Gen. 15:6). Here is a strong argument that a person could be accepted by God even though he was uncircumcised (i.e., a Gentile). Romans 5 and 6 discuss at various points how Christ's work undoes the problems created by the sin of Adam, the first human. While Adam's sin brought death, condemnation, and the power of sin to the whole world (e.g., 5:12), Christ brought life, acquittal, and the power of the Spirit (e.g., 5:16).

Romans 6 and 7 also discuss what role the Jewish Law plays in the life of the believer. On the most basic level, the Law informs a person of God's standard and expectation (Rom. 7:7). On a darker level, the power of sin uses the Law to make us fall to temptation (5:20; 7:8). The power of sin is such that a person wanting to keep the Law could not do the good things he or she wanted to do (7:15–24). What a dreadful state to be under the power of sin! Paul exclaims, "Oh, what a miserable person I am! Who will free me from this life that is dominated by sin?" (7:24 NLT).

Paul's answer is Jesus Christ, God's solution to the problem of sin. If Christ's death provides atonement, Christ's Spirit frees a believer from the power of sin (Rom. 8:2). A person with the Holy Spirit is a person who is not controlled by his or her "flesh," the earthly part of a person that belongs to the domain of Satan (e.g., 8:8). With the Spirit inside, we are potentially immune to the power of sin and thus able to keep the essence of the Jewish Law—love (8:4; 13:8–10). Eventually, even our flesh will be transformed into spirit, along with the rest of the created realm, which anticipates the day when it "will be liberated from its bondage to decay and brought into the glorious freedom of the children of God" (8:21).

We become a part of these incredible promises by uniting with Christ and what He has done. Symbolically, this union takes place when we are baptized. "For we died and were buried with Christ by baptism. And just as Christ was raised from the dead by the glorious power of the Father, now we also may live new lives . . . Our old sinful selves were crucified with Christ so that sin might lose its power in our lives. We are no longer slaves to sin" (Rom 6:4, 6 NLT).

What about Israel as God's Chosen People?

When you read Romans as a blueprint for how to get saved, chapters 9–11 seem somewhat out of place. It seems like Paul suddenly goes off on a tangent about Israel and the Gentiles. However, these chapters are anything but a tangent. They are the climax to which the first eight chapters have been leading; namely, the fact that the gospel as Paul preached it confirms God's righteousness and faithfulness.

Even back in Romans 3, Paul anticipated how a Jew might respond to his teaching. If salvation had nothing to do with keeping the Jewish Law, then what was the advantage of being a Jew (Rom. 3:1)? Had God just thrown away His special relationship with the Jews all of a sudden, as if He had divorced His older wife for a younger woman? What happened to the fact that God had elected, or chosen, Israel out of all the people of the earth (e.g., Deut. 7:6)? What about His promises to bless them if they kept the Jewish Law (e.g., Deut. 28)? By saying that God saved both Jew and Gentile in the same way, how could anyone really consider God to be righteous?

Romans 9–11 deals with this issue. Paul gives two basic answers: (1) God can do whatever He wants, and (2) God has not abandoned Israel as His chosen people. The second point is the most important in Paul's argument, for it is the one that defends God's faithfulness to Israel. Paul does not believe that God has done away with Israel as His special people, even though the Jewish Law could not make them acceptable to Him.

In fact, Paul says exactly the opposite: The "Jews are still his chosen people because of his promises to Abraham, Isaac, and Jacob. For God's gifts and his call can never be withdrawn" (Rom. 11:28–29 NLT). Paul even thinks that Israel will eventually come to accept Christ. He says, "And so all Israel will be saved" (11:26). At present, however, "not everyone born into a Jewish family is truely a Jew! Just the fact that they are descendants of Abraham doesn't make them truly Abraham's children" (9:6–7 NLT). Currently God had chosen only a select group of Jews to accept the message.

The idea that God chooses some and not others occurs frequently in these three chapters. This fact has led some denominations to teach the idea of predestination—the notion that God has predetermined who will believe and who will be saved. In this way of thinking, no person is really free to decide to have faith: either God has already programmed you to believe or He has not. If He has not, you will not believe. In particular, Romans 9 certainly sounds like it teaches this idea. Paul says, "God has mercy on whom he wants to have mercy, and he hardens whom he wants to harden" (Rom. 9:18).

However, it is important to read Paul's words in context. In general, he is not talking about which individuals God had chosen to save and which He had not. He is talking primarily about Jews and Gentiles, particularly the Jews who had rejected Christ. He is thinking far more about groups of people rather than about individuals. Paul argues that God can do whatever He wants. If He wants to open the door of salvation to the Gentiles by making the Jews reject Christ, God can do that—He's God (Rom. 9:16; 11:15).

Many of Paul's comments in these chapters emphasize the absolute authority of God as the creator of all, but in the process the picture of God can seem cold and unfeeling (Rom. 9:20–23). It is thus very important to keep these comments in proper perspective. Paul ultimately holds out hope for the very ones he said God had currently not chosen—the Jews. "Did they stumble so as to fall beyond recovery? Not at all! Rather, because of their transgression, salvation has come to the Gentiles to make Israel envious" (11:11). In other words, Paul holds out hope for the very people God had hardened!

Different Views of the "Righteousness of God" in Romans 1:17 (NRSV)

A young German monk by the name of Martin Luther once struggled deeply with Romans 1:17: "the righteousness of God is revealed" in the gospel. He did not feel like such a gospel was "good news" for him because he did not think he was good enough for God to accept him. Rather, he expected God to condemn him on the day of judgment. When Luther saw the words "the righteousness of God," he understood them to mean the "justice of God." The gospel revealed a God who would justly condemn him for his sins. To him, God was an exacting judge who one day would severely punish those who did not measure up to perfection. Luther feared such a day.

Then it occurred to him that the phrase "righteousness of God" in this verse could be taken in another way. What if it did not refer to God's righteousness—God's justice or rightness? What if the verse was talking about human righteousness—the possibility for humans to become right in the eyes of God? What if this verse was about how righteousness came from God by way of the gospel; about God making it possible for humans to be declared innocent of their sins? When Luther read the verse this way, the gospel truly became good news: what is revealed in the gospel is the acquittal of God, a way to be forgiven for our sins.

A load lifted from Luther's mind. Yes, he thought—in the courtroom of God's judgment, the "righteousness" in this verse was his "not guilty" verdict. God found him innocent of all charges, and he was not held accountable for his sins—not that he actually was innocent. Luther believed a Christian at all times was "both righteous and a sinner, as long as they are always repenting." The beauty of it all for Luther was that God found him "not guilty" even though He knew he was "guilty as sin." He only declared him righteous—acquitted in the court of heaven—even though he was really guilty.

God did this for him because of his faith in Jesus Christ. He was "justified," declared innocent or not guilty, because he trusted in what Christ had done. Jesus' righteousness counted as his righteousness. "Justification by faith" thus became the center of Luther's message, just as Luther thought it had been the center of Paul's. We might call this "imputed" righteousness.

Some two hundred years after Luther, another man by the name of John Wesley took Luther's line of thought one step further. He believed that this right standing we get from God was not just a legal fiction—something that was true in the eyes of the law but was not really true in reality. Wesley believed that God could actually make us righteous so that we did not sin all the time. For him, the righteousness God gave us became a reality, not just a legal decision—it was "imparted" righteousness. The righteousness revealed from God is the possibility of truly becoming righteous, a *goodness* from God that He actually makes possible for His people. For Wesley, God actually imparted righteousness to the Christian; He did not just impute it. Wesley believed that the Spirit of God gave the believer the power to do the right thing, truly to become righteous.

While all these positions have an element of truth to them, none of them precisely capture what Paul himself meant when he said that the righteousness of God was revealed in the gospel. In the light of the Old Testament (e.g., Isa. 42:6), as well as the Dead Sea Scrolls, the phrase "righteousness of God" in Romans 1:17 almost certainly refers to God's righteousness and not to ours. Thus, while the conclusions of Luther and Wesley were largely true, they have viewed Romans slightly out of focus.

Paul is not primarily talking about the predestination of individuals. He is talking about the people of Israel. We should be careful not to construct a wholesale doctrine of predestination when Paul himself held out hope to anyone who confessed Christ (e.g., Rom. 10:9). In the end, Paul's arguments aim to explain or describe what happened to Israel. Paul was not formulating a philosophy concerning how individuals come to be saved in general.

Paul's Instructions in Romans 12–15

Most of the instructions Paul gives in these chapters concern the need for Christians to show love, to be unified, and to live at peace with everyone—instructions that fit well with Paul's belief that Jew and Gentile are one in Christ. In Romans 12, for example, Paul explains how all Christians are part of the same body, the body of Christ (Rom. 12:5). He urges Christians to have sincere love (12:9) and to live at peace with everyone, letting God take care of judgment (12:18–19). In Romans 13, Paul explicitly points to love as the essence of the Jewish Law (13:10), and he encourages Christians to submit to those in authority over them (13:1). They should even pay their taxes (13:6–7)!

Romans 14 deals with another way Christians should show love—by acting in a way that does not hinder the faith of a fellow Christian. In particular, most of the things Paul mentions could apply to how Gentile Christians should behave around conservative Jewish Christians. For example, someone sensitive to another's beliefs might eat only vegetables, probably to avoid eating meat offered to idols (14:2). Others might observe the Jewish Sabbath (14:5). Paul indicates that both those who observe these aspects of the Jewish Law and those who do not are acceptable to God as long as they act out of faith (14:23). The one should not look down on the other (14:3).

A Letter of Commendation (Rom. 16)

Romans ends with what appears to be a letter of commendation from Paul to the Roman Christians on behalf of a woman, Phoebe. She appears to have been a patron or supporter (*diakonos*) of the church that met in a port village of Corinth—Cenchrea. She is probably the one who took the letter of Romans to Rome.

The chapter is mostly taken up with greetings both from Paul to various Christians in Rome and from various individuals in the Corinthian church. We learn that Priscilla and Aquila, a wife-husband ministry team, had returned to Rome and were hosting a church meeting in their house (Rom. 16:3–5). We learn of another husband-wife team, Andronicus and Junias, who were probably eyewitnesses of Jesus while He was on earth. Paul calls them both apostles, the wife as well as the husband (16:7).

Paul mentions Gaius, a man who must have been a rather wealthy member of the Corinthian church, for all the house churches of Corinth were able to meet in his house (16:23). Paul also mentions a man in Corinth named Erastus, whose name has been discovered on an inscription from Corinth. He was the city treasurer (16:23). Finally, Paul's amanuensis, the one who actually wrote down the words of the letter, gives his greeting. His name was Tertius (16:22).

Questions for Study and Discussion

1. What are some of the ways that Christians have interpreted the phrase "the righteousness of God"? Which one do you think is correct based on the text in this chapter?

2. In which part of a human being does Paul locate the power of sin? Who holds control over the domain in which that part of a person exists? Whose sin handed power over this domain to an evil power? What is God's antidote to the power of sin?

3. Do you agree with this chapter's approach to the meaning of Romans? Is Paul's main concern the question of salvation for Gentiles in the light of God's prior covenant with Israel?

Unity Problems

The Corinthian Letters

Like many churches today, the various Christians in Corinth
did not always get along as well as they should have.

House Churches and Division

When you hear about the church at Corinth, you might think of a large structure where lots of people can meet or perhaps a smaller church with a steeple on top. In reality, the earliest Christians did not have church buildings like we do. Such structures did not exist until the A.D. 300s—after the Romans stopped putting Christians to death. Instead, the churches to which Paul ministered met primarily in the homes of people in the community. Thus, when he referred to churches he

At a Glance

- The churches at Corinth had serious unity problems, mostly along social lines—some had a higher social standing than others.
- Some questioned Paul's authority in favor of other early Christian leaders like Apollos.
- Some thought they had superior knowledge and wisdom to that of other, weaker Christians.
- Some even did not believe in a resurrection.
- Some thought that sexual freedom demonstrated spiritual power; and others thought Christians should stop having sex altogether.
- Some boasted about the spiritual gifts God had given them, thinking themselves superior to others for this reason.
- Paul's solution to all this disunity was love, which he praised in 1 Corinthians 13.

did not refer to buildings, but to "assemblies" or groups of Christians joining together in worship.

A city like Corinth probably had more than one house church—a fact that might have contributed to the divisions among Christians in the city. When Paul mentions the household of a woman named Chloe (1 Cor. 1:11) or of Stephanus (1 Cor. 1:16; 16:15), it is possible that he is referring to various house churches in Corinth. Nevertheless, the main meeting place for the churches at Corinth was the house of a man named Gaius (Rom. 16:23). This man must have had a fairly large house to accommodate the whole church in this city. He was probably a person of some means.

Like many churches today, the various Christians in Corinth did not always get along as well as they should have. But their problems have worked to our advantage, for now we are able to study Paul's responses to their situations. The two letters called 1 and 2 Corinthians are full of information we simply would not have if Corinth had not been such a divided church.

The Situation in Corinth

We have more information about Paul's dealings with the church at Corinth than with any other single church. Acts tells us he made two visits to the city, and we have two letters that he wrote to the Christians there. We know further from Paul's own writings that he wrote at least two more letters that have not survived. He also visited Corinth an additional time that Acts does not mention.

Acts tells us that Paul spent a year and a half in Corinth when he founded the church (ca. A.D. 50–52). He then continued to watch its progress carefully from Ephesus, a city about two hundred and fifty miles east across the Aegean Sea. First Corinthians is actually the second letter Paul wrote to Corinth from Ephesus, and 2 Corinthians is Paul's fourth, written while he was en route.[1] At the time he wrote 2 Corinthians, he was traveling through the region of Macedonia, just to the north of Greece.

Paul wrote 1 Corinthians for at least two reasons. First, he had heard reports that the Christians in Corinth were divided and did not get along with one another. Some even questioned his authority and the validity of his message. The fundamental problem at Corinth, therefore, was disunity. It is no coincidence that 1 Corinthians 13, the love chapter of the New Testament, is in this book, for a lack of love was the heart of the Corinthians' problem.

Second, Paul was answering some questions that the Corinthian church had written to him. Many of these questions related to matters that were causing division in the Corinthian church—things like whether they should speak in angelic tongues, whether or not there is a resurrection, and whether they should eat meat that had been sacrificed to an idol. Paul used the second half of 1 Corinthians to address these issues.

Social Divisions at Corinth

First Corinthians 11 gives us a snapshot of the division in the Corinthian church. The last part of this chapter deals with what had been happening when the church partook of the Lord's Supper—the weekly meal early Christians had on Sunday to remember Christ's death. Although today we celebrate Communion or the Eucharist as a small part of a church worship service, the Christians originally had a meal together—much as Jesus did with His disciples at His Last Supper, the prototype of Christian Communion. This was the Passover meal, so it involved an entire meal.

Eating together in the ancient world was a very significant thing. Generally you only ate with people of your own sort, and having a meal often was calculated to increase your prestige according to who shared the meal with you. For Jews, eating was a highly religious event and a time when ceremonial purity was a chief concern. The issue of table fellowship, whom you should eat with, was thus a major issue that showed up time and again in Paul's writings.

In Corinth, the way Christians were eating together reflected their disunity. The wealthier individuals of the church ate sumptuously. They did not share their food with the less fortunate, nor did they wait for them (1 Cor. 11:21).

At the end of such meals, some of the wealthy would even be drunk from the amount of wine they had consumed, while others in the church went home hungry. It also seems likely that the wealthier group ate meat on such occasions—something most people could not afford. The likelihood that such meat came from one of the nearby pagan temples created yet another issue over which the church was divided.

This state of events was an atrocity to Paul. A meal that was meant to show the oneness and unity of Christians had become a matter of division and privilege. If you are going to do it that way, Paul writes, eat at home (1 Cor. 11:34).

In 1 Corinthians 1:26 Paul notes that the majority of the Corinthian church were not born with worldly power and influence, but he implies that some were. We know from Romans 16:23 that Erastus, a member of the church, was the city treasurer. Archaeologists have actually unearthed a stone indicating that a man with this name paid for a building in the city. This may very well be the same person. We have already mentioned that Gaius also must have been a well off individual, since his house apparently was big enough for the whole church to assemble inside.

While Paul was probably not on bad terms with Gaius and Erastus, a great deal of Paul's opposition probably came from this more powerful element in the Corinthian church. These are the ones likely to have favored the highly educated Apollos over Paul. These are the ones likely to have scoffed at the notion of physical resurrection and to have favored eating meat that had been offered to an idol. And surely the man who was sleeping with his stepmother was from this group or else he would not have been able to get by with it.

Questioning Paul's Leadership

Acts tells us that Paul was not the only Christian leader to serve at Corinth. A man named Apollos also ministered there in the period after Paul founded the church (Acts 18:27–28). Over time, there were some in the community, probably from the social elite, who used Apollos as a way to undermine Paul's authority, proclaiming him more educated and a greater intellect than Paul.

Acts tells us that Apollos was from Alexandria, a place where Jews were known for their knowledge of Greek philosophy (Acts 18:24–26). It is quite possible that he really did differ from Paul in his approach to some issues.

First Corinthians 1:12 describes the situation that resulted in the church: "One of you says, 'I follow Paul'; another, 'I follow Apollos'; another, 'I follow Cephas'; still another, 'I follow Christ.'" If some used Apollos's supposed "wisdom" to undermine Paul's instructions, others pointed to Peter as a real apostle, in contrast to Paul. Indeed, it is quite possible that Paul did not have the wholehearted support of Peter and the church in Jerusalem at the time he wrote 1 Corinthians.[2] Paul's opponents in Corinth probably used this fact to their advantage.

In what was a fairly common situation, Paul found himself needing to defend his authority to the Corinthians. He argues in 1 Corinthians 9 that he deserves just as much financial support as Peter, although he does not take advantage of this right. In 2 Corinthians 10–13 he later defends his apostleship even more vigorously, providing a kind of apostolic resume to the unconvinced in Corinth.

Paul also has some things to say to those who thought him an inferior speaker and thinker. He takes the first four chapters of 1 Corinthians to argue that human wisdom—such as his opponents claim to have—has nothing to do with God's wisdom. God's wisdom, Paul writes, was to send the Messiah to die on a cross—something the Greeks would consider ridiculous and something the Jews viewed as offensive.

The heart of the Corinthian problem, Paul writes, is that they are oriented around their flesh, the part of their person most susceptible to the power of sin and Satan (1 Cor. 3:1–4). They are thinking with their human, fleshly minds and not with the mind of the Spirit. When we are spiritual, we realize that all of us together make up the body of Christ and that no part of that body is unimportant (12:22–23). It is together that we are the temple of the Lord in which the Holy Spirit lives (3:16; 6:19).

Superior Wisdom and Knowledge

Paul's opponents in Corinth claimed to have superior wisdom and knowledge. Paul describes their attitude:

Already you have all you want! Already you have become rich! You have become kings—and that without us! How I wish that you really had become kings so that we might be kings with you! . . . We are fools for Christ, but you are so wise in Christ! We are weak, but you are strong! You are honored, we are dishonored (1 Cor. 4:8, 10)!

This attitude probably stood behind a number of issues about which the Corinthian church had questions. The bottom line for Paul was that "the foolishness of God is wiser than man's wisdom, and the weakness of God is stronger than man's strength" (1 Cor. 1:25).

One person in the community seems to have had "superior" wisdom on a sexual matter. Perhaps using Paul's teaching that Christians were not "under the law" (e.g., 1 Cor. 9:20), some at Corinth were proud of a member who was living with his stepmother in open violation of the Jewish Law (cf. Lev. 18:8). Paul says to such individuals: "And you are proud! Shouldn't you rather have been filled with grief?" (1 Cor. 5:2). Instead they were flaunting the slogan, "I am allowed to do anything" (see 6:12; 10:23 NLT).

One of the big questions Paul addresses in 1 Corinthians is the matter of meat that had been sacrificed to idols (1 Cor. 8–10). This issue was somewhat complex and involved a number of factors. First, there was the social issue, the fact that only the wealthy would have meat at all. Second, there was the fact that much of the meat available at the marketplace would have come from nearby pagan temples. Third, we must also consider the possibility that Apollos's teaching on this matter might have differed from Paul's.

All of these factors made the issue of meat offered to idols a divisive one. The "wise" at Corinth saw eating meat that had been sacrificed to a pagan god as an indication of their strong conscience. After all, they knew that "an idol is nothing at all in the world and that there is no God but one" (1 Cor. 8:4). They could eat such meat with full confidence that the gods or goddesses to which it had been offered did not really exist. It was just meat.

Paul does not completely contradict them, at least not initially. His tactic was not to deny the strength of their conscience but to remind them that the well-being of their brothers and sisters was far more important than their individual rights. He steers them toward an attitude of love: "If what I eat causes my brother to fall into sin, I will never eat meat again, so that I will not cause him to fall" (1 Cor. 8:13).

A final matter about which this group may have viewed themselves superior is in their view of the afterlife. Evidently some in the Corinthian church did not believe in a resurrection (e.g., 1 Cor. 15:12). It is hard to know exactly what they were saying, but one strong possibility is that they rejected the notion of a physical resurrection—a very strange idea for the Greek world. It is possible they believed that our spirits survived death, perhaps even that we were already reigning spiritually with Christ (cf. 4:8). However, Christianity taught resurrection, not the immortality of the soul. Paul's response is a combination of both: a spiritual resurrection. A body is involved, but it is a different kind of body. "Flesh and blood cannot inherit the kingdom of God" (15:50).

Divisions over Spiritual Gifts

Another point of division in the Corinthian church derived from their exercise of spiritual gifts, special abilities God had given them through the power of the Holy Spirit. The two most prominently discussed in 1 Corinthians are the gift of prophecy (the ability to present messages from God about the community and its future) and the gift of tongues (the ability to speak in angelic languages). While it is hard to know for sure how this division related to those who claimed superior wisdom, it is possible that these same people were some of the ones speaking in tongues. They would thus feel that they had a special channel to God. If this is the case, it would explain how they thought they were already reigning with Christ spiritually. Paul does not forbid speaking in tongues, but he limits its use in the Christian worship assembly (1 Cor. 14:27–28).

The exercise of prophecy in the church could bring disruptions as well, although Paul encourages it in worship (1 Cor. 14:1–3). Like tongues, Paul limits the use of prophecy to two or three individuals per service (14:29). He insists that women who pray and prophesy in such a setting have their heads veiled out of respect for their husbands (11:5), perhaps a reflection of ancient concerns for modesty. The worship of men and women together in such close quarters (a house church), with women taking prominent roles like praying or prophesying, probably created a somewhat awkward social situation. The veiling of the women probably helped ease such tensions.

Questions for Study and Discussion

1. Do you know of any contemporary churches that remind you of the Corinthian church? How often do churches today have cliques and divisions? What are some of the issues behind the cliques and divisions; e.g., different church leaders, matters of social status or wealth?

2. Are Christians today ever tempted to think themselves superior to other Christians? Do some denominations think they have more knowledge than others or that they are purer? Have you ever known a Christian to think he or she had a superior spiritual gift to another Christian?

22

Healing Relationships

2 Corinthians

Paul writes 2 Corinthians after a period of significant tension. With the tension largely resolved, Paul writes some of the most uplifting words in the entire New Testament.

A Touchy Situation

When reading through the first nine chapters of 2 Corinthians, it is clear that there had been a crisis in the Corinthian church and in Paul's relationship with that church. Paul had written a previous letter shaming the Corinthians, in part because they had not dealt properly with someone in the church who had wronged another Christian in the community (2 Cor. 7:12). Paul had evidently defended his authority in that previous letter (3:1) and had informed the church that he was coming himself to straighten things out. In the end, he

---

At a Glance

- Paul wrote more letters to Corinth than we have today, and he visited the city at least one more time than Acts tells us.

- It is possible that 2 Corinthians consists of two of Paul's letters to Corinth that have been put together (chapters 10–13 would then be from a letter Paul wrote before he wrote chapters 1–9).

- Second Corinthians 1–9 reflects that Paul and the Corinthians had been reconciled to one another. Paul rejoiced that because of a harsh letter he had sent, someone had repented of his sins.

- Second Corinthians 10–13 is a vigorous defense of Paul's authority. Some think these chapters are an excerpt from the harsh letter just mentioned.

had sent Titus instead (1:23–2:4, 13). Given the touchy situation, some of the leaders of the community perhaps felt that Paul had left them holding the bag and that he had talked out of both sides of his mouth. He said he would come but then did not follow through (1:17–18).

> "We are hard pressed on every side, but not crushed; perplexed, but not in despair; persecuted, but not abandoned; struck down, but not destroyed. We always carry around in our body the death of Jesus, so that the life of Jesus may also be revealed in our body."
>
> —2 Corinthians 4:8–10

Against this background, the first nine chapters of 2 Corinthians give us the rest of the story. The church had risen to the occasion and had taken appropriate action with regard to the wrongdoer (2 Cor. 2:6–7). More importantly for Paul, they reaffirmed their submission to his authority (2:9; 7:12). Paul was delighted when he met up with Titus and found out that the church was back on track (7:6–7). Second Corinthians 1–9 presents us with a comforting tale of reconciliation between Paul and the house churches at Corinth.

Given the warm and conciliatory tone of the first nine chapters of 2 Corinthians, the reader is immediately struck by the difference in 2 Corinthians 10. All of a sudden, Paul is back on the defensive, vigorously defending that he is an apostle. In 3:1 and 5:12 he leads us to believe he is not going to do that again. In fact, the content of 2 Corinthians 10–13 has much in common with what Paul implies was in the harsh letter he had previously written them. He mentions coming to visit them to straighten things out regarding sexual immorality (12:21). He is uncertain about their loyalty and goes to great lengths to demonstrate his authority. These are the things the first part of 2 Corinthians assumes have been sufficiently resolved.

For this reason, some scholars argue that 2 Corinthians 10–13 is an excerpt from the harsh letter Paul mentions in the first nine chapters. In this theory, the excerpt had been appended to the conciliatory letter as Paul's writings were being collected and passed around, perhaps as a point of reference for the other chapters. It is important to note that this view would not affect the Bible's inspiration, nor does it attribute error to the Scriptures in any way. We already know that the Bible's packaging as one book has nothing to do with the way these books were written or the order in which they first appeared. It would thus be quite a mistake to think that the Bible's authority is somehow connected with how its packaging appears. And, of course, it is possible that these chapters were originally part of the same letter anyway. Perhaps they were aimed at those in the Corinthian church who had not yet come around to accepting Paul's authority.

Getting Back Together: Chapters 1–9

The key idea in these chapters is comfort or encouragement, a word Paul uses in one way or another over twenty times in these first nine chapters. Paul writes to encourage the Corinthians after a period when significant tension had existed between them. With the tension largely resolved, Paul writes some of the most uplifting words in the entire New Testament.

We have already mentioned the basic circumstances of the discomfort. Someone in the Corinthian church had wronged someone else in the church. Some among the house churches of Corinth did not accept Paul's authority on the matter. Rather, they favored those whom Paul called "super-apostles" (2 Cor. 11:5).

As Paul travels around the Aegean Sea from Ephesus, to Troas, to Macedonia, he meets up with Titus, who was going around in the opposite direction. Titus reassures Paul that the church is still loyal to his authority and that the sinner has been dealt with. In the middle of telling the story of this meeting with Titus, Paul sidetracks for about five chapters to speak comforting words to the Corinthians. While things are not always going well on the outside, he says, we are inwardly being prepared for heavenly things to come.

Chapters 3–6 are filled with the contrast between how things look on the outside and what is really happening on the inside. "Though outwardly we are wasting away, yet inwardly we are being renewed day by day" (2 Cor. 4:16). The glory that Christians have in them comes from the Holy Spirit (3:18), and it is encased in a "jars of clay" (4:7). The jar is very breakable, but inside there is a transformation going on. The "earthly tent" we live in, our bodies, will eventually be destroyed, but God has another house for us that he will give us at the resurrection (5:1–5), the spiritual body of which Paul spoke in 1 Corinthians 15. Until then, the Holy Spirit in us is a guarantee of that body, as well as a down payment of the glory yet to come (1:22; 5:5). Paul even notes that we are already "being transformed into his likeness with ever-increasing glory, which comes from the Lord, who is the Spirit" (3:18). Even from the moment we become a part of Christ, we become a "new creation" (5:17).

The bottom line of Paul's ministry is reconciliation: getting humanity back together with God. Paul sees his job as that of an ambassador from God to people like the Corinthians. Ultimately, God is using Christ to bring humanity back to himself. He had Christ take on the sins of the world, so that Paul and ambassadors like him could bring an invitation to all people. Paul gives them the message plain and simple: "Be reconciled to God!" (5:20).

The final two chapters of this section deal with an offering that Paul and the churches he founded have been collecting for the church in Jerusalem. Paul holds up to the Corinthians the model of Christ: "Though he was very rich, yet for your sakes he became poor, so that by his poverty he could make you rich" (8:9 NLT). This offering was certainly "for the poor among the saints in Jerusalem" (Rom. 15:26), but it also may have been a peace offering between Paul and a part of the church with which he himself was at odds. As such he may have seen it as part of his own reconciliation to the church.

A Vigorous Defense: Chapters 10–13

Even if 2 Corinthians 10–13 was originally a part of the same letter as the first nine chapters, it was probably similar to the harsh letter Paul had sent previously. Paul tells them that he is coming for a third visit, during which he will settle some matter in dispute. He had warned them on his second visit. When he returns, he warns, "I will not spare those who sinned earlier or any of the others, since you are demanding proof that Christ is speaking through me" (2 Cor. 13:2–3). They had accused him of being timid when face to face with them, but bold when he was communicating with them by letter (10:1, 10; 13:3).

He felt compelled to boast about his qualifications as a minister. The better part of 2 Corinthians 11–12 presents excerpts from his resume. He illustrates in 2 Corinthians 11 the significance of his service to God by the many troubles he has faced. He has been thrown in prison, flogged, beaten, stoned, and shipwrecked. He has endured the dangers of travel by land and sea, and has faced the opposition of both Jews and Gentiles. When the governor of Damascus had the city gates guarded in order to arrest him, Paul escaped by being lowered in a basket from a window in the city wall (11:32–33).

> "God was reconciling the world to himself in Christ, not counting men's sins against them. And he has committed to us the message of reconciliation."
>
> —2 Corinthians 5:19

In 2 Corinthians 12, Paul verifies his spiritual qualifications in terms of the visions and revelations he has experienced. He tells how he had gone up to the third heaven, "caught up to paradise," where he had heard inexpressible things (12:4). His experiences were so tremendous that God had to give him a physical problem just to keep him from becoming conceited (12:7).

His conclusion is that while he might not have the standing of some of the "super-apostles" so valued by his opponents in Corinth, he is in no way inferior to them (11:5–6; 12:11). "The things that mark an apostle—signs, wonders and miracles," Paul does among them patiently (12:12). His warning to them is very serious indeed: "Examine yourselves to see whether you are in the faith; test yourselves. Do you not realize that Christ Jesus is in you—unless, of course, you fail the test?" (13:5).

Questions for Study and Discussion

1. Which model of Christ's death is most meaningful to you: (1) His death as a sacrifice for sins and to satisfy God's anger, (2) His death in your place, taking your punishment, (3) Christ's defeat over evil powers that enslave humanity, or (4) Christ as an ambassador from God to humanity to reconcile us to one another?

2. How angry is Paul in 2 Corinthians 10–13? Is he modeling an appropriate Christian response to his situation?

3. Would it affect the authority or inspiration of 2 Corinthians if it were actually two of Paul's letters that someone had joined together?

4. If someone were to find Paul's other letters to the Corinthians, should we put them into the Bible? Did God and the church already set the boundaries for the canon? What qualifies a book as Scripture?

Paul on the Defense

Galatians

Some Jewish Christians had taught the Galatians that
they would not escape God's judgment unless they
were circumcised and kept the Jewish Law.

A Slap in Christ's Face

Although some disagree about when Galatians was written, one solid suggestion is that Paul wrote it in the same general time period that he wrote 2 Corinthians and Romans. During his second missionary journey, some crisis forced Paul to spend some time with the non-Jewish Galatians (Gal. 4:13–15). Although they became Christians, he did not circumcise them. He had come to believe that Gentiles did not need to be circumcised in order to escape God's coming wrath. Christ's death alone atoned for their sins.

At a Glance

- Paul probably wrote Galatians near the end of his mission to Asia Minor and Greece (A.D. 53–57), not long before he wrote Romans. Some believe that it was the first letter he wrote (ca. A.D. 48–49).
- Paul wrote because some group was exerting pressure on the Galatians to be circumcised and to follow the Jewish Law.
- Paul formulates a different way for Gentiles to be acceptable to God: by faith rather than by keeping the Old Testament covenant.
- It is Christ's faithfulness and their faith in Christ that gives them a "not guilty" verdict in God's court.
- The result of this faith was incorporation into Christ, the presence of the Holy Spirit, and the resulting fruit (especially love).

Not long after Paul departed, some Jewish Christians came in and taught the Galatians that they would not escape God's judgment simply because they had been baptized and trusted in Christ's death to atone for their sins. They said that unless they also followed the Jewish Law by being circumcised, observing the Sabbath, and keeping the Old Testament covenant in general, they would still be found guilty when God judged the world. What is worse, the Galatians were buying it! Paul saw this teaching as a slap in Christ's face and a horrible perversion of the Christian message.

The letter to the Galatians was Paul's response. From some of his comments, we can tell that Paul was rather angry when he wrote this letter (e.g., Gal. 5:12). It is also the only one of Paul's letters without the standard introduction in which Paul gives thanks to God for those to whom he is writing. Instead, he gets right down to business after his greeting: "I am shocked that you are turning away so soon from God, who in his love and mercy called you to share the eternal life he gives through Christ" (Gal. 1:6 NLT).

Background

In the first two chapters of Galatians, Paul recounts some of the key events in his ministry, focusing primarily on the current disagreement. Paul strongly asserts that God chose him specifically to bring Christianity to non-Jews or Gentiles. From his mother's womb, God had chosen him for this mission (Gal. 1:15–16). His call to Christianity came by way of a direct revelation from God, after which he immediately went to Arabia. After three years, he traveled to Jerusalem to meet Peter and James. He makes it clear that he has never been under their authority.

His next visit to Jerusalem was fourteen years later. During this trip, which may very well be the Jerusalem Council of Acts 15 seen through Paul's eyes, Paul presented the message he gave to Gentiles. The Jerusalem Council, as you recall, decided the issue of whether Gentiles needed to be circumcised in order to escape God's wrath. But neither Peter, John, nor the Lord's brother, James, opposed his mission or the fact that he did not circumcise Gentiles. The uncircumcised Titus, Paul's helper, remained uncircumcised. The only thing the Jerusalem leaders added was concern for the poor, something Paul had already included in his ministry.

We might think that the Jew-Gentile matter was solved at this point. The church had agreed that Gentiles could escape God's coming wrath on earth without being circumcised. Some readers might be surprised, then, to see what happened next. Peter, Barnabas, and Paul were in the city of Antioch, where Jewish and Gentile Christians were eating together in fellowship. But when certain men came from James in Jerusalem, both Peter and Barnabas separated themselves and would not eat with the Gentiles anymore. Paul considered this to be hypocrisy, which at that time was understood to be a failure to discern God's will appropriately. In front of everyone, he corrected Peter.

It would be hard to underestimate the significance of this one event for Christianity. In the short term, this argument probably was part of why Paul and Barnabas went their separate ways on their second missionary journeys. But more important is the fact that Paul seems to have lost this argument. He almost certainly would have told us if Peter had come to agree with him on this occasion. The implication is that Paul suddenly found himself outside the mainstream of Christianity, out of favor with the apostles and leaders of the church. Now he would have to justify his authority in places like Galatia and Corinth. He had a long road ahead of him.

Ironically, this conflict may have been the catalyst for bringing the gospel to Greece and Rome, since it probably pushed Paul away from Palestine and its nearby regions. It may also have been the speck of dirt that resulted in the pearl Christians call "justification by faith." This event may have led Paul to formulate teachings that would eventually become some of the most significant doctrines in the history of the modern church.

Why did Peter and Barnabas stop eating with the Gentile Christians if they already believed the uncircumcised could be saved in the judgment? They probably stopped because they felt God still expected them to keep the Jewish Laws regarding purity and what foods to eat. The Gentiles might not die when God came to judge the earth, but this fact did not make them clean in the eyes of the Jewish Christians, nor did it place them on the same level of acceptability as the Jews before God. If the Gentile Christians were to eat with Jewish Christians, they would have to be clean in accordance with the Old Testament codes regarding holiness.

Justification by Faith

One reason Paul considered Peter's actions hypocritical is because Peter himself did not keep the Law perfectly. As Paul also says of the ones troubling the Galatians, "Even those who advocate circumcision don't really keep the whole law. They only want you to be circumcised so they can brag about it and claim you as their disciples" (Gal. 6:13 NLT). In fact, Paul did not believe anyone could keep the Law perfectly. Therefore, anyone relying on the Jewish Law in order to be accepted by God at the judgment was doomed: "All who rely on observing the law are under a curse, for it is written: 'Cursed is everyone who does not continue to do everything written in the Book of the Law'" (3:10).

After Paul had kept the Law as well as a Pharisee, the meager efforts of the Galilean Peter and the Jerusalem Christians to enforce the Law must have seemed almost ridiculous to him. As Paul says to Peter, "You are a Jew, yet you live like a Gentile and not like a Jew. How is it, then, that you force Gentiles to follow Jewish customs?" (2:14).

The day of judgment will be a day when the living come before the greatest judge of all, God. Everyone will be on trial, and everyone will either receive a verdict of "guilty" or "not guilty." Any Jew who depended on keeping the Jewish Law to escape a guilty verdict, Paul says, is doomed. Rather, the only way to be justified, to be found not guilty and innocent, to be acquitted of all charges and declared righteous—the only way for that to happen is by trusting or having faith in Christ's death. This idea is called justification by faith.

A number of scholars think that Paul refers in Galatians not only to our faith in Christ but also to Christ's own faithfulness. For example, Philippians 2:8

talks about how Jesus obeyed God to the point of dying. Those who think that Galatians and Romans focus on Christ's faithfulness argue that it is not even so much our faith that saves us as the fact that we put our trust in the faith Christ showed when He died for our sins and trusted God to raise Him from the dead (cf. Heb. 5:7).

Here is how Galatians 2:16 looks when interpreted in this way: "Since we knew that no one is considered 'not guilty' by keeping the Jewish Law unless declared innocent through the faith of Jesus Christ, we also had faith in Christ Jesus so that we might be declared innocent on the basis of Christ-faith and not by keeping the Law. By keeping the Law, no one will be found 'not guilty'" (author's translation).

The great thing about this interpretation is that it focuses on Christ rather than on the individual believer. It holds true to the fact that for Paul, it is being in Christ that saves us, the fact that we are part of the body of Christ. It also fits with the idea that all Christians share the same Spirit of Christ.

A balanced understanding of what Paul understands as justification by faith avoids some of the arguments different denominations have had over the years. For one thing, Paul is not exactly talking about whether we are saved by faith or by good deeds. Roman Catholics believe that God accepts us in part by the good deeds we do, while most Protestants vigorously argue that it is faith alone that saves us. Protestants and Catholics alike understand the faith versus works debate as a matter of faith alone versus good deeds alone saving us.

> "Since we knew that no one is considered 'not guilty' by keeping the Jewish Law unless declared innocent through the faith of Jesus Christ, we also had faith in Christ Jesus so that we might be declared innocent on the basis of Christ-faith and not by keeping the Law. By keeping the Law, no one will be found 'not guilty.'"
>
> —Galatians 2:16 (author's translation)

In these passages, Paul is not really talking about good works in general. Instead, he is talking about whether Jews are saved because of the way they keep the Old Testament Law, the Jewish Law. Paul is thinking mostly about the issue of circumcision facing the Galatians and the fact that they were observing the Sabbaths and festivals of the Old Testament (Gal. 4:10). The debate was not faith versus works in general; it was trusting in Christ's death versus keeping the old covenant.

For Paul, therefore, faith includes some works. As he writes, "For in Christ Jesus neither circumcision nor uncircumcision has any value. The only thing that counts is faith expressing itself through love" (5:6). Paul would thus agree with James 2:17 that faith without works is dead.

Living by the Spirit

The way we get into Christ's body is for God to get into us. Just as we are "in Christ," the Spirit of God is in us. In Paul's mind, to be a Christian was to have God's Spirit in our hearts (cf. Rom. 8:9). Paul expresses some of his thinking in Galatians and Romans by talking about two parts of a human being: body and spirit. When he is talking about how sin can have control of our bodies, he refers to our flesh, a word translated as our "sinful nature." Our spirit, on the other hand, is the part of us that most directly receives God's power by way of God's Holy Spirit. When God's Spirit is in us, it is as if God has put a little bit of heaven in us, even though we are still on earth in our fleshly bodies.

Paul clearly believes that sin and evil spiritual forces have virtually uncontained power over our flesh before we come to Christ (e.g., Rom. 7:18; Gal. 4:8–9). As he sees it, the Jewish Law is oriented around our physical existence on earth and constantly reminds us of our slavery to powers beyond our control. Freedom from these forces and the power to love comes from God's Spirit (Gal. 5:1, 13–14, 16). After the Galatians had started out with the Spirit, Paul could not comprehend why they would subject themselves all over again to the power sin had over the flesh (3:3). They had freed themselves from the spiritual forces that rule this earthly realm (4:9). The earthly Jerusalem, enslaved to Rome, was no longer their "mother." Now they were the children of the heavenly Jerusalem.

Paul encourages the Galatians to live by the Spirit, not to return to their days in the flesh. Relying on their flesh, they would simply find themselves doing things that would not gain them entrance into God's kingdom, things like sexual immorality, hatred, envy, drunkenness, and the like (Gal. 5:19–21). But under the power of the Spirit, they would yield the fruit of the Spirit: love, joy, peace, patience, kindness, goodness, faithfulness, gentleness, and self-control (5:22–23).

The Who's and When's of Galatians

Two different regions have emerged as possible destinations for the book of Galatians. One was located in north central Asia Minor and was called Galatia because of the Gauls who settled there. Scholars refer to this region as "ethnic Galatia." However, at the time of Paul, the Roman province of Galatia also included the area to the south of ethnic Galatia, an area that included a number of cities Paul visited. To which of these did Paul write the epistle to the Galatians?

Some scholars favor the south part of the Roman province of Galatia because Paul planted churches there. Those who argue for this destination usually date the writing of Galatians early among Paul's letters, often as the first New Testament letter he wrote (ca. A.D. 48–49). Some of the motivation for such an early date is to better fit events in Galatians with the way Acts presents Paul's life. In particular, Galatians 2 differs enough from Acts 15 for some to consider them two different events. If they were two different events, the meeting in Galatians 2 would need to have happened before the Jerusalem Council of A.D. 49. In addition, some think Peter and Paul would not have argued over eating with Gentiles after the Jerusalem Council.

However, we know that Paul passed through the area of northern Galatia, and we know that he did many things that were not recorded in Acts. Further, Galatians 2:1–10 may very well be Paul's version of the Jerusalem Council. In fact, most scholars equate the two. Those who argue for northern Galatia as the destination go with a later date like A.D. 53–57, placing the writing of Galatians at about the time Paul was writing books like 2 Corinthians and Romans. Indeed, those three books share many of the same themes. Finally, we have no reason to believe a physical illness brought Paul to southern Galatia as suggested in Galatians 4:13–15. On the other hand, we could easily picture such a providential layover in ethnic Galatia while Paul was on his way through during his second missionary journey.

Questions for Study and Discussion

1. What do you make of Paul's attitude in Galatians? Does it indicate that it is okay for a Christian to get angry?
2. Do you find it surprising that some early Christians believed they needed to continue to keep the Jewish Law after becoming Christians?
3. Does Paul indicate that a Christian's behavior changes after the Spirit is in his or her life? According to Paul, will a Christian give in to the desires of the flesh when he or she is walking in the Spirit?

Letters from Prison

Ephesians, Philippians, Colossians, and Philemon

Traditionally, Paul wrote the Prison Epistles during his imprisonment in Rome.

The four short letters to the Ephesians, Philippians, Colossians, and to the slave owner Philemon are often called the Prison Epistles. They are so called because in each letter Paul mentions that he is in chains as he writes (Eph. 6:20; Phil. 1:13; Col. 4:18; Philem. 13). Tradition has it that Rome was the place from which Paul wrote these letters, but Paul was also imprisoned in the cities of Ephesus and Caesarea, leading others to suggest one of these as the point of origin. Some also argue that Colossians and Ephesians are pseudonymous, written under the authority of Paul's name, but not by Paul himself.

At a Glance

- Ephesians, Philippians, Colossians, and Philemon are Paul's Prison Epistles.
- Traditionally, Paul is thought to have written them from Rome while imprisoned there.
- Ephesians celebrates the unity of the church, particularly between Jew and Gentile.
- Philippians is a letter of thanks to Philippi after the church sent support to Paul.
- Colossians warns Christians at Colossae about a false teaching involving the Jewish Law.
- Philemon is a letter asking a slave owner to receive back his slave, Onesimus, who had apparently run away.
- Some think Colossians and Ephesians are pseudonymous—written under the authority of Paul's name, not literally by Paul himself.

Ephesians

To a great degree, Ephesians is a celebration of the unity of the church as well as an argument for its unity. Obviously written to a Gentile audience (e.g., Eph. 1:13; 2:11, 19; 4:17), Ephesians is similar to Colossians (covered later in this chapter) in many respects. It incorporates Colossians' comments on the cancellation of the Jewish Law into a grand statement on how God has abolished the dividing wall of hostility between Jew and Gentile (Col. 2:14; Eph. 2:14–18). Ephesians builds on the imagery of Colossians regarding the mystery of how God has brought Jew

> "There is one body and one Spirit—just as you were called to one hope when you were called—one Lord, one faith, one baptism; one God and Father of all."
>
> —Ephesians 4:4–6

and Gentile together through Christ, a plan that "God did not reveal . . . to previous generations" (Eph. 3:5 NLT). The letter gives a tone of certainty to this plan by its strong language of election and predestination (Eph. 1:4–13), language that should be read as God's favor toward the Gentiles rather than as individual predestination.

In continuity with Paul's earlier writings, Ephesians mentions that the unified church is the body of Christ (Eph. 1:23; cf. 1 Cor. 12), a holy building and temple (Eph. 2:21; cf. 1 Cor. 3:10, 16). In a magnificent passage, Ephesians notes, "There is one body and one Spirit—just as you were called to one hope when you were called—one Lord, one faith, one baptism; one God and Father of all" (4:4–6). Within the unity of the church there are various roles to play: some apostles, some prophets, some evangelists, some pastors and some teachers (4:11). Even the household has its proper order: wives are to submit to their husbands (5:22); husbands are to love their wives (5:25); children are to obey their parents (6:1); and slaves are to obey their masters (6:5). You are to "make every effort to keep the unity of the Spirit through the bond of peace" (4:3).

Ephesians closes with a familiar encouragement to put on the armor of God; to be prepared for spiritual battle. In keeping with Colossians' heightened sense of evil spiritual powers, Ephesians notes that "our struggle is not against flesh and blood, but against the rulers, against the authorities, against the powers of this dark world and against the spiritual forces of evil in the heavenly realms" (6:12). To combat such forces, Ephesians encourages us to arm ourselves with the virtues represented metaphorically by a belt of truth, a breastplate of righteousness, shoes of readiness to preach, a shield of faith, a helmet of salvation, and a sword of the Spirit (6:14–17). This kind of armor will enable the believer to stand firm against the Devil's temptations (6:13).

A quick comparison of Ephesians and Colossians shows that the two are very similar indeed. In fact, at one point they have exactly the same wording for over twenty-five words (Eph. 6:21–22; Col 4:7–8). This paragraph is only the tip of the iceberg, however, for they share many other verses in common and have many common themes, although they do not always discuss those themes in the same way.

For those who believe Paul wrote both of these letters, the similarity is usually explained by the fact that they are both written at about the same time to two different churches. Many traveling preachers preach the same basic message in different locations. Since the earliest manuscripts of Ephesians leave out the words "to Ephesus," some scholars have suggested that this letter was actually the letter of Laodicea mentioned in Colossians 4:16.

Ephesians does not explicitly address a specific problem or situation. For this reason some have suggested it was written to circulate widely without having a specific destination in view—a "circular letter." One scholar even suggested it was a cover letter written as a kind of preface for all of Paul's writings as they began to be collected.[1] Whatever we decide on such issues, Ephesians does have a different feel and tone than Paul's other letters and, like Colossians, its imagery differs as well. It even seems to be built out of the letter to the Colossians, although it has a much grander style and artfully fills out what are sometimes very "bare bones" statements in Colossians.

Philippians

Paul wrote Philippians partially in response to aid he had recently received from the church at Philippi. This aid was sent by way of a man named Epaphroditus (Phil. 4:18). The letter presents a Paul who is in prison, yet at peace with his sufferings. If Paul was in Rome as he wrote this letter, it appears that near the end of his ministry he achieved a certain peace about those who opposed him personally. He no longer seemed to be bothered that some preached Christ "out of envy and rivalry" rather than with "goodwill" (1:15). He was just pleased that Christ was being preached (1:18). Rejoicing is a key theme in the epistle, even in the face of suffering.

Paul's reflections on his sufferings indicate someone who is prepared to die. If he lives, he has a job to do in spreading the gospel. But to die, he says, is better (Phil. 1:21). To be with Christ is something he finds very desirable, but he also feels that he still has some work to do on earth. For this reason he believes that God will set him free from his chains. In either case, he has learned to be content in whatever situation he finds himself (4:11–12). He is trusting in God to supply his every need (4:19).

Philippians reflects traces of themes found in some of his other letters. He warns the Philippians about the "dogs," an ironic way of referring to those Jewish Christians who insisted Gentile converts to Christianity become circumcised (3:2). The irony is that many Jews referred to non-Jews as dogs specifically because they were uncircumcised. Paul, on the other hand, gave up his earthly Jewish credentials for Christ, although he formerly was a Hebrew of Hebrews and a strict Pharisee who kept the Law blamelessly (3:5–6). Philippians 3:9 echoes Paul's teaching elsewhere that acceptability with God comes on the basis of faith and not by keeping the Jewish Law.

If the recent gift of the Philippians provides Paul with a reason to write this letter, Paul takes the opportunity to address some of his concerns about the Philippians, concerns like the Judaizers mentioned in the preceding paragraph. Paul also wishes to encourage the Philippians to be joyful in

---

Shifts between Paul's Earlier Writings and Ephesians

Earlier Writings	Ephesians
1. all things not yet under Christ's feet (1 Cor. 15:27, 28; cf. Heb. 10:13)	all things already under Christ's feet (1:22)
2. Christians will be raised With Christ (Rom. 6:5; 8:11)	Christians already raised with Christ; seated with Christ (2:6)
3. Christians have been justified; will be saved (Rom. 5:9)	Christians have been saved (2:8)
4. works of Jewish Law (Gal. 2:16)	works (2:9)
5. Paul, least of apostles (1 Cor. 15:9)	Paul, less than the least of all the saints (3:8)
6. body of Christ (1 Cor. 12:27)	body of church; Christ as head of body (1:22–23), but also body of Christ (4:12)
7. Christ did not abolish the Law; upheld it (Rom. 3:31)	Christ abolished the Law (2:15)
8. foundation is Christ (1 Cor. 3:11)	apostles and Christian prophets are foundation; Christ is cornerstone (2:20)
9. Satan (1 Cor. 5:5)	the devil (6:11)
10. *church* refers primarily to specific congregations	*church* refers consistently to all Christians everywhere

---

the persecution they were experiencing (Phil. 1:25, 29). He urges them to imitate his attitude toward suffering (3:17—4:1) and to rely on God for their needs (4:19). In the process, he encourages them to remain unified—an indication that those who opposed them would be destroyed in the end (1:28). He encourages them to press on and make their way together toward their eventual salvation on the day of Christ (2:12; 3:12–16).

Paul sums up the appropriate attitude of a Christian in an early Christian hymn about Jesus (Phil. 2:6–11). This hymn tells how Christ did not take advantage of his royal identity but instead played the role of a servant, emptying himself of his divine prerogatives. He obeyed God and suffered death as a result, but God consequently exalted him as Lord of the universe. Here is some of the most exalted language of the New Testament regarding Christ, as well as one of the clearest indications in the New Testament that Christ existed before he became a human being.

Colossians

Paul and Timothy seem to have written the letter to the Colossians to warn those at Colossae about a philosophy (Col. 2:8) they believed might potentially threaten their faith. It seems likely that some in the audience had already accepted its claims (cf. 2:19–20). While scholars disagree over the nature of this philosophy, it clearly had Jewish components. As was the case with the Galatians, the Colossians might have felt pressure to keep aspects of the Jewish Law. The philosophy insisted on the observance of Jewish festivals and Sabbaths (2:16) and adherence to the Old Testament food laws (2:21). The Colossian males might also have felt pressure to become circumcised (3:11).

Yet the situations in Galatia and Colossae differed significantly from one another. Paul's opponents in Galatia were Jewish Christians compelling the Gentile Galatians to become Jews as a part of their conversion to Christianity. In Colossae, on the other hand,

---

Christ Jesus . . .

Who being in the form of God,
Did not consider equality with
God something to plunder;
But he emptied himself,
Taking the form of a servant.

Having become in the likeness of men,
And having been found in form as
a man,
He humbled himself,
Having become obedient to death . . .

Therefore God highly exalted him,
And gave him a name above all
names
That at the name of Jesus every
knee should bow . . .
And every tongue confess that Jesus
Christ is Lord . . .

—Philippians 2:6–11 (author's translation)

the philosophy in question did not seem to be Christian at all. In fact, many suggest it was not really Jewish either, but a highly syncretistic movement—a mixture of Judaism with the pagan religions of the region, the Lycus valley.

If the followers of this philosophy literally worshiped angels (Col. 2:18), it would have been unacceptable to the overwhelming majority of Jews. After all, the cornerstone of Jewish religion is monotheism—the worship of Yahweh to the exclusion of all other gods. For some scholars, the incredible strangeness of such a mixture of ideas makes them wonder if the phrase "the worship of angels" is an exaggeration of this philosophy; i.e., angels simply played an extremely important role in the philosophy in question, but no one actually worshiped them.

A better suggestion is that the phrase "the worship of angels" was not about worshiping angels at all, but about angels worshiping. In other words, the philosophy in question was a form of mystical Judaism that highly valued visions of the heavenly realm. One who had such a vision mystically entered into the divine world and participated in heavenly worship. Several worship texts from the Dead Sea Scrolls indicate that the Essenes desired to participate with the angels in the heavenly worship of God. Another mystical movement within Judaism called "Merkabah mysticism" also aimed at participation in the worship of heaven around the divine throne of God. Some have argued that Paul's vision of the third heaven in 2 Corinthians 12:2 and his claim to speak in tongues more than all the Corinthians (1 Cor. 14:18) indicate that he too was acquainted with such mystical practices.

If this philosophy were a form of Jewish mysticism, it would explain some of the differences between Colossians and Paul's earlier letters. For example, while Paul's opponents in Galatia disagreed with him over how to escape God's wrath in the future, those in Colossae may not have even anticipated a coming judgment at all. For them, the issue seemed to be about how to attain spiritual wisdom by entering into the angelic realm. They believed that keeping the Jewish Law and certain ascetic practices—matters of extreme self-discipline (e.g., Col. 2:18, 23)—qualified you for access to the heavenly realm alongside the angels, thus providing true wisdom (e.g., 2:18).

Paul's response is highly appropriate. First, he connects both the Jewish Law and the spiritual forces admired in this philosophy with the created realm rather than with heaven and God's presence. This move was natural because the Jews believed that angels had delivered the Jewish Law to the earth (e.g., Acts 7:38, 53; Gal. 3:19; Heb. 2:2) and that they functioned as God's ambassadors to the creation (e.g., Heb 1:5, 14). By associating the Jewish Law and angelic powers with the created realm, Paul locates the elements of this Jewish philosophy in exactly the opposite position in which its proponents place it. While they claim their practices will lead to heaven and spiritual wisdom, Paul argues that their practices are wholly associated with the earthly.

In contrast, Paul locates Christ and Christians squarely in the heavenly realm. Paul's normal orientation around coming salvation and the coming kingdom have shifted somewhat to focus on the current participation in heaven and its kingdom. That is, while his earlier writings are largely horizontal in orientation—focused on the future in relation to the present, Colossians is more vertically oriented—focused on the heavenly in relation to the earthly. Thus Paul says that we have already been raised with Christ (3:1), and he speaks of us already being in the kingdom of the Son (Col. 1:13).

Further, he makes it clear that angels and other spiritual forces are not the highest authorities in the creation, nor are they the means by which atonement takes place. In a majestic hymn (1:15–20), Paul clearly gives Christ the supreme place over the creation. "By him all things were created: things in heaven and on earth, visible and invisible, whether thrones or powers or rulers or authorities; all things were created by him and for him. He is before all things . . ." (1:16–17). In Christ "are hidden all the treasures of wisdom and knowledge" (2:3), unlike those who try to attain wisdom by their heavenly visions. And while the Essenes may have believed that angels offered the true sacrifices of atonement in a heavenly temple,[2]

Colossians clearly notes that it is through Christ that "we have redemption, the forgiveness of sins" (1:14).

Like the hymn in Philippians, the Colossian hymn also presents Christ in some of the most exalted language of the New Testament. The first half of the hymn probably existed before Colossians was written and sounds like what any Jew might have said about God's wisdom or Word. It is prob-

---

Christ

Who is the image of . . . God,	**Who is** the beginning,
The firstborn of all creation.	**The firstborn** from the dead . . .
Because in him were created all things . . .	**Because in him** [God] desired the fullness to dwell
All things through him and for him were created.	And **through him** to reconcile **all things** to him.
And he is **before all things**,	[That He might become **supreme in all things**,]
And all things in him **became united** . . .	**Making peace** through the blood of his cross.

—Colossians 1:15–20 (author's translation)

---

ably no coincidence that the gospel of John begins by calling Jesus God's "Word," just as other parts of the New Testament also indicate that Jesus is God's wisdom.

If the first half of the hymn refers to Christ as the supreme wisdom of God for the creation, the second half similarly presents Christ as the supreme Savior of all things. The second half may also have existed before Paul wrote Colossians. If the world came together through God's wisdom, so in Christ all things also have come together and have become reconciled to God. The hymn powerfully brings out the close relationship between creation and salvation. As Paul says in 2 Corinthians 5:17, our reconciliation to God makes us a "new creation."

As we mentioned in our discussion of Ephesians above, Colossians and Ephesians have a great deal of material in common, leading some scholars to believe they were both written at about the same time. Those who believe Paul wrote them think he was in Rome at the time. Those who believe Ephesians to be pseudonymous usually argue that Colossians was written first. One reason is that while Colossians addresses a specific problem in Colossae, Ephesians does not seem to have a particular situation in view.

A good number of scholars believe Colossians to be pseudonymous as well, although fewer scholars suggest this for Ephesians. The vocabulary and style of Colossians differs from what Paul uses elsewhere. He also applies some of his typical imagery from earlier letters differently in Colossians. For example, while Paul talks of all Christians together making up the body of Christ—some are eyes, some are ears (e.g., 1 Cor. 12:16–17)—Colossians talks of the body of the church, with Christ as the head. Christ is thus no longer the whole body, but a part of it.

Since Timothy is also one of the authors of Colossians (1:1), others have suggested that he is the primary author of the letter. Paul thus would have known what Timothy wrote and agreed with it, but its style and imagery would represent Timothy's way of thinking more than his own. In this scenario, Timothy would be somewhat of a ghostwriter for Colossians—he wrote the words but its authority came primarily from Paul. Many conservatives find this suggestion attractive because it preserves Paul's authorship while also explaining the differences between Colossians and Paul's earlier letters.

Ghostwriting in the New Testament?

People are surprised to learn that some of the New Testament books might have been ghostwritten, despite the widespread prevalence and acceptance of ghostwriting today. Here are some key thoughts about pseudonymity and ghostwriting in the ancient world:

- The ancient world was an oral culture—oriented around hearing rather than reading.
- A pseudonymous writing is one that is written under the authority of a dead figure from the past to address a contemporary situation.
- In general, Paul and the ancients used amanuenses (or secretaries) to put their words down on paper.
- Some writings in the New Testament may have been ghostwritten—composed by coauthors and then approved by those we think of as the primary authors (e.g., Paul or Peter).
- Many scholars argue that some writings like Ephesians, 1 Timothy, Titus, and 2 Peter are pseudonymous, and that they were written after the deaths of both Paul and Peter.

Philemon

One of the shortest books in the New Testament, Philemon is a letter that Paul sent to a slave owner of the same name. One of Philemon's slaves, Onesimus, had somehow become alienated from his owner. Perhaps he had been somewhere on business and ran off with his owner's money or property. Whatever the cause of the separation, Onesimus seems to have sought out Paul in prison in the hope of being reconciled to his master. In the process, he became a Christian and a help to Paul.

Paul wrote Philemon so that Philemon would receive Onesimus back, forgiving him for running away as well as for whatever other wrongs he might have done. "If he has harmed you in any way or stolen anything from you, charge me for it" (v. 18 NLT). While receiving back a runaway slave without serious penalty was not unheard of in the ancient world, Paul was asking a rather large thing of Philemon. To support this desire, Paul leans on Philemon by calling in the spiritual debt Philemon owes Paul—"I won't mention that you owe me your very soul!"(v. 19 NLT). Further, while the issue was a private matter between Onesimus and Philemon, Paul wrote to the entire church (v. 2), putting Philemon on the spot. The whole church would see how he responded to Paul's authority!

Interestingly, Paul never tells Philemon to free Onesimus, although Christians often presume that this is what the letter is about. Rather, Paul only tells Philemon to "welcome him as you would welcome me" (v. 17). Indeed, Colossians, which Paul may have sent at the same time as the letter to Philemon, says nothing about freeing slaves, even though it mentions master and slave relations and even Onesimus himself (Col. 3:22—4:1; 4:9). It only commands slaves to obey their masters in everything they do (3:22).

Philemon seems to have lived in Colossae, since the letter shares almost all the names found in Colossians. Indeed, Colossians indicates that Epaphras and Onesimus were from Colossae, both major players in the letter to Philemon (Philem. 10, 23). While Paul may not have commanded Philemon to set Onesimus free, it is interesting that a man named Onesimus became the bishop of Ephesus in the years that followed.[3] If this is the same man, then it seems Philemon finally did release him from slavery. Paul hints in Philemon that he would prefer to keep Onesimus with him rather than send him back (v. 13). Perhaps Philemon set Onesimus free so he could return to help Paul.

Questions for Study and Discussion

1. Identify one major theme from each of the Prison Epistles by which to remember them. What aspect of each one stands out the most to you?
2. How might Christians today model the unity celebrated in Ephesians?
3. How would you explain the unique shifts in Paul's imagery in Ephesians, especially since they do not appear in letters reputedly written at the same time or afterward?
4. What can we learn from Philippians about how to suffer? What attitude did Paul have toward life and death?
5. Christians often revere the Ten Commandments as a part of the Jewish Law still in force today. What does Colossians have to say about Gentiles and keeping the Sabbath?
6. Does Paul hint in Philemon that Philemon should set the slave free, or is this idea simply what we want to hear Paul say?

Paul's Earliest Preaching

1 and 2 Thessalonians

*Paul's message of judgment and salvation did not focus
on the dead but on the living, since Paul expected
this judgment to occur in the near future.*

The New Testament has thirteen letters that bear Paul's name, letters sent to various places around the ancient Mediterranean. Of these, 1 Thessalonians was probably the first he wrote.[1] If so, it was probably also the first New Testament book written.

It is sometimes hard for us to imagine what Christianity would have been like without a New Testament. The Bible Paul used was what we call the Old Testament—it was the whole Bible for him! Paul knew some of the things Jesus had said while He was on earth, but perhaps not too many. He rarely quoted Jesus or referred to His teaching.

At a Glance

- First Thessalonians was probably the first book of the New Testament to be written.
- Paul wrote 1 Thessalonians from Corinth on his second missionary journey (ca. A.D. 51).
- Paul wrote the book as Timothy returned from Thessalonica with the good news that the Thessalonians were remaining true to Paul and to their faith.
- In his first letter to them, Paul reminds the Thessalonians of appropriate Christian sexuality, brotherly love, and diligent work.
- First Thessalonians also deals with what happens to Christians who die before Christ returns—they will rise from the dead.
- Second Thessalonians deals with things that will take place before Christ's return, including the coming of a "man of lawlessness."

He also had heard what some of Jesus' earliest followers were preaching, but what was most important for him was the revelation he had received directly from God. He was convinced that God had appointed him as an ambassador to non-Jews. This belief led him to travel thousands of miles on foot during his lifetime, preaching the good news of Jesus around the Mediterranean world.

Paul first visited the city of Thessalonica on his second missionary journey. It is one of the first cities he visited in Europe. About one hundred miles west of Philippi, Thessalonica was on the main road that crossed Macedonia, the region north of Greece. As the capital of Macedonia, Thessalonica was a somewhat large city. Accordingly, it was a logical place for Paul to stop and preach the gospel.

> "It is God's will that you should be sanctified: that you should avoid sexual immorality; that each of you should learn to control his own body in a way that is holy and honorable, not in passionate lust like the heathen, who do not know God."
>
> —1 Thessalonians 4:3–5

Acts gives us the impression that Paul did not stay very long in Thessalonica because of some fierce opposition that arose toward him in the Jewish synagogue. But he probably was with them longer than two or three weeks (e.g., 1 Thess. 2:9). Philippians 4:16 tells us that he stayed there long enough to receive help from the Philippian church "again and again."

No matter the exact length of time, he is forced to leave town in the face of strong opposition (1 Thess. 2:1–2). The Christians send him away to Berea under cover of nightfall (Acts 17:10). Similar things happen there as well, leading Paul to travel south to Athens, Greece. But he remains concerned for the infant churches he left in Macedonia. Finally, he sends Timothy back to Thessalonica to strengthen and encourage the Christians there in their faith, and to make sure that the opposition he faced has not discouraged their commitment to his message (1 Thess. 3:2).

By the time Timothy returns to Paul, Paul has moved even farther south to the bustling city of Corinth. Timothy brings good news: the Thessalonians continue to hold Paul and his teaching in high regard. It is in this context that Paul writes the first letter of the New Testament, 1 Thessalonians. He writes both in celebration of the good news he has just received from Timothy and to give them some basic reminders of how to live. Perhaps of greatest interest to us is his instruction about Christ's coming return to earth from heaven.

Miscellaneous Instructions

Jews associated two sins in particular with Gentiles: idolatry and sexual immorality. They took both of these to be signs of ignorance on the part of such non-Jews. Thus, it is no surprise that sexual immorality is one of the main issues Paul deals with in his letter to the Thessalonians. While Paul does not specify the exact nature of the particular sexual sins he has in mind, adultery certainly would qualify as one that would "wrong his brother or take advantage of him" (1 Thess. 4:6). Paul might also have in mind someone who slept with a virgin promised to him.

Paul also encourages the Thessalonians to show brotherly love to one another (1 Thess. 4:9). Later in the letter he tells them to live peaceably with each other, to respect their hardworking leaders, and to be patient and kind to everyone (5:12–15). The letter closes with a number of miscellaneous exhortations, including some words to those who are lazy (5:14)— a theme continued in 2 Thessalonians.

What about Christians Who Die?

First Thessalonians 4:13—5:11 might not strike a modern Christian reader as odd at first. These verses present us with some basic teaching on Christ's return to earth and the resurrection of the dead that will take place at that time. Paul tells the Thessalonians that Christians who had died will rise from the dead to meet Jesus in the sky (1 Thess. 4:14–16). Then those who are still alive will also ascend into the sky to meet Jesus—an event Christians often call "the rapture" (see 4:17).

In explaining when this would happen, Paul uses the analogy of a pregnant woman (5:3). On one level, such a woman can feel that the time is approaching; she experiences labor pains. In that sense, Christians who are "sons of the light and sons of the day" (5:5) will be ready for Christ's parousia, his arrival back to earth (5:5–11). On the other hand, the day of the Lord is also like the coming of a thief—it is unannounced (5:2). So it is also with the birth of a child. While the mother knows it is coming soon, the exact hour comes unexpectedly.

Conservative Christians talk a lot about the rapture, and certainly most Christians believe that death is not the end of our existence. But Paul wrote these things to Christians he had taught for several weeks, perhaps several months. How could the Thessalonians be ignorant (1 Thess. 4:13) about what happens to Christians after they die if Paul had spent several weeks with them?

For many Christians, Christianity is all about heaven and hell. One approach to evangelizing non-Christians is to ask them where they would go if they were to die suddenly. Would they go to heaven or hell? However, Paul does not mention anything about Christians going to heaven or sinners going to hell in 1 Thessalonians. Indeed, none of his writings even mention hell; we get only a few hints in his writings that Christians might go to heaven when they die.[2] When he was in Thessalonica for all those weeks, Paul apparently said little or nothing about what happened to Christians after death.

Thus, while Paul likely believed in heaven and hell, he had quite a different focus than we do today. As with many Jews, Paul thought much more in terms of the future resurrection of bodies than in terms of the immortality of the soul. He spoke of the time between death and this future resurrection as a time of sleep (1 Thess. 4:13–15). At the resurrection, not before, God will provide us with spiritual bodies (1 Cor. 15:44) and will clothe us with a heavenly "tent" (2 Cor. 5:1–2).

What was Paul thinking about, then, when he spoke about salvation—is not salvation about going to heaven? First Thessalonians powerfully demonstrates that Paul's early preaching concerned the coming day of the Lord, the day when God will come to judge the earth. Accordingly, Paul's message of judgment and salvation does not focus on the dead but the living, since Paul expected this judgment to occur in the near future (cf. 1 Cor. 7:29; Phil. 4:5). Salvation for Paul meant that Christ had made it possible for the Christians on earth to escape God's wrath when He came to judge the world. The fate of the dead may have been an afterthought—Paul probably did not expect many Christians to die before that day came.

With these things in mind, we can reconstruct the situation in this way. Paul comes to Thessalonica with the message that God was soon going to judge the world for its sins—both Jew and Gentile. To a Jew, this message might not have been very surprising. However, Paul proclaims that through Jesus Christ, God has provided a way of escape. He probably preaches that Jesus' death was like a sacrifice that atoned for sins. Many Jews may even have found this message acceptable.

> "Be joyful always; pray continually; give thanks in all circumstances, for this is God's will for you in Christ Jesus.
>
> "Do not put out the Spirit's fire; do not treat prophecies with contempt. Test everything. Hold on to the good. Avoid every kind of evil."
>
> —1 Thessalonians 5:16–22

Where Paul probably got into trouble with the Jews of the city was preaching that this sacrifice was valid both for Jews and Gentiles. The Gentiles do not need to become circumcised or start following the Jewish Law to escape punishment, he says. Paul, Silas, and Timothy no doubt ate with Gentiles and crossed boundaries of purity, which might have infuriated some Jews. He may also have attracted a group of Gentiles that the book of Acts calls "God-fearers," Gentiles who were sympathetic to Judaism but for whatever reason did not fully convert. If Paul drew such individuals away from the local synagogue, we can see even more reason for the Jews of the city to be angry with him.

If Paul's message were primarily about God coming to judge the world, the fate of the dead might not come up. Paul wrote 1 Thessalonians at least in part to address the question of Christians who might die before Christ returned. Interestingly, however, Paul never discusses the fate of the wicked in any of his writings, nor does he address the question of those who died in the Old Testament—he writes only of the dead "in Christ." These are important things to consider. They help us realize the extent to which we read our beliefs into the Bible rather than get our beliefs out of Scripture.

One final instance of this practice comes with 1 Thessalonians 4:17. This verse comes after Paul tells his audience that the dead in Christ will rise to meet Him in the sky. Paul then says, "After that, we who are still alive and are left will be caught up together with them in the clouds to meet the Lord in the air. And so we will be with the Lord forever." Most Christians assume that the place where we remain with Christ forever is heaven. This conclusion may indeed be correct, but it illustrates how often we fill in the blanks of Scripture with things that are not exactly said by the text of the Bible. First Corinthians 6:2–3 indicates that Christians will help Christ judge the world—both humans and angels. As mentioned earlier, we will meet in the air for battle and then come back to earth as an army. Paul never says where we will remain forever.

2 Thessalonians

The second letter to Thessalonica in the New Testament is very similar to the first. Its opening language and style often mirror 1 Thessalonians, as do some of its topics. The last chapter of 2 Thessalonians deals with the problem of laziness just as 1 Thessalonians does. It is in 2 Thessalonians that we find what is sometimes known as the Protestant work ethic: "If a man will not work, he shall not eat" (2 Thess. 3:10).

Second Thessalonians contrasts slightly with 1 Thessalonians regarding Christ's second coming. While 1 Thessalonians talks about Christ returning at any time, like a thief at night, 2 Thessalonians talks about a series of events that need to happen before He can return. The first letter implies that the Thessalonians should be prepared now for Christ's return; the second argues that things are not yet ready. Of course, these two emphases do not necessarily contradict each other. As we saw above, 1 Thessalonians uses the imagery of a pregnant woman to discuss Christ's parousia (1 Thess. 5:3). She may not know the exact day or hour, but she can sense that it is coming soon.

What is interesting about 2 Thessalonians is the fact that some evidently thought the day of the Lord had already occurred (2:2). In our current Christian mind-set, it is difficult to imagine how anyone could mistake something for judgment day or Christ's return to earth. Some popular Christian images of the rapture involve driverless cars crashing into one another or airplanes plummeting to earth because their pilots have suddenly vanished. If the day of the Lord is like this, you will hardly be in doubt about whether it has happened or not.

The people 2 Thessalonians mentions must have viewed the day of the Lord somewhat figuratively. To them it must have referred to some cataclysm or to some horrific event that had already taken place. They interpreted such an event or events as the judgment of God on the world or on Israel. Clearly, they must not have interpreted the kingdom of God as a transformation of their bodies or of the world. Perhaps they viewed it as a spiritual matter, something inside a person rather than something that would literally come to the earth. They remind us a little of the people mentioned in 2 Timothy who believed that the resurrection had already taken place (2 Tim. 2:18).

Paul warns the Thessalonians not to be alarmed by teaching of this sort. He tells of some events that must happen before judgment day arrives, events that have not yet happened. Unfortunately, the letter is very cryptic and vague about what these events actually are. The audience clearly understood what Paul was talking about (e.g., 2 Thess. 2:5–6), but he does not make things very clear for those of us who are listening in on their conversation.

The letter says, for example, that a rebellion must come before the day of judgment, and during this rebellion a "man of lawlessness" will be revealed (2 Thess. 2:3–4). This person will set himself up in the God's temple as if he were a god. He will perform counterfeit miracles and signs (2:9). Paul affirms that the Thessalonians know about these things, in addition to knowing what was keeping the man of lawlessness from coming (2:5–6).

It is here that the letter reaches its most cryptic point. Paul says that they know what was now keeping this man from being revealed (2 Thess. 2:6), but after he was taken out of the picture, the man of lawlessness would be revealed (2:7). In the course of two verses, the thing holding the man of lawlessness back changes from an "it" to a "he." Many suggestions have been made about what this mysterious it/he might be, but scholars have never reached any clear agreement.[3]

> Salvation for Paul was primarily about the fact that Christ made it possible for the Christians on earth to escape God's wrath when He came to judge the world.

Christians often relate the man of lawlessness in 2 Thessalonians to the beast of Revelation 13 or an individual called the Antichrist (based on a particular interpretation of 1 John 4). However, we should be very careful because it is not clear that these verses all refer to the same thing. First John, for example, never speaks of a single Antichrist—it speaks of many antichrists who were around back in John's day (1 John 4:3). These were people who believed Jesus had not taken on human flesh (4:2), possibly members of a heresy called *Docetism*, which believed that Jesus had only seemed to become human. Ironically, the Bible never uses the word *antichrist* in the way we do today.

When Revelation talks about various beasts, on the other hand, it is speaking highly symbolically and may not even be referring to specific individuals. For example, many scholars think that the second beast of Revelation 13 is a symbol for Roman emperor worship and that the first beast represents the Roman emperor, perhaps Nero. Nevertheless, since the first beast has some interesting traits in common with the man of lawlessness in 2 Thessalonians, some relationship could exist between the two.

One final issue relates to the statement that the man of lawlessness would set himself up in the temple. Certainly no Jew would do anything like this, although we know of several instances in history when a Gentile ruler did. In 167 B.C., for example, the Syrian ruler Antiochus Epiphanes desecrated the temple by having a pig sacrificed there—the event to which Daniel 9:27 probably refers. The Roman general Pompey similarly violated the temple in 63 B.C. In A.D. 40 the Roman emperor Caligula tried to have a statue of himself set up in the temple but thankfully died before this order could be carried out. Finally, in A.D. 70 the temple was destroyed. During this invasion, the Roman soldiers sacrificed to the Roman gods within the precincts of the temple, perhaps the event to which Mark 13:14 refers.

The problem with the passage in 2 Thessalonians is that for someone to set himself up as a god in the temple, there has to be a temple. For this reason many Christians think that someday the Jews will rebuild the temple in modern-day Jerusalem. Unfortunately, when read in its original context, very little in the Bible seems to relate to this issue. We can find prophecies that relate to its destruction in A.D. 70, but not to its reconstruction.

In fact, the book of Hebrews indicates strongly that no earthly temple could ever have God's future approval—Christ's death has definitively put an end to all earthly sanctuaries and sacrifices (Heb. 8:1–2; 10:5–9, 26). Therefore, if we are to maintain the truthfulness of 2 Thessalonians, we probably will have to take its reference to a temple as symbolic or relate it to one of the events mentioned in the previous paragraph.[4]

Questions for Study and Discussion

1. Do you agree that Paul has very little to say about heaven or hell in his writings?
2. What do you think the "day of the Lord" is? When do you think it will occur?
3. Do you think that the Jewish temple will ever be rebuilt or has the situation about which Paul was writing already occurred?

Passing on the Torch

1 and 2 Timothy, and Titus

The Pastoral Epistles give advice to two pastors
about how to shepherd their flocks.

Paul's two letters to Timothy and the letter to Titus are customarily called the Pastoral Epistles because they give advice to two pastors about how to shepherd their flocks. Timothy and Titus were Paul's traveling companions and were useful to him in his extensive missionary activities. More than once he sent them in his place to take care of problems in the churches of Greece and Macedonia. Timothy served as Paul's representative on various occasions to Thessalonica and Philippi (1 Thess. 3:2; Phil. 2:19). Titus similarly went to Corinth on Paul's behalf (2 Cor. 7:6; 8:16–18).

At a Glance

- First and 2 Timothy and Titus are called the Pastoral Epistles because of their focus on how to lead the church.
- Their main focuses include the correction of false teaching and the order of relationships in the church (not least the qualifications of church leaders).
- Most conservative scholars believe these three letters were written in the last days of Paul's life, before and during a second imprisonment in Rome.
- Other scholars believe they were written pseudonymously to address Pauline communities of the late first and early second century.

In the Pastoral Epistles, however, Paul has a different mission in mind for Timothy and Titus—directing the church after he was no longer around. The majority of conservative scholars believe that Paul gave this message in the very last year or two of his earthly life. If Paul was the literal author of these letters, he probably wrote them just before and during his final imprisonment and subsequent death in Rome. Accordingly, these letters show a strong concern for the church to maintain sound teaching in the days to come.

However, many other scholars believe these letters were written to invoke Paul's authority a number of decades after his death. In this scenario, some of Paul's churches have gone astray in their beliefs, leading someone to write under his name to redirect them toward sound teaching.

Whoever the author, the Pastoral Epistles present Paul as the supreme model of Christian faith. While he often encourages his churches to view him as a model to follow (e.g., 1 Cor. 4:16; 11:1; Phil. 3:17; 4:9), in these letters he speaks of himself as a prototype. In 1 Timothy, he speaks of his conversion as the supreme example of God's graciousness (1 Tim. 1:16)—he had been the worst sinner of all. In 2 Timothy his teaching is the supreme model to follow (2 Tim. 1:13), teaching he is trusting Timothy to guard and pass on accurately to future generations.

Paul's primary role in these letters is thus as a teacher (1 Tim. 2:7; 2 Tim. 1:11)—something he never calls himself in his earlier writings. His primary concern is accordingly that Timothy and Titus faithfully preserve his teaching. All three Pastoral Letters may address the same basic heresy or false teaching. Titus addresses a Jewish teaching that involves keeping aspects of the Jewish Law (e.g., Titus 3:9). The false teaching Paul refers to in 1 Timothy seems similar and involves asceticism—an extreme form of self-discipline (e.g., 1 Tim. 4:3). Second Timothy mentions some Christians who believe that the resurrection has already taken place (2 Tim. 2:18). In opposition to the false teaching, the Pastoral Epistles show a strong concern for orthodoxy (correct belief) to prevail in the days after Paul passes from the scene.

A second main concern of the Pastoral Epistles is for proper order in the church—an understandable issue, whether penned by Paul just before his death or written several years later by someone else. On the one hand, the pastorals are the only New Testament writings to provide extensive qualifications for specific kinds of church leaders. Yet they also give extensive directions for individuals like older men and women, young men, widows, and slaves. Indeed, one of the most infamous verses in the New Testament regarding the role of women appears in 1 Timothy (1 Tim. 2:12). We see in the pastorals the plotting of a course that would eventually grow into the church as an institution with established roles and well-defined boundaries.

1 Timothy

We have already mentioned the dual emphases of the Pastoral Epistles: they warn against false teaching and give instructions for appropriate order in the church. Certainly 1 Timothy reflects both emphases.

In contrast to Paul's sound teaching, 1 Timothy hints at some false teaching of a Jewish nature. Paul mentions a preoccupation with "myths and endless genealogies" (1 Tim. 1:4) and seems to connect it with the Jewish Law (1:8). Beyond these comments, we are not told the nature of these stories or genealogies. Whatever this heresy was, it forbade marriage and involved certain restrictions on what one could eat (4:3). Perhaps some teachers of this heresy took money for their instruction, perhaps even from churches. For whatever reason, the situation leads Paul to warn, "the love of money is a root of all kinds of evil" (6:10).

Most of 1 Timothy relates to the appropriate roles of various individuals in the church. First Timothy discusses the qualifications of an overseer—what would later be known as a bishop (1 Tim. 3:1–7). Given the organization of churches today, it would be tempting to see this role as that of head minister over an individual congregation, what some churches call a senior pastor and others a priest. However, a good argument can be made that Paul did not have in mind a single individual but a group of several men who together would lead a house church (e.g., 1 Tim. 5:17; Titus 1:5).

It seems certain that Paul or the author of 1 Timothy had only men in view as the leaders of a church. This is in contrast to what we might assume from Paul's earlier writings and the book of Acts. He strongly asserts, "I do not permit a woman or to have authority over a man; she must be silent" (1 Tim. 2:12). Somehow it seems significant that this statement appears in a book that is strongly concerned with false teaching. Since the author views women through the lens of Eve (2:14)—whom many Jews considered the prototypical gullible woman—this prohibition has everything to do with the belief that women are easily misled and thus make bad teachers.

Another church role addressed in 1 Timothy is deacon, meaning someone who serves. Paul refers to a woman named Phoebe by this term in Romans 16:1 (although women seem excluded from this role in 1 Timothy), perhaps implying that she was one who provided material support for the church in Cenchrea, the port village of Corinth. Many of the qualifications for a deacon are the same as those for an overseer. Men in both roles were to manage their households and children well (1 Tim. 3:5, 12). They were to have only one wife (3:2, 12); and any drinking should be done with moderation (3:3, 8; cf. 5:23). In general, they were to be respectable first-century individuals (cf. 3:2, 8).

First Timothy has interesting things to say about other individuals in the church, most notably widows. Paul draws a distinction between "true" and "false" widows. Evidently, when a woman agreed to be supported by the church as a widow, she committed herself never to remarry. Many young widows, Paul points out, did not keep this vow but remarried because of their physical desires (1 Tim. 5:11). Paul tells Timothy to wait until a widow was sixty before being "put on the list of widows" requiring assistance (5:9). Her female relatives should take care of her (5:8, 16) until she remarried (5:14).

The social roles that 1 Timothy encourages differ little from what non-Christians of the first century in general believed to be respectable behavior—there is little that is distinctively Christian about them. While this fact is clearest with regard to the subservient role women play throughout the letter, it is also apparent with regard to slaves. Far from encouraging

Christian masters to free their slaves, 1 Timothy urges slaves to work even harder because they are benefiting a Christian (1 Tim. 6:2). While comments like these may have been appropriate for the audience of 1 Timothy, it is hard to read them today and not believe that God intended for us to move the church forward on such issues—as it were, putting the spirit of Galatians 3:28 into action.

2 Timothy

Second Timothy has the most concrete feel of all the Pastoral Epistles and differs the least from Paul's earlier writings. It mentions more names and specific situations than both 1 Timothy and Titus combined. Second Timothy reads like Paul's last will and testament, his farewell letter. As Paul victoriously says in 2 Timothy 4:7–8, "I have fought the good fight, I have finished the race, I have kept the faith. Now there is in store for me the crown of righteousness, which the Lord, the righteous Judge, will award to me on that day."

The setting is Rome (2 Tim. 1:17). Paul has already successfully passed his first defense before Nero, but almost all his associates have deserted him (4:16). Demas, mentioned in Philemon 24 and Colossians 4:14, especially seems to have turned his back on Paul, perhaps even on Christianity (2 Tim. 4:10). Others from Asia, Phygelus and Hermogenes, have similarly abandoned him (1:15). Perhaps even Crescens and Titus have left Rome to escape persecution (4:10). Only Luke remains with Paul (4:11).

Of the two preoccupations of the pastorals—sound teaching and order in the church—2 Timothy focuses primarily on the first. It does, however, give us hints at how a proper chain of authority helps to maintain truthful teaching. Paul notes that he himself has laid hands on Timothy so that he could receive the Holy Spirit (2 Tim. 1:6–7). Paul says that Timothy knows "all about my teaching, my way of life, my purpose, faith, patience, love, endurance, persecutions, sufferings" (3:10–11). The implication is that Timothy is an authorized bearer of Paul's authority—he knows Paul's mind

Some Shifts between the Pastorals and Paul's Earlier Writings

Pastorals	Paul Elsewhere
Paul considers himself the prototypical sinner (1 Tim. 1:15), the worst ever.	Paul considers himself blameless in keeping the Law before coming to Christ (Phil. 3:6), rarely uses words like *repentance* or *forgiveness*, speaks of his prior accomplishments as a Jew rather than his failures (Phil. 3:7,13).
Paul primarily refers to himself as a teacher (*didaskalos*; e.g., 1 Tim. 2:7), his teaching as prototypical doctrine (*didaskalia*; e.g., 2 Tim. 1:13); he emphsizes "sound" teaching (1 Tim. 1:10) and "trustworthy sayings" (e.g., 1 Tim. 1:15).	Paul never refers to himself as a teacher or to his thought as doctrine; he never uses the terms *sound teaching* or *trustworthy sayings*.
Law refers to moral core— don't murder, commit adultery, lie (1 Tim. 1:8–10).	*Law* refers to practices that divide Jew and Gentile (e.g., circumcision, food laws).
Paul says women cannot teach or have authority over men; the shame of Eve's sin remains in force until a woman bears children (1 Tim. 2:12–15).	Paul speaks of a female deacon (Rom. 16:1) and probably apostle (16:7); presumes that women prophesy in church (1 Cor. 11:5); blames Adam for sin and notes that in Christ the distinction male or female does not apply—at least in regard to sin or sonship (Gal. 3:28).
Paul tells Timothy that he is not lying about the fact that he is an apostle (1 Tim. 2:7).	Timothy is perhaps Paul's most frequent associate as an apostle—why would he feel a need to reassure him of this fact?

and can speak for Paul. Paul encourages Timothy to pass on this same teaching to "reliable" people (2:2).

As we have already mentioned, Paul's teaching in 2 Timothy is considered the prototype of Christian truth (2 Tim. 1:13). It is a deposit (1:12, 14) that he is trusting both God and Timothy to guard after he has passed from the scene. He encourages Timothy to be a "good worker, one who does not need to be ashamed and who correctly explains the word of truth" (2:15 NLT). Timothy knows the Scriptures and he knows that "all Scripture is God-breathed" (3:16).

In contrast to Paul's deposit of truth and the correct teaching passed on through Timothy, Paul also warns Timothy about false teaching. For example, two individuals named Hymenaeus and Philetus were teaching that the resurrection had already taken place (2 Tim. 2:17–18). Second Timothy, on the other hand, affirms that salvation and resurrection are both yet to come (2:10–11; 4:1). These two men are examples of engaging in "godless chatter, . . . those who indulge in it will become more and more ungodly" (2:16). Timothy is encouraged not to quarrel with such individuals. Rather, those are people he should "gently instruct, in the hope that God will grant them repentance leading them to a knowledge of the truth" (2:25).

Paul notes that we should expect false teaching like this to rear its ugly head "in the last days" (2 Tim. 3:1). At that time people "will not put up with sound doctrine. Instead, to suit their own desires, they will gather around them a great number of teachers to say what their itching ears want to hear. They will turn their ears away from the truth and turn aside to myths" (4:3–4). If 2 Timothy is pseudonymous, these comments no doubt picture the writer's own time in the late first and early second century, and he was writing to invoke Paul's authority against these perversions and misinterpretations of the Scriptures.

Titus

The book of Titus has much in common with 1 Timothy and presents some of the same basic advice for proper order in the church. Elders, leaders of a church who are called overseers in 1 Timothy, are similarly allowed only one wife and should have obedient children (Titus 2:1–3). As in 1 Timothy, older men and women are given advice on how to conduct themselves, as well as on how to train younger men and women (2:4–8). Slaves are encouraged not to talk back to their masters (2:9–10) and, just as in 1 Timothy, people are told to obey the political authorities (3:1).

Titus may also have the same heresy in mind as 1 Timothy does, although it is clearer about the Jewish nature of the false teaching. It makes warnings about the "circumcision group" (Titus 1:10) and connects the heresy with the Jewish Law (3:9). Like 1 Timothy this teaching involves myths (cf. 1 Tim. 1:4), although we hear in Titus that they are Jewish in nature (Titus 1:14). A preoccupation with genealogies is also common to these heresies (1 Tim. 1:4; Titus 3:9), as is the prospect of financial gain in some way (1 Tim. 6:5; Titus 1:11).

One difference between 1 Timothy and Titus, however, is the audience addressed. The context of 1 Timothy is Ephesus (1 Tim. 1:3) while that of Titus is the island of Crete (Titus 1:5). This difference might imply some distinction between the heresy of 1 Timothy and that of Titus. In particular, Titus quotes a Cretan proverb that would not seem to apply very well anywhere else: "Cretans are always liars, evil brutes, lazy gluttons" (Titus 1:12). In a manner consistent with ancient group culture, Paul affirms that this saying is true.

Perhaps the most significant contribution that Titus makes to us as Christians has to do with the way it refers to Christ. This letter seems to refer to Christ as "God our Savior" four times (Titus 1:3; 2:10, 13; 3:4; cf. 1:4; 3:6). The best example is Titus 2:13 where Paul says, "We wait for the blessed hope—the glorious appearing of our great God and Savior, Jesus Christ." This direct equation of Jesus with God is one of the clearest statements of Christ's divinity—the fact that He is God—in the New Testament. The New Testament often refers to Christ as the Son of God, but very rarely does it directly equate Jesus with God in such a straightforward way.

The Authorship of the Pastorals

We have already mentioned that scholars debate whether Paul wrote the Pastoral Epistles or whether they are pseudonymous. We have discussed some of their unique characteristics and noticeable shifts from Paul's earlier writings. While both of these viewpoints can fit with the belief that the pastorals are inspired and authoritative, they do lead to slightly different interpretations of these letters and possibly to somewhat different ways of applying them today. Our respect for the Bible and its authority for the church today should lead us to consider the options carefully.

One of the challenges the pastorals give us comes from the book of Acts. How do the various places Paul mentions in these three letters fit with his life as Acts presents it? The majority of those who argue for Paul as the literal author suggest that after the two years of house arrest mentioned in Acts (Acts 28:30), Paul was released from prison and continued with his ministry. Perhaps Paul did make it to Spain as he intended (Rom. 15:24). Perhaps he returned to the East, visited Crete (Titus 1:5), and saw Ephesus once more—even though he had been so sure he would not (cf. Acts 20:25). He then traveled through Macedonia again (1 Tim. 1:3) and wintered at a place called Nicopolis (Titus 3:12).

Following this hypothesis, however, Paul did not fare so well when he returned to Rome. He was imprisoned again, and some of his closest associates deserted him (2 Tim. 4:16). But Paul was ready to die for Christ. In some of the most confident language in the New Testament he says, "I have fought the good fight, I have finished the race, I have kept the faith. Now there is in store for me the crown of righteousness, which the Lord, the righteous Judge, will award to me on that day" (2 Tim. 4:7–8).

This reconstruction accounts well for various comments scattered throughout the pastorals. The strongest objection to it is the impression Acts gives us that Paul did not return to the East after his trip to Rome. We mentioned in chapters 12 and 16 of this text that it was very likely Acts was written after the destruction of Jerusalem in A.D. 70 because of how Luke presents Jesus' prophecy of Jerusalem's destruction. Luke thus would have known what happened to Paul in the years after his house arrest in Rome. Therefore, if Paul returned to Ephesus, it is a little surprising that Acts would record Paul telling the Ephesians that "none of you among whom I have gone about preaching the kingdom will ever see me again" (Acts 20:25). This difficulty is not insurmountable, but it does cast some doubt on Paul's return to the East in the time period after Acts.

Throughout our discussion in this chapter, we have noted a number of shifts in the language of the pastorals from Paul's earlier writings. For example, Paul never refers to himself as a teacher elsewhere (cf. 1 Tim. 2:7; 2 Tim. 1:11), and he never refers to his instruction as a body of teaching (e.g., 1 Tim. 6:1; 2 Tim. 3:10) or a deposit (1 Tim. 6:20; 2 Tim. 1:12) like the pastorals do. While he considers himself an example for others to follow, he never speaks of his teaching as the prototype (2 Tim. 1:13) of true teaching or his conversion as the greatest example of God's mercy (1 Tim. 1:16). These words and others like them either do not occur at all in Paul's earlier writings, or Paul never uses them in the same way. However, they occur consistently throughout the Pastoral Epistles.

Several shifts seem to go beyond style and language. For example, Paul does not think of himself as the greatest of all sinners in his earlier writings (cf. 1 Tim. 1:16), as we have seen in earlier chapters. On the contrary, he believes himself to have kept the Law blamelessly (Phil. 3:6) before his vision of Christ. Although he believes with his head that everyone is a sinner, the absence of terms like *repentance* and *forgiveness* from his writings probably reveals that he had not experienced in his own life a sense of moral failure. Even in his most famous discussion on the inevitability of sin, he lets himself off the hook—"I am not really the one doing it; the sin within me is doing it" (Rom. 7:20 NLT). In the end, it is not his sin that he lays aside as he presses on as a Christian—it is his honorable accomplishments as a Law-keeping Jew that he sets aside as worthless in comparison to Christ (Phil. 3:7–8). The statement of 1 Timothy 1:16 thus presents an unknown side to Paul or a significant change in his attitude toward his previous life.

Another difference between 1 Timothy and Paul's earlier writings seems to be the role of women in the church. Those who believe that women cannot teach men often note how absolute Paul's prohibition seems in 1 Timothy 2:12. He bases his argument on the story of creation rather than on a problem in a specific community. Yet in Paul's earlier writings women seem to have done the very things Paul is forbidding here. In 1 Corinthians 11:5, for example, women appear to pray and prophesy in the presence of men. While 1 Timothy 3:12 allows only men to be deacons, Romans 16:1 refers to a woman named Phoebe as a deacon, using the same masculine form of the word that appears in 1 Timothy. Paul mentions a woman named Priscilla before he mentions her husband in Romans 16:3, calling her a "fellow worker." Later on in the chapter, he even seems to refer to a woman named Junias as an apostle (16:7).

One interesting shift in the pastorals is the ever so slight change from viewing truths in a context to viewing them on universal terms. The things for which Paul argues in his earlier letters relate consistently to specific churches with specific situations and issues. Even Romans, Paul's most systematic letter, carries with it the sense of his concrete struggle between his Jewish heritage and the inclusion of Gentiles as full Christians.

In the pastorals, however, not only Paul's teaching but Christian teaching in general has become a body of belief, a set of standardized ideas rather than ideas fitted to specific contexts. While we have seen that early Christianity was a somewhat diverse movement consisting of a number of different groups with contrasting ideas, the pastorals assume that the boundaries of Christian belief are relatively set. We can now clearly distinguish sound doctrine from heresy.

> **Paul's Later Writings and Society**
> - For the most part, the New Testament does not aim at changing the structures of ancient society, but addresses respectable Christian behavior within them.
> - New Testament social teaching may at times reflect a defensive strategy to avoid persecution.
> - The New Testament assumes the existence of slavery, but it values freedom.
> - The roles the New Testament lays out for women and children are very similar to how non-Christians in the ancient world viewed these roles.
> - Even more than we see demonstrated in the New Testament, it may be possible for us today to move society's structures closer to what they will be in heaven.

Those who argue that Paul wrote these letters believe that these shifts took place within Paul and Peter's lifetime, or even that true teaching was clear from the very birth of Christianity. Those in favor of pseudonymity believe this shift took place decades after Peter and Paul had passed from the scene. When these men were alive, they might say, the strength of Paul's personality and his personal experience of the risen Christ provided the authority for his teaching. It was after the death of such figures that a body of standardized belief and practice emerged. In the absence of such foundational personalities, a set of teachings became the standard (cf. Eph. 2:20; 2 Pet. 3:2).

We could mention a host of smaller items in the debate. Why would Paul need to assure Timothy that he really was an apostle? After all, Timothy was a convert of Paul's and a long-time coworker. Yet after mentioning his role as apostle, Paul says, "I am telling the truth, I am not lying" (1 Tim. 2:7). Were the roles of elder and deacon this well defined in Paul's lifetime? We certainly know they existed well before Paul's death (cf. Phil. 1:1). And what about the clarity with which Titus refers to Christ as God (e.g., Titus 2:13)? Only the gospel of John, traditionally dated in the 90s of the first century, approaches such a clear understanding of Christ's divinity.

No single argument seems decisive against Paul as the actual author. A person's style can change over time or in a different setting. Or perhaps Paul used a different amanuensis to write these letters and gave that person a good deal of freedom. Yet we must admit that the weight of all these factors taken together is significant. We can understand why most scholars have concluded in favor of pseudonymity. But the vast majority of conservative scholars insist that Paul is the literal author. Individuals will have to make up their minds in terms of their own faith and understanding.

Questions for Study and Discussion

1. In what way do the Pastoral Epistles address the need for order and a chain of authority in the church?

2. What aspects of the Pastoral Epistles relate to the need for correct doctrine in the church?

3. Do you think that the Pastoral Epistles are pseudonymous? Which arguments are most convincing to you?

Hebrews, General Letters, and Revelation

Don't Give Up the Race

Hebrews

Despite the uncertainties of Hebrews' background, its basic
message is clear enough: keep going, stay
confident in Christ, remain faithful, do not drift away.

A great deal of mystery surrounds the book known as the epistle to the Hebrews. We do not know the identity of its author, where it was written, or to whom it was sent. Without specific knowledge of the situation it addresses, Hebrews has been the playground of speculation. Scholars have suggested almost every conceivable situation to explain its unique mixture of imagery without reaching any definite conclusion. Despite these uncertainties, the basic message of this early Christian sermon seems clear enough: keep going, stay confident in Christ, remain faithful, do not drift away.

At a Glance

- Hebrews was probably a sermon written to encourage a particular community to stay faithful to its Christian commitment.
- This community may have faced potential persecution and wavered at the prospect.
- The primary alternative to faith seems to be reliance on the Old Testament sacrificial system for atonement.
- Hebrews proclaims that Christ is a high priest whose single offering in the true, heavenly sanctuary has definitively cleansed sin once and for all.
- Conversely, the Old Testament system of atonement was only a shadowy example of the reality provided by Christ.

The Bottom Line

A number of times, Hebrews encourages its audience to remain true to its confession (Heb. 3:1; 4:14; 10:23). This letter may actually be referring to a specific Christian confession the believers made when they were baptized, something like "Jesus is the Son of God." Whether or not it was a specific confession, however, it is clear that the author of Hebrews wishes his audience to stay true to Christianity, to keep going, to lay aside anything that might hinder them from finishing the Christian race.

Hebrews is somewhat vague about what might have been hindering its original audience. Were they facing persecution? Were they beginning to doubt that Christ was really going to return to earth? Were certain Jews or Jewish Christians tugging at them in some way, perhaps denying that Jesus' death on the cross was enough to take away all their sins? Some even suggest that they simply had not matured as Christians and needed to move on to the next level in their understanding.

The bottom line is that these believers were lacking confidence in their faith (e.g., Heb. 10:35). This lack of confidence seems to have stemmed from questions about what was true, as well as the pressure they were experiencing from outside their community. As far as their questions about truth, they were wondering whether Christ's death was enough to take care of all their sins. At the same time, some element in their environment was raising the stakes of being a Christian. Perhaps persecution was looming on the horizon or perhaps they had become outcasts in the eyes of their families and friends. Whatever the specific context, the author of Hebrews affirms powerfully that they have something secure to trust in and that they can boldly approach God for help because of what Christ has done.

> "What is man that you are mindful of him, the son of man that you care for him? You made him a little lower than the angels; you crowned him with glory and honor and put everything under his feet."
>
> —Hebrews 2:6–8 (quoting Ps. 8:4–6)

The Basic Story of Salvation

The basic point of Hebrews—keep going—appears throughout this early Christian sermon. Every so often the author will stop his argument and remind the audience of this bottom line. The argument itself, however, is focused on the superiority of Christ. Throughout Hebrews the author shows the audience that what Christ has done is far superior to anything possible in the days of the old covenant—the Old Testament time when the Jewish Law was in force. If the audience's basic need was to have confidence, Hebrews meets this need by showing that what Christ did was something absolutely dependable, and that God guaranteed it with oaths and promises.

The second chapter of Hebrews provides an overview of the whole story of salvation by way of Psalm 8. This psalm, as many early Christians understood it, indicates that God initially intended humanity to rule the earth. God's intention was for us to have "glory and honor" in His creation, for everything to be in submission to us (Heb. 2:6–8). Unfortunately, this was no longer the case (2:8). Presumably because of sin, only do we not rule, but we are slaves to death and to the one who holds power over death, the devil (2:14).

According to Hebrews, Christ took on flesh and blood to defeat the power of the devil (Heb. 2:14–16). He became lower than the angels for a little while (2:9), partook of the human experience with its temptations, yet did not sin (4:15). He became the sacrifice to end all sacrifices (10:14), a merciful and faithful high priest for God's people (2:17). Now He can lead us to the glory we were supposed to have in the first place (2:10).

With this basic story in mind, it is appropriate that Hebrews begins by celebrating Christ's superiority over the angels. While Christ's mission to save us required Him to become lower than the angels for a little while, He has now returned to heaven, and God has enthroned Him as king of the universe. Hebrews 1 is like an opening hymn that celebrates the fact that Christ has now made salvation possible. It reads like the announcement of the old newspaper salesperson standing on the corner shouting, "Extra,

extra, read all about it!" Today's paper reads, "Christ accomplishes salvation—God exalts Him above the angels!"

Christ, the High Priest

As we mentioned in the previous section, the way Hebrews reinforces the confidence of the audience is by showing the superiority of Christ. By the time the author finishes his main argument, he has shown that Christ is greater than angels, Moses, Old Testament priests, and Old Testament sacrifices—not to mention the fact that He has entered into a superior sanctuary. When we look closely at these individual contrasts, we see that they all connect to Hebrews' overall contrast between the old covenant (the Jewish Law) and the new covenant brought about by Christ.

It is important to notice that Hebrews does not just argue that Christ is great in general. It argues that Christ has canceled and replaced the old covenant. Under the Jewish Law, atonement—the process of getting right with God by offering Him something—involved an endless number of animal sacrifices. Only certain priests were qualified to offer such sacrifices to God; namely, individuals who descended from Levi, one of the twelve sons of Jacob. They offered these sacrifices in a single, authorized location, which at the time of Moses was a portable tent, a sanctuary we sometimes call the wilderness tabernacle.

The Israelites worshiped God at this tabernacle while they wandered in the desert for forty years. The tabernacle had two basic chambers: an outer room called the Holy Place or the "Holies," and a smaller inner room, the Most Holy Place or the "Holy of Holies." Although priests from the tribe of Levi—Levitical priests—entered the outer chamber on a

> Hebrews is the only book in the New Testament that refers to Christ as a priest.

regular basis, only one priest was qualified to enter the innermost room of the tent. This individual was the high priest, the highest office of priest, and he entered that room only once a year on the Day of Atonement.

Hebrews indicates that Christ is the decisive replacement of all these elements of the old covenant with its system of sacrifices. In fact, Hebrews argues that none of these things actually got you right with God even in the time of the Old Testament! They could not truly atone for sins; they could not clean them or take them away (Heb. 10:1, 4). According to Hebrews, the sacrificial system of the old covenant simply provided shadowy illustrations of what Christ eventually was to do for real (3:5; 8:5).

The fact that Hebrews reinforces the confidence of the audience in such a specific way—arguing for the superiority of Christ over the Jewish sacrificial system—makes us suspect that this sacrificial system was part of their problem. The Jewish sacrificial system

> Hebrews 11 is the "faith chapter" of the New Testament.

must have been the main competition to the audience's reliance on Christ. For this reason, some think the audience consisted of Jews who were tempted to return to mainstream Judaism. Or perhaps they were God-fearing Gentiles who had associated with Jewish synagogues before they accepted Christ. Whichever the case, the author of Hebrews found a way to argue that Christ is the reality behind every component of the old covenant.

Angels and Moses

Of all the contrasts Hebrews makes, the contrasts of Christ with angels (Heb. 1) and with Moses (3:1–6) seem least relevant. However, when we remember that Moses delivered the Jewish Law to Israel, we see that a contrast between Moses and Christ—the giver of a new law (8:6, 10; 10:16)—fits in well with the old and new covenant contrast. While Moses was a servant in God's house and his words were prophecies about Christ (3:5), Christ is God's Son (3:5–6).

Similarly, many Jews at the time of Christ believed that angels had brought the Law to Moses (Heb. 2:2; cf. Acts 7:38, 53; Gal. 3:19) and that they were its enforcers and guardians on the earth (cf. 1 Cor. 11:10; Col. 2:20–21). Like Moses, they were also servants of God (Heb. 1:7, 14), not a Son like Christ

(1:5). Under the old covenant they served as God's ambassadors to the world, God's principal messengers and mediators—God's go-betweens.

Now, Hebrews indicates, Christ has become the new mediator between God and humanity (Heb. 8:6). When the first chapter of Hebrews shows that Christ is superior to the angels, it announces powerfully that salvation is now possible. Christ became lower than the angels for a little while (2:9) and offered the sacrifice to end all sacrifices (10:14). Now Christ has taken His place as king next to God in heaven, far superior to the servant angels of the old covenant (1:3–4).

Levitical Priests, Sacrifices, and Sanctuaries

Christians long before the time of Hebrews had considered Christ's death to be a sacrifice (Rom. 3:25). A crucifixion was quite different from killing an animal and sprinkling its blood in a temple. It was an act of capital punishment, putting someone to death. More recent forms of capital punishment have included electrocution, lethal injection, or hanging. At the time of Christ, the Romans crucified non-Roman criminals and enemies to make an example of them. They nailed such people to crosses and hoisted them up so everyone could see the shameful result of opposing the Romans and their laws.

From very early on, Christians began to see Christ's crucifixion metaphorically as a sacrifice. The normal or literal use of the word *sacrifice* was about offering animals in a temple or on an altar—usually a stone, table-like structure on which the animal was killed. People made offerings to a god to secure his or her goodwill or to atone for something that might have made the god angry. The early Christians saw Christ's death in this way—it was like a sacrifice that atoned for Israel's sins and thus would bring restoration to God's people.

However, Hebrews is the first Christian writing that clearly considers Christ not only a sacrifice, but a priest as well. Again, this is a metaphor—the words are not being used in their normal, literal way. Try to picture Christ both as the one sacrificing and as the one being sacrificed. Hebrews creates this metaphor to show that Christ is the reality behind every aspect of the Old Testament system of atonement and sacrifices. The old covenant had priests, individuals from the tribe of Levi. Hebrews demonstrates that Christ is also a priest, but a far superior priest to any of the Old Testament priests.

Hebrews shows Christ's superiority by way of another priest mentioned in the Old Testament; in fact, the very first priest mentioned in the Bible. This priest's name was Melchizedek, and Genesis 14 tells how he blessed Abraham after a battle. Since he lived at the time of Abraham, he existed before the time of the Levitical priests. After all, Levi was Abraham's great-grandson. Hebrews argues that since Melchizedek was a priest to Abraham, he was a greater priest than any descendant of Levi could be (Heb. 7:4, 7, 9).

The main characteristic of a priest after the order of Melchizedek seems to be that he never dies (Heb. 7:3, 8, 16, 25). A great deal of debate has surrounded this figure in Hebrews. Is this appearance of Christ in the Old Testament a christophany? Is he an angelic being, such as the figure mentioned in one of the Dead Sea Scrolls?[1] What makes it hard for us to understand Hebrews 7 is the fact that the author is using a method of Jewish interpretation that seems strange to us.

In asking what constitutes a priest like Melchizedek, Hebrews turns to Genesis 14 and focuses not so much on what the text says as what it does not say. For example, Genesis does not say that Melchizedek came from a priestly family, like the Levitical priests did (Heb. 7:3, 6). Genesis does not mention Melchizedek's death either. Therefore, Hebrews can conclude that a priest like Melchizedek does not have a priestly genealogy and does not die. Christ fits such a role perfectly.

> "Now faith is being sure of what we hope for and certain of what we do not see."
> —Hebrews 11:1

Hebrews 7 now comes to its bottom line. The old covenant and the Jewish Law were founded on the system of sacrifices and atonement provided by Levitical priests (Heb. 7:11). If God turned from the Levitical priests to a priest like Melchizedek, Hebrews argues, then the entirety of the old covenant and its Law has been replaced (7:12). Thus, since Christ has arrived, the Old Testament sacrificial system has come to an end. While the blood of bulls and goats could not take away sin (10:4), Christ has offered His own blood through the eternal Spirit (7:24–25; 9:14), actually cleansing us.

For this extended metaphor to work, Christ must be not only a priest, but He must also have a sanctuary in which to offer himself. Hebrews speaks of a heavenly tabernacle in which Christ offered himself—the model on which the earthly tabernacle was based (Heb. 8:5). A great deal of debate has surrounded this heavenly sanctuary. Is it similar to what Plato called the ideal models behind the shadowy things in the world? Is it like the heavenly temples we read about in some Jewish literature, actual buildings up in heaven? Or is it the universe itself, with heaven as the Most Holy Place?

> "Therefore, since we are surrounded by such a great cloud of witnesses, let us throw off everything that hinders and the sin that so easily entangles, and let us run with perseverance the race marked out for us. Let us fix our eyes on Jesus, the author and perfecter of our faith."
>
> —Hebrews 12:1–2

This last option probably comes closest to what Hebrews means—Christ's entrance into heaven was like a high priest entering into the Most Holy Place on the Day of Atonement.

Hebrews is thus unique in the New Testament because not only does it consider Christ to be a priest, but it also considers Him to be a high priest. And while the New Testament elsewhere compares Jesus' death to the Passover sacrifice (e.g., 1 Cor. 5:7) or to a sacrifice in general (e.g., Col. 1:14), Hebrews is the only place where Christ's death is clearly compared to the sacrifice made on the Day of Atonement. Just as that sacrifice was only offered once a year, Hebrews argues that Christ's sacrifice also was only offered once (Heb. 9:25–26). That one sacrifice has effectively done what no other sacrifice has ever done—it has taken away sins forever.

Following Good Examples

One of the ways in which Hebrews both encourages its audience to keep going and discourages them from turning away is by giving examples of each alternative. For instance, Abraham is a good example of someone who kept going even though he would die before his descendants inherited the Promised Land (Heb. 11:8). Moses could have enjoyed all the privileges of royalty in the palace of Pharaoh in Egypt, but he chose instead to be faithful to God and to suffer with God's people (11:25). Hebrews 11 is filled with examples of individuals who faithfully kept going, even though "they did not receive the things promised" (11:13). They endured in faith, even though the things they were trusting God to fulfill were invisible to them.

Hebrews also provides its audience with scary examples of individuals who turned away from God. The most obvious are the Israelites who died in the desert after they escaped Egypt with Moses. These individuals had left Egypt under God's protection; they had been given the assurance that they would enter the Promised Land (Heb. 3:16). But in the end they did not make it due to of their lack of faith (3:19). Hebrews' audience did not miss the point. You have become Christians all right, and God has extended to you the promise of entering into His rest at that heavenly city (4:2; 11:16; 12:22). But if you abandon your faith, God will judge you just as He judged them.

There are several times that Hebrews notes the possibility of becoming a Christian and yet not making it to the end (e.g., Heb. 3:14; 6:4–8; 10:26–27; 12:16–17). In fact, Hebrews seems to teach that once you have crossed a certain line, it is even impossible to return. Christians of all denominations find it hard to accept this teaching. For some, the idea that you could lose your salvation is unacceptable. For others, the idea that you cannot return after losing it is unacceptable. Whatever our interpretation of Hebrews, we can take comfort in the fact that mainstream Christianity has always affirmed that anyone who wants to come to Christ can—whether for the first, second, or fiftieth time. It is not just any sin in general that the audience of Hebrews was in danger of committing; they were in danger of publicly shaming Christ by rejecting Him and the atonement He has provided.

The Who's, When's, and Where's of Hebrews

Hebrews provides much fuel for guessing games. Who was its author? To whom was it sent? We simply do not have enough information to answer questions like these with certainty.

For over a thousand years, the church believed Paul wrote Hebrews; almost no scholar would argue for Paul today. Hebrews' style is quite different from Paul's known writings. Some key words in Hebrews are also used differently than Paul used them. When Paul talks about the Law, he largely refers to things like circumcision and dietary laws; Hebrews almost exclusively refers to the Law's sacrificial system. When Paul talks about faith, he generally means trust; Hebrews speaks primarily of faithfulness. One of the strongest arguments against Paul as author is the fact that Paul likely would not have said that he heard Christ's message of salvation from the apostles (Heb. 2:3), as if he were not an apostle who had seen and heard from the Lord himself!

Although the church probably accepted Hebrews into the Bible because it agreed on Paul as its author, other names had been suggested earlier, like Barnabas. In the end, an early Christian named Origen put it best when he wrote, "Who the author is, God knows." While the author probably knew Paul and may have been in his circle of ministers, it is unlikely that any new evidence will surface to settle this question once and for all.

The fact that the author was with some Italians and that he included them in his greetings to the recipients of this letter or sermon might provide us with a little more basis for guessing this sermon's destination, but not much more (Heb. 13:24). It could mean the author was writing from somewhere in Italy and those with him sent greetings to the audience, or it could mean that the author was writing back to Italy from somewhere else. The fact that Timothy had been in prison nearby could indicate the sermon was written from Asia Minor, perhaps Ephesus (13:23). The letter is first quoted from Rome, which might tip the scales in favor of Italy as the destination.[2] Once again, we simply do not know for sure.

A man named Clement quoted Hebrews in the late A.D. 90s, so it must have been written before then. The mention of leaders who had apparently died may indicate a time after Peter and Paul were put to death in Rome in the mid-60s (Heb. 13:7). Scholars are divided over whether Hebrews was written before or after the Jerusalem temple was destroyed. Hebrews refers to the offering of sacrifices in the present tense (e.g., 9:9; 10:2), but never refers to the temple in Jerusalem. Other Jewish authors after

> "It is impossible for those who have once been enlightened, who have tasted the heavenly gift, who have shared in the Holy Spirit . . . if they fall away, to be brought back to repentance, because to their loss they are crucifying the Son of God all over again and subjecting him to public disgrace."
>
> —Hebrews 6:4, 6

A.D. 70 write in the present tense about offering sacrifices, making it difficult to pin a date regarding the comments in Hebrews. Overall, our opinion is that the flavor of Hebrews better fits the period after the temple was destroyed than before, but it is difficult to conclude for certain.

Questions for Study and Discussion

1. What strategy does Hebrews use to demonstrate that Christ has replaced the entirety of the Old Testament sacrificial system?

2. Do you think Hebrews goes one step further in its understanding of the significance of Christ's death than do the writings of Paul and the rest of the New Testament? Does the author of Hebrews differ in his understanding or does he have the same understanding, expressing it in different imagery?

3. Do you think it is possible to lose your salvation, that is, to go from being saved to unsaved? Why or why not?

The General Letters
James, 1 and 2 Peter, 1–3 John, and Jude

The General Epistles are a group of miscellaneous writings
by important early church figures like James, Peter, and John.

The letters mentioned in the title of this chapter are often called the "General" or "Catholic" Epistles because they address much broader audiences than Paul's letters. In this context, the word *catholic* means *universal*, implying that these letters were addressed to everyone, not to specific churches. Of all the books in the New Testament, these were debated most vigorously by the church about whether to include them in the canon.

However, most of these letters do not have universal audiences in view. According to one interpretation, James was addressed to "the twelve tribes

At a Glance

- The books of James, 1 and 2 Peter, 1–3 John, and Jude are called General Epistles because they address broader audiences than Paul's letters.
- James deals with the temptation to rely on those who are rich and on earthly things. This letter affirms that God is our only legitimate patron.
- First Peter addresses Christian suffering. It encourages its audience to be holy and to exercise respectable conduct on earth.
- Second Peter addresses skeptics who question whether Christ is going to return again.
- First John encourages a community that has lost a significant number of members.
- Second and 3 John encourages a fellow church and a man named Gaius.
- Jude addresses false teaching and heresy.

scattered among the nations" (James 1:1). First Peter addressed "exiles of the Dispersion in Pontus, Galatia, Cappadocia, Asia, and Bithynia" (1:1 NRSV)—perhaps referring to individuals the Romans had literally sent into exile from Rome. Third John is written to a single individual, a man named Gaius (3 John 1:1). In the end, the General Epistles are really a group of miscellaneous writings authored by important figures in the early church. If for no other reason, they fit together because they do not go with any other group of writings in the New Testament.

James: Who Is Your Real Boss?

At first glance, the book of James appears to be a collection of loosely related advice to a Jewish Christian audience. If we look a little more closely, we see that most of its teaching relates to the fact that "every good and perfect gift is from above, coming down from the Father of the heavenly lights" (James 1:17). Because God is the true source of everything we need, we should not rely on the rich. James reads like instructions to various Christians, telling them to have their priorities in order.

One of the reasons we might not see how James's teachings fit together is because the world of James was structured around the relationships of patrons to clients. Patrons were the haves and clients the have nots. As such it was customary for the haves to supply some of the basic needs of the have nots. In return, the have nots showered the haves with praise and honor. In this way clients received their basic needs while patrons gained prestige and glory through their generosity. We won't fully appreciate New Testament words like *grace* and *gift* until we understand the ancient patron-client relationship.

When we look at James from this perspective, we can see that it primarily addresses the matter of who should be our patrons and clients. Clearly God is the one on whom we are to depend, in contrast to the rich and their reliance on the world. On the other hand, the poor and downtrodden are those to whom we should show favor. When we have priorities like these, we will likely face trials and hardships from the rich (e.g., James 1:2; 2:6–7).

It is hard to be teachers and leaders under such circumstances (cf. 3:1). But God promises wisdom to the person who remains resolved and committed to the right priorities (1:5; 3:17).

The Rich

The New Testament has almost nothing good to say about money. In a world where goods were exchanged more than money, those who relied on money were often seen as greedy and selfish. As the Arab proverb goes, "Every rich man is either a thief or the son of a thief." Further, the ancients thought in terms of a limited amount of goods in the world. When you look at possessions from this perspective, the only way to gain is to take from someone else.

It is no surprise, therefore, that the New Testament virtually equates wealth with sin and evil. James is no different: "[the rich] will pass away like a wild flower" (James 1:10). James presents a hypothetical situation in which two men come into a synagogue, one who is rich and one who is poor (2:2). The temptation, James indicates, is to give the rich man the finest seat and make the poor man stand. To do so, however, would be wrong. James asks, "Is it not the rich who are exploiting you . . . dragging you into court?" (2:6).

James probably has temptations like these in mind when he says that God never tempts us (James 1:13). Such temptations, James says, come from their own "evil desire" (1:14). The focus of such desires is clearly possessions and worldly gain. "You ask, . . . that you may spend what you get on your pleasures" (4:3). "You want something but don't get it. You kill and covet, but you cannot have what you want" (4:2). In contrast, James encourages his audience to "submit yourselves . . . to God. Resist the devil, and he will flee from you. Come near to God, and he will come near to you" (4:7–8). The bottom line is that "friendship with the world is hatred toward God" (4:4).

The Poor

Back in the 1500s, the father of Protestantism, Martin Luther, called the book of James "an epistle of straw." He did so not only because it says very little about Christ, but also because it appears to indicate that good deeds are necessary to be acceptable to God. Since Luther interpreted Romans to mean that we become acceptable to God by faith alone, he did not like the book of James. In fact, he did not even translate it into German at first. His interpretation of Paul hardly fit together well with statements like James 2:24: "You see that a person is justified by what he does and not by faith alone."

It is difficult for many to read James and Paul's writings without concluding that these two men flatly disagreed with each other. James says we are made right with God by what we do, our works in addition to our faith. In contrast, Paul says that "people are declared as righteous, because of their faith, not because of their work" (Rom. 4:5 NLT). Indeed, both men use the same Scripture to draw opposite conclusions. Genesis 15:6 says that "Abram believed the LORD, and the LORD declared him righteous because of his faith" (NLT). For Paul this verse means that we get right with God by faith (e.g., Rom. 4:3; Gal. 3:6). For James it is the fact that Abraham did the right thing when God told him to sacrifice Isaac (James 2:23), not some abstract faith that did not show itself in his actions.

> "Now listen, you rich people, weep and wail because of the misery that is coming upon you . . . You have lived on earth in luxury and self-indulgence. You have fattened yourselves in the day of slaughter."
>
> —James 5:1, 5

In the end, we probably take both Paul and James out of context when we read Luther's debate into their words. For example, Paul's argument is not primarily about whether good deeds in general can get us right with God, whether we can earn our salvation. Rather, it is keeping the Jewish Law that Paul says cannot make anyone right with God (Rom. 3:20).

Further, Paul never teaches that a Christian may simply believe and never produce any fruit in his or her life (cf. Gal. 5:22–23). In fact, Paul indicates he could be disqualified at the end of the race if he did not conduct himself appropriately (1 Cor. 9:27). If it is necessary for Paul to live a certain way in order to attain salvation in the end, then even he believes that works of a sort are involved in salvation. He is thus not really that far from James when James says, "Faith without deeds is dead" (James 2:26).

We also need to keep the broader context in mind to correctly understand James's comments. James addresses the person who thinks only of how to increase possessions, doing nothing to benefit those who are in need. The rich person says, "Today or tomorrow we will go to this or that city, spend a year there, carry on business and make money" (James 4:13). This attitude does not give God His proper place or acknowledge that God is in control of such things. Such a person claims to have faith, but his or her life doesn't show it.

James soundly rebukes such a person. "You believe that there is one God. Good! Even the demons believe that—and shudder" (2:19). On the other hand, "Religion that God our Father accepts as pure and faultless is this: to look after orphans and widows in their distress and to keep oneself from being polluted by the world" (James 1:27). The true concern of an individual submitted to God is not accruing possessions or staying on good terms with the rich. The proper concern is with the poor and downtrodden of the world. "Christians who are poor should be glad, for God has honored them" (James 1:9 NLT).

James in Context

Although the author of James does not clearly identify himself, it seems almost certain that he was the half brother of Jesus (cf. Mark 6:3). This James became the leader of the church in Jerusalem (cf. Acts 15:13, 21:18) until he was martyred in A.D. 62. The flavor of the book fits very well with the Jewish Christianity of which James was a part. If this James wrote it, we should probably date it sometime in the A.D. 50s.

1 Peter: Christians and Suffering

Like James, 1 Peter also addresses an audience that is suffering. "Do not be surprised at the painful trial you are suffering," Peter says (1 Pet. 4:12). He thinks of their sufferings as the beginning of God's judgment on the earth: "For it is time for judgment to begin with the family of God; and if it begins with us, what will the outcome be for those who do not obey the gospel of God?" (4:17). The bottom line is for believers to "commit themselves to their faithful Creator and continue to do good" (4:19).

Because 1 Peter was written in the context of persecution and suffering, it might seem defensive in nature—it encourages Christians to live in ways that most ancients thought were respectable. When someone is watching you closely, just waiting for an excuse to pounce on you, you try to do what will keep you from being pounced on. Accordingly, 1 Peter encourages Christians to live in an orderly, respectable way. Christians were to "live such good lives among the pagans that, though they accuse you of doing wrong, they may see your good deeds and glorify God on the day he visits us" (1 Pet. 2:12).

The Living Hope

First Peter expresses a fervent expectation that Christ's return is near, just as Paul's writings do (e.g., 1 Pet. 4:7; cf. Phil. 4:5). The fact that the audience was suffering heightened the hope that He would return soon. Like Hebrews, Peter encourages his audience to think of themselves as "aliens and strangers" on the earth (2:11; cf. Heb. 11:13), individuals who do not really belong down here. Rather, our inheritance is in heaven, and we are just waiting for our salvation—our escape will appear when Jesus is revealed on earth for a second time (1 Pet. 1:4–9).

Nevertheless, the audience had been born again, this time by God's Word. If they drank the milk from this Word, they would grow up to have salvation (1 Pet. 2:2). God redeemed us, paid for our freedom, by way of Christ's blood (1:19). "He [Jesus] bore our sins in his body on the tree, so that we might die to sins and live for righteousness" (2:24). As a result, Christians were to "be holy in all you do" just as God is holy (1:15). We are to act as if we belong to God, which means we must not slip back into our old ways of doing evil (1:14).

First Peter presents us with some unique images of Christians as a "holy priesthood" (1 Pet. 2:5). We are a "spiritual house," Peter says (2:5), with Christ as the cornerstone (2:6–7; cf. Eph. 2:20). Peter redefines God's people in terms of Christians in general, not just Jews. The Gentile Christians of the audience were a "holy nation" of a new sort (2:9–10). Martin Luther used some of these verses to speak of a priesthood of all believers, the notion that all Christians are priests, not just specific individuals. While 1 Peter does not really address such issues directly, it does indicate that all Christians are priests who offer spiritual sacrifices to God.

Submit to the Proper Authority

After Peter tells his audience to live model lives for non-Christians to see, he gives a number of examples of what that might mean. For example, he encourages Christians to submit to Caesar and his governors (1 Pet. 2:13–17). He tells slaves to submit to their masters—even those who are harsh (2:18)—giving Christ as an example of someone who suffered undeservingly (2:21). He says that wives should submit to their husbands (3:1)—they should call their husbands master, as Sarah did to Abraham (3:6). Husbands were encouraged to be considerate of their wives as the "weaker partner" (3:7).

It is in passages like these that we see clearly how connected 1 Peter is to its context in the ancient world. If we followed these words without considering ancient culture and the defensive position in which Peter's audience finds itself, we would have to say that the American Revolution was immoral and that we had no real basis for abolishing slavery in America. Still closer to home is the implication that wives whose husbands abuse them are to submit to them so they will be "won over . . . when they see the purity and reverence of your lives" (1 Pet. 3:1–2). God's Spirit has rightly led the church to recognize that these verses should not be applied in these ways today.

Yet the principles of mutual respect and submission to authority are certainly things we should continue to encourage. Peter tells his audience, "Humble yourselves, therefore, under God's mighty hand . . . Cast all your anxiety on him because he cares for you" (1 Pet. 5:6–7). They are to "live in harmony with one another; be sympathetic, love as brothers, be compassionate and humble. Do not repay evil with evil or insult with insult, but with blessing, because to this you were called" (3:8–9). These instructions relate to the very core of Christian values.

The Who's, When's, Where's of 1 Peter

The traditional understanding of 1 Peter flows rather easily from the text. The apostle Peter identifies himself in the first line and mentions in 5:1 that he witnessed Christ's death. Peter probably wrote from Rome, since he says in 5:13 that the church in "Babylon" greets the audience. It is very likely that "Babylon" here is a nickname for Rome, both because we have no reason to believe Peter ever traveled so far east to the site of Babylon and because we know some Jews referred to Rome in this way. Like Babylon, Rome destroyed Jerusalem and its temple.

The audience of 1 Peter was made up of "God's chosen people who are living as foreigners in the lands of Pontus, Galatia, Cappadocia, the province of Asia, and Bithynia" (1 Pet. 1:1 NLT). All these places are in Asia Minor, modern-day Turkey. At least one scholar has argued that these individuals were literally exiled from Rome, taking the word *foreigners* in its more literal sense, *exiles* (e.g., NRSV).[1] Since Peter apparently wrote it from Rome in a time of persecution, the mid-60s seems an appropriate date for the letter. According to tradition, Peter was crucified upside down in Rome during the reign of Nero.

Some scholars have argued that 1 Peter is pseudonymous, based largely on its excellence use of Greek. But the fact that the letter is written in good Greek is not relevant. Although Peter the Galilean fisherman probably could not have composed such good Greek, the Greek-speaking Silas—whom 1 Peter 5:12 tells us was Peter's amanuensis in writing the letter—no doubt could have. We should look to Silas thus as the one who actually composed most of the words of 1 Peter.

The strongest argument that 1 Peter is pseudonymous comes from the reference to Rome as "Babylon." If Jews called Rome "Babylon" mainly because Rome had destroyed Jerusalem, the letter would have to date from after A.D 70 when Jerusalem was destroyed. Peter died several years before this event. If pseudonymous, this letter was written at some point after Peter's death to encourage Christians who were suffering. The author would have used Peter, therefore, as an appropriate voice to address such individuals, since Peter had died as a martyr to the faith. On the other hand, it is certainly possible that Jews referred to Rome as Babylon even before Jerusalem was destroyed. If this was the case, then we have no significant reason to think the author is anyone other than Peter.

2 Peter: The Lord Is Not Slow

Second Peter has a number of interesting features. For example, Peter draws most of the second chapter of 2 Peter from the book of Jude. Second Peter is the only New Testament book to refer explicitly to New Testament writings by other authors. Not only does it refer to a collection of Paul's letters, but it considers them to be Scripture—the first reference we have to a New Testament book as Scripture (2 Pet. 3:15–16). Second Peter alone speaks of the destruction of the world by fire (3:10), although Hebrews may imply this end as well (Heb. 12:29). Because of these unique features, this short book has much to offer us.

The main focus of 2 Peter is false teaching, particularly with regard to the future judgment of the world. Second Peter indicates that some had begun to doubt whether Christ was ever going to come back and if there really was going to be a judgment of the earth. "Where is this 'coming' he promised? Ever since our fathers died, everything goes on as it has since the beginning of creation" (2 Pet. 3:4).

> "Always be prepared to give an answer to everyone who asks you to give the reason for the hope that you have."
>
> —1 Peter 3:15

In response Peter reminds his audience that "with the Lord a day is like a thousand years, and a thousand years are like a day" (2 Pet. 3:8). "The Lord is not slow in keeping his promise, as some understand slowness" (3:9). Rather, Peter indicates that God is being patient so that as many as possible could be saved—"He is patient with you, not wanting anyone to perish, but everyone to come to repentance" (3:9). Assuredly, though, he would come unexpectedly, like "a thief" (3:10). On that day, "the heavens will disappear with a roar; the elements will be destroyed by fire, and the earth and everything in it will be laid bare" (3:10).

The majority of conservative scholars affirm Peter as the author of this book. As such they would date it to the late A.D. 60s. The majority of scholars in general believe it is pseudonymous, perhaps even the last book of the New Testament written. These individuals would date it sometime in the early second century (the A.D. 100s).

1–3 John

1 John

Although the gospel and epistles of John are technically anonymous, they share enough in common to suggest that they come from a common source. For example, compare 1 John 4:9 to John 3:16. Both share an emphasis on believing in Jesus as the Christ (e.g., 1 John 5:1; John 20:31), and both emphasize that the consequence of such belief is eternal life (e.g., 1 John 5:13; John 3:16). While the New Testament authors probably agree with John on this issue, none of them put it quite this way. It is thus reasonable to assume that the gospel of John and 1, 2, and 3 John all come from the same basic community and that the same authority figure stands behind all four documents.

The Situation

First John gives us several hints about the situation it addresses. It mentions that a number of individuals have departed from John's community. "They went out from us, but they did not really belong to us. For if they had belonged to us, they would have remained with us" (1 John 2:19). The reason John gives for their departure is that they did not believe that Jesus was the Christ (2:22).

It seems fairly likely, however, that they did believe Jesus was the Christ in some way—just not in a way that John found acceptable. If they had not at least been Christians in some sense, it is hard to explain why they would have joined with John in the first place. It is important, therefore, to look more closely at what John means when he says that Jesus is the Christ.

First, to John it is very important for someone to believe that Christ had truly been human. According to John, anyone who does not believe that "Jesus Christ has come in the flesh" (1 John 4:2) is an antichrist. The gospel reflects this same concern when it says, "The Word became flesh and made his dwelling among us" (John 1:14). Related to this concern is the stress 1 John 5:6 puts not only on believing that Christ came "by water"—presumably that Jesus was Christ at his baptism—but also by "blood," that the Christ shed His blood on the cross.

Many scholars see similarities between what John was combating and what another Christian named Ignatius challenged in the early second century (A.D. 100s). Ignatius said, for example, "What benefit does someone bring me if he praise me and blaspheme my Lord by not acknowledging that he wore flesh?"[2] And, "He suffered all these things for us . . . not as some unbelievers say—that he seemed to suffer."[3] Indeed, when writing to Ephesus, the traditional location of John's community, Ignatius mentioned that some individuals with evil teaching had stayed there for a while (cf. 2 John 10). He commended the Ephesians for the fact that they did not listen to such individuals.[4]

Scholars have suggested that "proto-Gnosticism" could have been the false teaching mentioned in many of the New Testament books, including 1 John. In Gnostic belief, matter is evil and spirit is good. Therefore, salvation is a matter of freeing our spirits from our bodies so they can soar to the spiritual realm. This salvation comes by way of true knowledge and wisdom. While Gnosticism did not become a fully developed movement until the second century, some of these ideas are evident in the first century in much more basic forms.

Two early forms of Gnostic teaching that are frequently mentioned when discussing 1 John are Docetism and the teachings of Cerinthus. Docetism was the heresy that Ignatius addressed in the quotes above. The word *Docetist* comes from a Greek word that means "to seem" (*dokeo*)—a name given to the Docetists because they believed that Jesus had only seemed to have flesh. Because they believed that flesh was evil, they did not accept the idea that Christ had truly taken on flesh.

Cerinthus was also one of the earliest Gnostics. A Christian named Irenaeus passed on a story that John had refused to bathe at the same bathhouse as this man because of his false teaching.[5] Cerinthus made a sharp distinction between the human, fleshly Jesus and what he thought of as the spiritual "Christ." He taught that the spiritual Christ had descended on Jesus at His baptism but had left Him before He suffered on the cross.

> "This is how God showed his love among us: He sent his one and only Son into the world that we might live through him."
>
> —1 John 4:9

It is reasonable to think that the "antichrists" of 1 John believed something similar to what Cerinthus or the Docetists taught, although it is hard to be completely certain. Cerinthus held a number of strange beliefs that 1 John says nothing about. Docetism seems to have had a strong Jewish element that we also hear nothing of in 1 John. What we know is that these false teachers did not believe that Christ had taken on flesh, and they did not think that they needed His death to cover their sins (cf. 1 John 1:8–10). They seem to have departed from John's community with a spirit of hatred toward those who disagreed with them (cf. 2:9–10).

The Message

The key claim with which 1 John leads off is the statement that "God is light; in him there is no darkness at all" (1 John 1:5). First John has one of the strongest statements about Christians and sin to be found in the New Testament: "No one who is born of God will continue to sin, because God's seed remains in him; he cannot go on sinning, because he has been born of God" (3:9). One of 1 John's main points is to urge its audience not to sin as 2:1 says, "My dear children, I write this to you so that you will not sin."

However, it is important that we know just exactly how John defines sin. On the one hand, he gives us two general definitions: "Sin is lawlessness" (1

John 3:4) and "all wrongdoing is sin" (5:17). But if we really want to understand what the heart of sin is to John, we will have to look at his repeated command to love one another. For John, as for the rest of the New Testament, love sums up everything that God requires of us.

The "new" command John gives in this letter is the "old" command that Jesus also gave and lived while He was on earth—love your brother (1 John 2:5–10). Those who left the community did not love their brothers—they were like Cain who killed his brother (3:12). Those who were in the light, on the other hand, were like Jesus, who laid down His life for us (3:16). Those who left were the ones who loved the world (2:15). They were the sort of people who do not help their brothers and sisters in need (3:17). One of the best-known passages in 1 John sums it up nicely: "Dear friends, let us love one another, for love comes from God. Everyone who loves has been born of God and knows God. Whoever does not love does not know God, because God is love" (4:7–8).

First John gives us many statements that can become skewed if we do not think of them in context. John's repeated commands to love surely relate to the fact that some had just left the church in a most unloving way. John's words against sinning thus were his pleas for Christians not to act like some so-called Christians had just acted. His commands were not so much abstract theological statements about Christians and sin; they come out of the divisive conflict from which his community had just emerged.

Similarly, some Christians ironically have taken John's comments about sinning in a way that actually contradicts John's overall message. First John 1:8 says, "If we claim to be without sin, we deceive ourselves and the truth is not in us." First John 1:10 also says, "If we claim we have not sinned, we make [God] out to be a liar." John would be shocked to know that some Christians think these verses teach that we cannot help but sin every day in word, thought, and deed—exactly the opposite point he was making in his overall message!

The false teachers who left John's community did not believe that Christ had come in the flesh or had suffered on the cross. They did not believe that Christ had come "by . . . blood" (1 John 5:6). Therefore, they did not think they needed the atoning death of Jesus to make them acceptable to God. It was as if they were saying they had no sin for Christ to cleanse.

Far from affirming that all Christians continue to sin, 1 John 1:8 and 10 relate to individuals who did not believe they needed Christ's atoning death—they thought they had no sin for Him to cleanse. First John certainly does not teach that Christians are helpless against sinning. On the contrary, John's desire is that those who have already trusted in Christ will not continue sinning (2:1; 3:9). "But if anybody does sin, we have one who speaks to the Father in our defense—Jesus Christ, the Righteous One. He is the atoning sacrifice for our sins" (2:1–2).

2 John

Second John is a short letter addressed to "the chosen lady and to her children" (v. 1). While some take this lady to be some unknown female, it seems more likely that John is addressing a sister church.[6] Once again, the author does not give his name, although he does refer to himself as "the elder," a title that may help us determine the identity of the author.

Much in 2 John is similar to the message of 1 John. For example, it mentions the "new" command that we had from the beginning, to "love one another" (2 John 5; cf. 1 John 2:7–10). It warns against false teachers who do not believe Christ came in the flesh and calls such a person an antichrist (2 John 7; cf. 1 John 4:2–3).

However, some scholars believe that 2 John was written before such individuals had fully left the communities under John's influence and, thus, that 2 John was written before 1 John (see 2 John 10). Second John gives us the impression that these individuals were traveling teachers who went from place to place. With such little information to go on, it is difficult to know for sure.[7]

3 John

Third John is a personal letter from John the elder to an individual named Gaius, although once again the letter is technically anonymous. While some have suggested that false teaching is still the problem, the letter is far from clear on this. More important, John writes to encourage Gaius to receive into his home individuals that John had sent, "even though they are strangers to you" (3 John 5).[8] The letter urges hospitality (v. 8) toward traveling teachers who receive no help from non-Christians, but rely on Christians alone for their food and living (v. 7).

Apparently, a man named Diotrephes rejected these traveling teachers and the authority of John himself (v. 9). It is not clear that he rejected them because he disagreed with their teaching, although this is possible. More likely, he saw himself as the leader of his church and believed that John and these teachers were intruding on his authority. Many think that 3 John was written at a time when single, authoritative men were increasingly becoming the leaders of individual churches. In the early 100s, the Christian Ignatius wrote, "Clearly we must consider the bishop to be like Christ himself."[9] Perhaps we are seeing in 3 John the growing conflict at the turn of the century between traveling teachers and prophets and local church leadership.

Who Was John?

Since the earliest centuries of the church, Christian tradition has held that the gospel of John and the three letters we call 1, 2, and 3 John all come from John the apostle, the son of Zebedee, the beloved disciple of John 13:23. Unfortunately, none of these letters actually name John as the author. The only clues we have are the mention of the "beloved disciple" in the gospel and the fact that he calls himself "the elder" in 2 and 3 John. Nevertheless, the strength of early Christian tradition is enough for some to affirm that the author is John, the son of Zebedee.

On the other hand, a good case can be made that the author is another John who had also been a follower of Jesus, just not one of the twelve core disciples. For example, there is the fact that Jesus seems to prophesy the martyrdom of John, the son of Zebedee in Mark 10:38–39. The author of John, on the other hand, seems to have died of old age (John 21:22–23). The use of the term "the beloved disciple" in and of itself is somewhat curious in the gospel, especially since the sons of Zebedee are mentioned in John

21:2. It is almost as if the gospel is deliberately ambiguous about who this beloved disciple was.

The matter gets even cloudier when we realize that Jesus had more than one follower named John. The Christian Papias, writing in the early 100s, mentioned not only John the apostle, but also someone he called John the elder. The fact that John actually identifies himself in 2 and 3 John as "the elder" makes this possibility particularly enticing. The Christian Eusebius, writing in the early 300s, noted the differences in style between the gospel of John and the book of Revelation and brought up the two individuals named John we have just mentioned. Although he preferred to think of the apostle as the author of the gospel (he did not like Revelation), he suggested that John the elder had written 2 and 3 John.[10] Perhaps he was correct.

Jude

The short book of Jude is directed against individuals who were teaching false things in the church. These individuals were participating in the activities of the church—they had "secretly slipped in among you" (Jude 4). They eat "with you without the slightest qualm," perhaps a reference to Communion or the Eucharist, but they spoiled these meals (v. 12). In fact, they tried to "shepherd" the churches, perhaps meaning that they claimed to have authority (v. 12). Perhaps they were traveling teachers similar to the ones we saw in 1 and 2 John. Maybe they were the false teachers mentioned in 1 Timothy.

In contrast to them, Jude encourages his audience to "contend for the faith that was once for all entrusted to the saints" (Jude 3). These individuals apparently had "evil desires" (16) and used the idea of God's grace as an excuse for immorality (4), perhaps of a sexual kind (7). One curious aspect of their belief involved slandering angelic beings in some way (8).

A number of Jude's features are interesting. First, there is the name Jude itself. Jude tells us that he is "a brother of James." Most likely, he is telling us that he is the brother of James, the leader of the Jerusalem church, and thus the half brother of Jesus himself (cf. Mark 6:3). It is also interesting that 2 Peter seems to have used almost all of Jude in the composition of its second chapter, although we should not conclude from this fact that the false teaching it addresses is the same as what Jude attacks.

One of the most interesting things about Jude is the way it seems to quote non-biblical writings as authoritative. It seems to treat as history a story told in a writing known as the Assumption of Moses. It also quotes a book known

> "For God so loved the world that he gave his one and only Son, that whoever believes in him shall not perish but have eternal life."
>
> —John 3:16

as 1 Enoch, whose various parts were written over the period from about 200 B.C. to the first century A.D. Not only does it seem to quote Enoch as Scripture, but it also treats Enoch's words as if Enoch really said them. At the very least this shows us that we can find truth anywhere. It may also affirm to us that God reveals truth to us from within what we understand— He does not always correct us on the details.

Questions for Study and Discussion

1. What is the bottom line for each of the General Epistles? Can you summarize each one in a sentence or two?

2. How well do you think the ancient patron-client system or the concept of limited good helps us to better understand the message of the New Testament?

3. First Peter advocates submission to oppression rather than civil disobedience or social reform. When we can actually have an impact on our society and social structures, do you think God would still advocate passive submission?

4. Why do you think God has allowed two thousand years to pass without sending Christ back to earth?

5. What do you make of the fact that Jude seems to consider books that are not in the New Testament as authoritative? Did God work around Jude's misunderstanding or was the church wrong not to include such books?

Jesus Revealed!
The Apocalypse

While so much of Revelation is difficult to follow, its bottom
line comes through loud and clear: God wins in the
end, and He wins through Jesus Christ.

The Genre of Revelation

Very early in the book of Revelation, you realize how different it is from the rest of the New Testament. Its fantastic images of dragons, beasts, and destruction are unparalleled in the other books, as is its author's heavenly trip. Yet it still has many features in common with other New Testament books. Like Paul's writings, Revelation addresses specific situations in specific churches (Rev. 2–3). Like some of the gospel material, it contains prophecies of the future (1:3).

At a Glance

- Revelation fits three genres: (1) a circular letter, (2) a prophetic writing, and (3) an apocalypse.
- There are several basic approaches to Revelation, ranging from the belief that it was written about ancient Rome, to the belief that Revelation deals completely with things yet to come.
- Some think its middle section lays out a series of chronological events, while others think it portrays the same basic messages over and over.
- Its basic images relate to (1) a time of great trouble for Christians, (2) forces that will persecute Christians, and (3) the ultimate salvation of the persecuted and judgment of the persecutors.
- The author of Revelation is a man named John, perhaps not the author of the gospel of John.

Part of its uniqueness is that it uses more than one genre.[1] It is both a letter and a book of prophecy. However, the things that puzzle us most about Revelation arise from its third genre, apocalypse. For this reason, Revelation sometimes is known as "The Apocalypse."

There are still several existing apocalypses from the ancient world. The main point of an apocalypse is to reveal what is going on in heaven and what is about to happen on earth. Apocalypses typically begin with a visit from a heavenly being such as an angel. They are usually written during a time of crisis and aim to bring hope to their audiences and a certainty that everything will soon be all right. While Revelation probably is not pseudonymous, most apocalypses are. Their writers adopt the voice of a past authority figure to talk about the present. They imagine this historical figure having a vision of the author's time.

The book of Revelation shares many of these features with the other apocalypses of the period. In Revelation, Jesus is the first "heavenly being" who visits the earth (e.g., Rev. 1:9–20), followed by another angel who leads John into heaven (e.g., 17:1). The book reveals visions of heaven and the future (e.g., 4:1), and a time of great trial that is on its way (e.g. 3:10). Despite the trials to come, it emphatically proclaims that good will triumph in the end (e.g., ch. 20–22). The only feature Revelation does not seem to share with other apocalypses is that of pseudonymity. Most scholars believe that the John who identifies himself in Revelation 1:4 is the author of the book.

Revelation is one of the most difficult books of the New Testament to interpret. There are four basic approaches to its meaning. Preterists believe that all or nearly all of the prophecies of the book are directed at the time period in which they were made. In other words, the book describes events occurring in the late first century A.D. Futurists, on the other hand, believe that almost all its prophecies are still to come and relate to the end of time. Historists combine these two positions; they believe that Revelation prophesies about events from the past and the future, including events throughout the last two thousand years. Idealists believe the book is mostly about the continual struggle between good and evil. Its images thus are symbolic of all time rather than predictions of specific events in history.

The Revelation of Jesus Christ

You can often tell what a book is about by the way it starts and ends. The same is true of the book of Revelation. While so much of its imagery is difficult to follow, its beginning and conclusion come through loud and clear with the bottom line of the book: God wins in the end, and He wins through Jesus Christ.

The first sentence of the book may have had a double meaning: "The revelation of Jesus Christ" (Rev. 1:1). Jesus reveals a number of things throughout the book, so it presents revelations from Jesus Christ. On the other hand, some talked about Jesus' second coming as the time when He would be revealed (e.g., 1 Cor. 1:7; 1 Pet. 1:7, 13; 4:13). The phrase "the revelation of Jesus Christ" might have made readers think of Christ's return to earth, when He would be revealed.

Revelation both begins and ends with mention of Christ's return (Rev. 1:7; 22:7, 12, 20). In a time of crisis, Jesus reassures the churches of Asia that He will soon come back to earth and everything will be set straight. No matter how we interpret the various pictures the book gives us of God's salvation and judgment, we should not forget that it is primarily about what God has done, and will do, through Christ.

Christ has already died as a sacrifice for God's chosen people. The image of Christ we see most often in Revelation is the Lamb of God (e.g., Rev. 5:12). Because He died, Jesus is worthy to set in motion the judgment. Because He died, He is qualified to rule the world.

It is also interesting the way in which Christ is worshiped (e.g., Rev. 5:14). Revelation presents us with the worship of Jesus more clearly than any other book in the New Testament. Yet even here, God is the primary object of worship (e.g., 19:10; 22:9). In a scene that reminds us of Isaiah 6, Revelation 4 depicts four living creatures worshiping God, saying, "Holy,

holy, holy is the Lord God Almighty, who was, and is, and is to come" (4:8). This set of three "holys" is sometimes called the *trisagion*—calling God "holy" three times.

Some of the most fantastic images of Christ in Revelation, however, are those that depict Him coming to the earth in judgment. Revelation 14:14–16, for example, pictures Jesus sitting on a cloud with a crown on His head and a sharp sickle in his hand, with which He reaps the earth. In 19:11–16, He is the Word of God riding on a white horse. Jesus' eyes blaze with fire and He has many crowns on His head (19:12). A sharp sword comes out of His mouth (19:15), and the titles "King of Kings and Lord of Lords" are written on His robe and thigh (19:16). As He comes, He treads the "winepress of the fury of the wrath of God almighty" (19:15), an allusion to the blood that will flow on the day of judgment.

There are two important conclusions. First, these two images of Christ probably refer to the same event—Christ's second coming to the world with salvation and judgment. For this reason, we cannot assume Revelation offers a chronological sequence of events. Instead, it gives us several different pictures of the same basic events—judgment and salvation. It offers a kaleidoscopic view of judgment rather than a storyline of how each event will unfold.

Second, John clearly does not intend this imagery to be taken literally. He doesn't give us a literal picture of what Jesus will look like on judgment day or even of what He looks like now in heaven. Surely no one thinks that Jesus really looks like a slain lamb with seven horns and seven eyes (Rev. 5:6). With this comes a strong word of caution about how literally we take Revelation's imagery of such things as beasts and marks on foreheads. We cannot rule out the possibility that these are symbols for things like governments and allegiances.

Signs and Seals

Although a great deal of debate surrounds the meaning of the images in the central part of Revelation, they seem collectively to make three points, each of which shows up several times: (1) a time of great trouble is coming, (2) evil will oppress Christians in an unparalleled way, and (3) eventually Christ will return, bringing judgment to the wicked and salvation to the righteous. Revelation unfolds this message by a series of different images.

Seven Seals

After John's spirit goes up into heaven and sees God on His throne (Rev. 4:1), he witnesses a crisis. There is a scroll that symbolizes the solution to the problems of the world and of God's people, but no one is worthy to open it. John weeps to think that the world's problems will not be solved, but is consoled when someone in heaven points out Jesus to him (5:4–5). Because of Jesus' death as the Lamb of God, He is worthy to open the scroll!

The next two chapters (Rev. 6–7) involve a number of images of judgment that take place as Jesus opens each of the seven seals on the scroll—seven pieces of wax keeping the scroll shut—one by one. After Jesus opens the sixth seal, John witnesses 144,000 Jews on earth (7:5–8), probably a symbolic rather than an actual number. "A great multitude that no one could count, from every nation, tribe, people and language" (7:9), follows the 144,000. All these individuals are right with God, although they have experienced "the great tribulation" on the earth (7:14).

The nature of this great tribulation is highly debated among Christians. Many Christians think of this as a specific seven-year period at the end of time during which a figure they call the Antichrist will rule on the earth. While we cannot say that they are wrong about how God will end things, it is important to realize that Revelation itself nowhere discusses such a seven-year period. While it does mention a three-and-one-half-year period when Jerusalem will undergo siege (11:2–3) and a three-and-one-half-year period when God's people will be protected from Satan (12:6, 14), these seem to be the same period of time. Not only is this a time when God's people are protected (not persecuted, as in the great tribulation), but Revelation never associates the beast with this time of persecution. The idea of a seven-year period actually comes from the book of Daniel (Dan. 9:24–27)—it does not feature in the teaching of Revelation.

Further, modern Christian prophecy often uses a number of terms differently from their original use in the Bible, if these terms appear at all. For example, the word "antichrist" appears in the New Testament in 1 John 2:18, but it does not refer to the evil figure of Revelation or the "man of lawlessness" mentioned in 2 Thessalonians 2:3. In 1 John it is used in the plural to refer to a number of individuals who deny that Jesus Christ came in the flesh, false teachers who lived at the end of the first century A.D. The phrase *the antichrist* used by many translations (e.g., NIV, NLT) does not actually appear in the Greek. The original does not put *the* in front of antichrist.

Another non-biblical term often used in relation to this hypothetical seven-year period is the *rapture*, the "seizing" of Christians from the earth as mentioned in 1 Thessalonians 4:17. Some futurists think that the vast crowd of Revelation 7:9 refers to the rapture of Christians from the earth before a seven-year period of tribulation begins, a pre-tribulation rapture. Others think that since these individuals have come out of the great tribulation, Christians will be removed from the earth three and one-half years into the seven-year period, a mid-tribulation rapture. Still others do not see Revelation as a straightforward sequence of events and so believe that these people are removed from the earth—if they manage to survive—after the tribulation, a post-tribulation rapture.

> The great tribulation in Revelation is a period during which God's people will undergo a time of intense suffering on earth.

It is important to realize how little this contemporary language really connects with the book of Revelation. While it is possible that God has inspired modern prophecy teachers to see the future correctly by reading the Bible "spiritually," Revelation itself did not involve any of these schemes. The great tribulation in Revelation is a period during which God's people will undergo a time of intense suffering on earth. The book does not give a specific amount of time for this suffering, nor does it give us any reason to think that the removal of Christians from the earth will take place at any point other than when Christ returns in judgment. In other words, we have no reason to believe that Revelation gives us any different message with regard to Christ's second coming than the other books of the New Testament.

Seven Trumpets

After the seventh seal is opened, a series of events featuring seven trumpets begins (Rev. 8–11). Once again, some interpret the events that accompany each trumpet blast as things that will take place sequentially, following the events of the seven seals. Indeed, the devastating things that happen as the trumpets are sounded are worse than the destruction that accompanies the opening of the seals. However, others believe that these images have the same basic meaning as the opening of the seven seals; namely, that things will get worse and worse as the final judgment approaches.

After the sixth trumpet sounds, just as happened after the opening of the sixth seal, Revelation stops to give us several pictures of the witness, persecution, and triumph of God's people. In Revelation 11, two witnesses appear on earth. These two individuals prophesy while the Gentiles trample on Jerusalem for forty-two months (three and one-half years). At the end of the forty-two months, a beast rises from the dead and kills them (11:7). But the two witnesses are also raised from the dead (11:11), leading to the final trumpet (11:15). After the final trumpet, Revelation once again makes us feel that we have reached the point of salvation and ultimate judgment.

A great deal of debate surrounds the meaning of the two witnesses of Revelation 11. Because the miracles the two witnesses perform are things that Moses and Elijah did (Rev. 11:6), some futurists believe that Moses and Elijah themselves will literally return to the earth during the first half of a seven-year tribulation. On the other hand, some preterists believe that Revelation is referring to Peter and Paul, both of whom were put to death by the emperor Nero, a popular suggestion for the identity of the beast. Indeed, the Romans did lay siege to Jerusalem for a period of forty-two months in the years between A.D. 66–70. However, Peter, Paul, and Nero all died well before this siege was over.

Another interpretation that fits more with the idealist interpretation is that these two witnesses symbolize the church, modeled after the Jewish sense that two or three witnesses were essential to assure the certainty of something (e.g., Deut. 19:15; cf. 2 Cor. 13:1). Indeed, in Matthew 18:20 Jesus says, "For where two or three come together in my name, there am I with them." In this interpretation, the two witnesses represent all Christians who faithfully preach Christ's return to earth. Revelation indicates that they will undergo a time of intense persecution.

Dragons and Beasts

Before the final series of sevens, Revelation presents us with more controversial images. The first is a woman and a dragon (Rev. 12). The dragon is clearly Satan (12:9), and the woman appears to represent the people of God—initially Israel but later the whole church. The woman is protected from Satan for three and one half years. A preterist might see this as a picture of the protection the Christians of Jerusalem enjoyed during the time that Rome laid siege to the city in A.D. 66–70. According to tradition, they fled to a desert city called Pella (cf. 12:6).

Revelation 13 continues with more evil forces that are the enemies of God's people. The "beast from the sea" and the "beast from the land" have given rise to much speculation among Christians. According to futurists, they refer to the Antichrist of the end times and a "false prophet" (e.g., Rev. 16:13) who will set up a world religion around the Antichrist, forcing everyone everywhere to worship him. Unless you have the "mark of the beast" on your right hand or on your forehead, you will not be able to buy or sell (13:16–17).

Preterists, on the other hand, see this imagery in relationship to the Roman Empire and emperor worship. Asia Minor, the area to which Revelation was written, was particularly known for the way it worshiped the Roman emperors, sometimes even while they were still living. In the years that followed the writing of the New Testament, Christians sometimes got into trouble for refusing to offer sacrifices to the emperors—a refusal that was seen by non-Christians as disloyal and unpatriotic.

One interesting preterist interpretation of the mark of the beast is that it refers figuratively to the use of Roman money. Some of the Roman coins in John's day celebrated the divinity of the emperor whose face they bore. It is understandable that some Christians may have struggled with using such coins, effectively keeping them from buying or selling unless they had the "mark of the beast" in their "right hand."

Since Revelation seems to revisit the same themes over and over, it is no surprise that Revelation 17 returns to the topic of the beast, this time in more detail. Revelation 13 speaks rather vaguely about this figure, mentioning ten horns and seven heads, a fatal wound that had healed, and the "number of his name . . . 666" (Rev. 13:17–18). Revelation 17 expands on the first two images, equating the seven heads with seven hills and the ten horns with ten kings.

In Revelation 17, a woman is sitting on a scarlet beast. This woman has on her forehead: "MYSTERY BABYLON THE GREAT, MOTHER OF PROSTITUTES AND OF THE ABOMINATIONS OF THE EARTH" (Rev. 17:5). Even if you believe the beast to be a figure yet to come in history, a good case can be made that John was thinking of ancient Rome as he wrote these chapters about the beast. For example, his readers almost certainly would have thought of Rome when they read that the "seven heads are seven hills on which the woman sits" (Rev. 17:9). The starting point for understanding the woman of Revelation 17, therefore, is the Rome of John's day.

One clue that this woman represents Rome is the fact that John refers to her as "Babylon" (Rev. 17:5). After the Romans destroyed Jerusalem in A.D. 70, Jews began to call Rome "Babylon" (cf. 1 Pet. 5:13), since the Babylonians had also destroyed Jerusalem several centuries previously. In fact, some have unfortunately identified the woman of Revelation 17 with the Roman Catholic Church and the beast with a future pope. While this hateful identification is most certainly wrong, it shows how clearly Revelation's imagery connects with the city of Rome.

Given that John's readers had Rome in mind, they almost certainly would have thought of Roman emperors when he mentioned seven kings in association with the seven hills. Since Revelation was written in the Asia Minor area, it made sense to think of Rome as "from the sea" (Rev. 13:1)—Rome was in that direction. John says, "Five kings have already fallen, the sixth now reigns, and the seventh is yet to come" (17:10 NLT). The scarlet beast, John tells us, "that was, but is no longer, is the eighth king" (17:8, 11 NLT). What is startling is that this eighth king was also one of the first seven (17:11), an individual who had been fatally wounded (13:3, 12).

Although a great deal of debate surrounds the meaning of these statements, the view that commands the most support is that John was referring to the emperor Nero. A good case can be made that even if the beast represents someone still to come, Nero provided John with the prototype of this individual. On one reckoning, the five dead emperors were: (1) Augustus, (2) Tiberius, (3) Caligula, (4) Claudius, and (5) Nero. If we omit the tumultuous year A.D. 69, during which Rome had three different rulers, the sixth would be Vespasian and the seventh Titus. If we take the number eight straightforwardly, Domitian becomes the eighth king—the emperor reigning at the time John wrote Revelation according to tradition.

This approach raises a number of questions. Is it valid to omit the emperors of A.D. 69? Should we start with Julius Caesar rather than Augustus? Must we then re-date Revelation, since the imagery places its writing during the time of Vespasian? Or is Revelation pseudonymous after all, placed back in time for stylistic reasons? Does John wish us to view Domitian as the beast?

Nevertheless, the idea that Nero was the basis for the symbolism of the beast fits well with other imagery Revelation gives us. For example, Nero committed suicide in A.D. 68, which corresponds to the fact that the beast was fatally wounded (Rev. 13:3, 12). Nero was also a fitting prototype of one who persecutes the church, since he was the first to put Christians to death on any large scale.

The figure of 666—the "number of the beast" (Rev. 13:18)—has long been intriguing to those interested in Revelation. Before the symbols we now use for our numbers existed, languages used their letters for numbers as well as for letters. You could thus add up the letters of a word. Christians have long pointed out that the name Caesar Nero adds up to 666 if you use Aramaic letters. Of course, Christians have also found ways to make the names of everyone from U.S. presidents to Catholic popes fit as well. Given the context of Revelation, however, Nero seems a fairly probable candidate for the origins of the 666 number.

A final factor makes Nero the most likely prototype for the beast. A legend existed in John's day that Nero would return one day with armies from the East to exact his revenge on Rome (cf. Rev. 16:12). A writing called the Sibylline Oracles tells of Nero fleeing "Babylon" (Rome) for the eastern empire of Persia. Eventually, he would return and exact judgment on the Roman world, including Asia Minor: "All Asia, falling to the ground, will lament for the gifts she enjoyed from you . . . But the one who obtained the land of the Persians will fight, and killing every man he will destroy all life so that a one-third portion will remain for wretched mortals."[2]

If this legend stands behind the puzzling imagery of Revelation 13 and 17, we do not need to think that John thought Nero himself would literally return from the dead. A futurist might see Nero simply as the prototype for the Antichrist to come. Similarly, a preterist might say that John thought of Domitian as a Nero-type individual. An idealist might suggest that figures like this have revived throughout history and will continue to appear from time to time.

The Final Showdown

In between the two chapters on the beast that we have just discussed, Revelation gives us one last picture of its basic themes. Revelation 14, for example, again mentions the 144,000 righteous, those Jews who have remained faithful to God throughout persecution.

Following this mention of the 144,000, we have two more series of seven. The first involves six angels and Christ, who is placed in the middle of the series. Christ and the last three angels are pictured harvesting the earth (Rev. 14:16), which seems in this instance to be a harvest of judgment, since blood flows from the harvest (14:19–20). The actions of the angels and of Christ all seem to be pictures of the same event, the final judgment.

Revelation 16 gives us the final series of seven—seven bowls of wrath. After the sixth bowl, the dragon and two beasts gather for the final battle at a place called Armageddon. It is not clear exactly what place John might have had in mind by this name. There is an important place called Megiddo in Palestine, but it is a valley, not a mountain. Thus, we cannot say for certain where Armageddon is located. John may not even have had a specific location in mind.

Final Salvation and Judgment

Revelation 16–19 supports the idea that what we have been seeing throughout the book over and over again is the same event of final salvation and judgment. If you thought Babylon had fallen in 16:19, you might be surprised to find her falling again in 18:2—and again in the final battle with the beast in 19:19–21. Christ rides a white horse in judgment in 19:11 and performs the same judgment already pictured in 14:16.

Revelation 18 has the starkest picture of Babylon's fall. It makes clear that economic sins are a part of her offenses. John rails against the orientation of Babylon around wealth (e.g., Rev. 18:19) and against all the merchants who take advantage of the opportunities she brings (18:11–13). These comments remind us of how severe the book of James is on the rich, as well as the merchant who goes from place to place in search of money (James 4:13). A preterist might find in these verses a critique of how the materialism of Rome brought hardship on the everyday person of Asia Minor.

Yet the preterist interpretation runs into some of its greatest difficulties in Revelation 18–22, events that hardly seemed to be fulfilled in John's own day. Unless you are willing to conclude that John's prophecies did not come true, the historist, futurist, and idealist perspectives become attractive from this point on in Revelation. A historist, for example, might understand Revelation 18 to be about the fall of Rome in A.D. 410. An idealist might say that all such persecutors of Christians will fall—not just Rome but any oppressive empire. A futurist might say that regardless of the overtones of the Roman Empire, the truest fulfillment of these words will take place at the end of time.

Revelation 20 is yet another chapter where a great deal of debate has occurred. This debate has centered largely on the nature of the millennium—a period of a thousand years mentioned in Revelation 20:2, 4, and 7. After the dragon (Satan) is destroyed, he is thrown into the Abyss for a thousand years. At this time, all those killed for their faith come back to life in the first of two resurrections from the dead. It is quite possible that this group includes the 144,000 and the others in Revelation 7:14 who come out of the great tribulation. These individuals reign with Christ for a thousand years on earth.

After the thousand years is over, Satan is released for one more battle. He loses, of course, and is consigned to a lake of fire forever. At this point, all the dead from all of history are raised and brought before a great white throne for judgment. Following this event, God makes a new heaven and earth, then a new Jerusalem comes down to that earth from heaven (Rev. 21:1–2). There is no temple in that city, for God almighty and Christ are its temple (21:22). Similarly, there is no need for a sun or moon because of the light these two bring (21:23). Interestingly, Revelation does not picture Christians going off to be in heaven forever—rather they find their place on a renewed earth on which there is no longer a curse (22:3). The book concludes with Christ's promise that the time for all these things is near (22:10).

The most natural reading of Revelation's millennium is futurist. Revelation seems to imply that things will get really bad for Christians in a time when most of those Christians will die for their faith. These individuals will be raised when Christ returns in judgment and they will rule on earth for a thousand years—perhaps not an exact number but a number symbolic of a very long period of time. This perspective is called a premillennial view because it would say that the millennium is still to come.

On the other hand, Revelation would likely have given its original readers the sense that it was speaking of Rome and that all these things would happen soon. "The time is near," Jesus says to the audience of this ancient time (Rev. 22:10). For this reason, most Christians up until about the 1800s were postmillennial in their view—they believed that Christ's rule roughly corresponded to the rule of the church on earth. In this view, the millennium is either something we are currently experiencing if we are part of God's church or it concluded some time ago. Unlike premillennialism, postmillennialism tends to believe that things will get better and better until Christ finally returns.

The difficulties with the two positions we have just mentioned have led others to what we might call an amillennial view—the view that Revelation is not really about a specific period of time that will take place in history. Rather, Christ rules at any point when His people are serving Him faithfully. It is important to remember that Christians of all stripes, both liberal and conservative, have been able to hold to all of these positions. That is to say, you cannot presume a person to be liberal or conservative simply on the basis of which interpretation he or she takes. We should not use "end time" views as a litmus test for whether or not a person is a Christian.

The Who's, When's, and Where's of Revelation

The traditional view of Revelation's background is very specific. According to this view, the apostle John wrote Revelation while he was exiled on the island of Patmos during the reign of the emperor Domitian in the 90s. Several aspects of the traditional view are far from certain.

Some have suggested that John might have written Revelation much earlier than the 90s. If one connects the seven kings of Revelation 17 with the emperors of Rome, then John would have written during the time of Vespasian (Rev. 17:10). On this reckoning, John wrote Revelation just after the Romans had destroyed Jerusalem.

Since the earliest years of the church, various Christians have also realized that the style and orientation of Revelation are quite different in many respects from that of the gospel of John. A man by the name of Dionysius noted as early as the 200s that the style of Revelation was dramatically different from that of John's gospel, as did the church father Eusebius in the 300s. This difference does not seem connected to the imagery of Revelation; the book simply seems to come from one for whom Greek is a second language.

Further, Revelation seems to have a strong sense of imminent judgment and salvation. The gospel of John, on the other hand, has very little emphasis on Christ's second coming and focuses more on the presence of God's Spirit on earth at that time. For these reasons, while most scholars accept that the author was a man named John from Asia Minor, a man on the island of Patmos at the time of writing, many do not think this John was the same individual responsible for the gospel and Johannine epistles.

At the same time, Revelation does share a number of commonalities with John's gospel. Both seem to come from Asia Minor, traditionally from about the same time period. Both uniquely use the image of Jesus as the Lamb of God and Christ as the source of living water. They both make reference to Christ as the Word of God; Jesus also makes "I am" statements in both. It is thus difficult not to see some connection between Revelation and the gospel of John.

Questions for Study and Discussion

1. Do you think Revelation is about John's time, the end of time, all time, or some combination of these possibilities?
2. Notice that Revelation uses very few of the terms associated with the interpretation of the book. Does this fact imply that most of our interpretations of Revelation have little to do with the book itself?
3. Does Revelation support the idea of a seven-year tribulation with an Antichrist and a rebuilt temple?

Epilogue
Where Do We Go From Here?

The Bible was not written in our categories of understanding,
but in those of the people to whom it was first written.

The Bible as Scripture

If you have read much of this book, you realize that the Bible's original meaning is not something you can arrive at very easily without knowledge of ancient language, history, and culture. In other words, without this knowledge you would only get a superficial sense of what Matthew, Paul, or any of the other writers of the Bible were really trying to say, even if you have an excellent English translation. In fact, there are enough gaps in our knowledge of the historical context of the Bible for even

> At this point we can no longer question that what Paul and his audiences understood his words to mean was a function of what words and ideas could mean two thousand years ago.

scholars to often disagree on its original meaning. These observations seem to contradict the belief of many Christians that anyone can understand the Bible correctly with a good translation.

For some, the Bible becomes less relevant and less meaningful when they begin to read it for what it meant originally. In most religions, the very idea of Scripture is that the words hold direct and immediate authority over you: "God said it; I believe it; that settles it for me." But when you begin to read Paul's words in the light of the situations he was addressing, it becomes less clear that his words are actually directed at you. You may begin to feel that you are reading letters written to someone else in a faraway place and that you are just looking over someone else's shoulder.

At this point in the game we cannot question that Paul's words were in fact written to the audiences of ancient times and that they addressed situations at the various places to which he wrote. We cannot question that what he and his audiences understood his words to mean was a function of what words and ideas could mean two thousand years ago. Nor can we now question that frequently there are significant differences between what our words mean and what theirs did.

In other words, if you have read very far into this book at all, you have crossed a bridge you can never go back over. You recognize the difference between then and now. You know that, at least in the first instance, the words of the Bible were written to someone other than you and that they were written in their categories of understanding rather than in yours. Is this the end of the Bible as Scripture? Does the Bible now become a dated book? Or is there a way to achieve what one philosopher called a "second naïveté," a way to see the Bible once again as a word to me directly?[1]

> Many conservative scholars believe that while the Bible was indeed written to ancient contexts, the way it addresses those contexts reflects certain timeless principles and the timeless character of God.

I would say, "Yes!" Most conservative scholars have reclaimed the Bible for today by slightly modifying their understanding of what it means to call it Scripture. Many conservative Christians would say that while the Bible was indeed written to contexts quite different from ours today, the way it addresses those contexts reflects certain timeless principles that in turn reflect the timeless character of God. In other words, while the specific commands and statements of the Bible may not always relate directly to today (e.g., the command not to eat pork), the principles behind those commands and the unchangeable nature of God always apply directly to us today.

For some this approach is enough to maintain the Bible as Scripture. For others, it may still seem like a lot of work and thinking—more work than you would expect of a message directed at you. Still others may ask whether the various portraits of God in the Bible even reflect the worldviews of ancient culture at times. To put it another way: Will we always be able to find a principle behind every command? Or does much of it boil down to the fact that God always meets people wherever they are—and within whatever understanding of the world they have?

The Bible as a Witness to Saving Events

In some ways, crossing the bridge to the Bible's original meaning does us a favor—it potentially places our faith on something far more solid than words. Words mean different things to different people in different contexts. But when we read the Bible in context, we begin to see Jesus, Peter, and Paul not as words on a page, not as characters in a story, but as real people who lived in history. We shift from words to events.

Surely the rock bottom foundation of Christianity, at least traditional Christianity, is the saving death and victorious resurrection of Jesus Christ. Ironically, the focus of so many Christians on the words of the Bible can sometimes cause them to lose sight of Jesus as a real person who really lived and who really rose from the dead. It is on this event in history that Christianity stands, not on the words about that event.

When we read the Bible in context, we begin to see its books as a part of God's constant workings in history, just a few examples of the way He has repeatedly met His people wherever He might find them. Each of its books represents just one instance of His ongoing relationship with the world. When we read the Bible in context, the story of this relationship becomes much bigger than the stories within the Bible. Rather, we see that the books of the Bible are within the story of God's relationship with the world. We might say that the individual books of the Bible are in the story of God even more than that the story of God is in the Bible.

Reading the New Testament in this way leads us to some important breakthroughs in our understanding. For example, when we read the Bible out of its historical context, we usually view it as a single book with a single message. To a high degree, we assume that each book has fully arrived at a final understanding of truth. For example, some Christians even have difficulty listening to the New Testament when it has a different perspective from the Old!

However, reading these books in their historical context leads us to wonder whether there is not in fact some dialogue that takes place within them. Do Matthew and Ephesians represent two different groups of Christians, each listening to God as they seek what He requires of them? Do genuine developments in understanding sometimes take place in the course of its pages? It is just possible that reading the Bible out of context causes us to miss the richness of God helping His people unpack the momentous events they had witnessed.

We know that the early Christians themselves experienced these events as such a process. Take Peter, for example. You would have expected him, of all people, to have it all figured out from the very beginning. After all, not only had he been with Jesus for His whole ministry, but he was also one of the chief apostles, one of the first witnesses to the resurrection. Yet we see him struggling with the most fundamental issues of Christian truth throughout the New Testament.

Take the matter of Jewish food laws. Mark tells of an incident in Jesus' ministry in which Jesus implies that "all foods [are] 'clean'" (Mark 7:19). Yet this truth apparently was not obvious to Peter, who decades later refused food that God offered him in a dream. "Surely not, Lord!" he told God. "I have never eaten anything impure or unclean" (Acts 10:14). Still later Peter would refuse to eat with Gentiles, in order to preserve his ritual purity (Gal. 2:12). Although I think Peter probably came around eventually, we have no hard evidence to prove it. Indeed, it is possible that Peter never fully agreed with the idea that Christ's death had ended "the system of Jewish law that excluded the Gentiles" and made "peace between Jews and Gentiles by creating in himself one new person from the two groups" (Eph. 2:15 NLT).

What we see is that the people in the Bible were real people who did not always have it all figured out. When we view the books of the New Testament as moments in a process of God helping His people to figure it all out, we at least have to consider the possibility that at points these books, rather than being the final word itself, are on a trajectory toward the final word. Take the notion of the Trinity. It took several hundred years after the books of the New Testament were completed for

> The rock bottom foundation of traditional Christianity is the saving death and victorious resurrection of Jesus Christ—real events in history rather than words about events.

Christians to work out the details of what was appropriate to believe about the divine status of Jesus and the Holy Spirit. The seeds for these beliefs are in the New Testament, but they are far from worked out.

The New Testament in no way questions the institution of slavery. Contrary to popular belief, Paul did not tell Philemon to free Onesimus the slave—he only told Philemon to take him back after he had run away (Philem. 17). Paul affirmed the goal of freedom but did not consider it a high priority (1 Cor. 7:21). Far from encouraging civil disobedience or anything like an Underground Railroad, 1 Peter 2:18–25 commands slaves to submit to masters even when these masters beat them unjustly. Yet surely we would all agree that the abolition of slavery has moved human culture just a little closer to what the Bible implies heaven will be like.

These observations lead us to realize just how important the church and the Holy Spirit are for us today. When we read these books for their original meaning, we realize that they say different things in different contexts. But if they say different things, then we need some way of prioritizing and connecting them to our situations. This process is bigger than any one individual. We dare not trust ourselves to apply the Bible appropriately without other Christians around to make sure the Holy Spirit is with us.

The Bible as Sacrament

I mentioned earlier in this chapter that I believe it is possible to attain a kind of "second naïveté" with regard to the Bible. I believe it is possible for its words to speak directly to us today even after we have passed them through the fires of their ancient meanings. Of course, not all Christians want to go back to reading the Bible without a view to its original, historical contexts. They may prefer to look for principles behind the things God commanded back then and then reapply the principles directly to today. Indeed, because of the historical orientation of our Western culture, it may be very difficult for some to suspend the idea of context long enough to read the Bible in this way again.

It is possible, however, to view the words of the Bible sacramentally. Baptism is considered a Christian sacrament—a divinely appointed way of meeting God in which some ordinary medium like water comes to have extraordinary significance. God may have set up the words of the Bible to work in this way.

> Each book of the Bible represents just one instance of God's ongoing relationship with the world. We might say that the individual books of the Bible are in the story of God even more than that the story of God is in the Bible.

Words are ordinary things—we use them all the time. In a sense, God could speak to you through any words, anywhere. Potentially, you could hear God's voice through the words of a newspaper. Yet, the history of the church seems to tell us that God has set aside these particular words of the Bible as a place where He can meet His people.

How the Holy Spirit accomplishes this feat is, of course, a mystery, and we know many people claim to hear God's voice when they probably do not. But if we are open, if we are in tune with God through prayer, who is to say that God will not authentically speak to His people through these words by way of the "dictionaries" in their heads, regardless of how close their understandings come to the original meanings? It is indeed possible for us to see ourselves in the stories of the Bible, regardless of what those stories meant to their original audiences. The very process of trying to understand the Bible's words in English leads us to hear them in ways that make sense to us in our lives.

Because the Bible treats the most important topics of human existence—the meaning of life, the possibility of existence after death, the problem of evil in the world—its words consider the very questions for which we are seeking answers. Because by faith we believe that the One with the answers was the One inspiring the people in its pages, we believe its words are the most appropriate place to go to hear the right answers. The Holy Spirit, working through individuals and the church, can do the rest.

Questions for Study and Discussion

1. As you finish this book, to what extent do you think the Scriptures were written for their own times and to what extent do you think they were written for all times?

2. What is the best way to read the words of Scripture? In terms of their original meaning? Prayerfully, in whatever way the Spirit leads you? In terms of your church's interpretations?

3. Does any particular teaching in Scripture give the "final word" on any specific belief or practice? To what extent is it legitimate and/or necessary to move beyond its words? Regarding things the Scriptures originally prohibited, is it legitimate to allow these things in new contexts? Regarding things the Scriptures originally allowed, is it legitimate to prohibit these things in new contexts?

Notes

Chapter 2: How to Read the Bible as a Christian

1. I will occasionally refer to God in this book by way of masculine pronouns such as He or Him. I do so because this is the most typical way the Bible itself refers to God, not because God is literally male. The Old Testament in particular makes it clear that God does not have genitalia of any sort.

Chapter 3: An Overview of the New Testament

1. The term *Apocrypha* most often refers to the seven books included in the Roman Catholic Bible but not in most Protestant Bibles: Tobit, Judith, 1 and 2 Maccabees, the Wisdom of Solomon, Ecclesiasticus (also known as Sirach), and Baruch. In addition, the books of Esther and Daniel in the Catholic Bible include extra material. A few other books appear in early manuscripts of the Greek Old Testament (e.g., 1 Esdras, 3 and 4 Maccabees, Odes of Solomon). Sometimes these books are also considered apocrypha.

Chapter 7: The Story Behind the Story: From Promised Land to No Land

1. J. D. G. Dunn, *The Partings of the Ways Between Christianity and Judaism and Their Significance for the Character of Christianity* (Philadelphia: Trinity, 1991), 18–36.

2. For example, N. T. Wright's *The New Testament and the People of God* (Minneapolis: Fortress, 1992) and *Jesus and the Victory of God* (Minneapolis: Fortress, 1996). These are volumes 1 and 2 respectively of the *Christian Origins and the Question of God* series.

Chapter 9: The Life and Teachings of Jesus: An Overview

1. *Christ* is the Greek translation of *Messiah*, which is a Hebrew term meaning "anointed one."

Chapter 10: Jesus, the Son of David: The Gospel of Matthew

1. Quoted by the early church historian, Eusebius, *History of the Church* 3.39.16.

2. Technically, Papias said that Matthew wrote in the Hebrew language, but he probably meant Aramaic, which was the "Hebrew" spoken in Palestine at the time of Christ (cf. Acts 22:2).

Chapter 11: Jesus, the Suffering Messiah: The Gospel of Mark

1. See also Mark 5:43, 7:36, and 8:26.

2. Examples of Jesus commanding the demons to be silent concerning His identity include Mark 1:25, 34; and 3:11–12.

3. The overwhelming majority of scholars believe the gospel of Mark originally ended at 16:8 and that the verses that follow in some Bibles were later added.

4. William Wrede (1859–1906) wrote his revolutionary *Messianic Secret in the Gospels* in 1901.

5. See E. P. Sanders, *The Historical Figure of Jesus* (New York: Penguin, 1993), 120, 238–48.

6. Eusebius, *Hist*. 3.39.14–15.

Chapter 12: The Beginnings of Jesus' Mission: The Gospel of Luke

1. For example, the Greek translation of Genesis 10 gives seventy-two as the number of all the nations of the world.

2. Repentance is also a significant emphasis in Luke-Acts.

Chapter 13: Stories Jesus Told: The Parables

1. The gospel of John records no parables, although it is filled with metaphors. See chapter 14 of this text.

2. Very similar to the parable of the lost son are the parables of the lost sheep and the lost coin, both in Luke 15 (the parable of the lost sheep is also in Matt. 18:12–14).

Chapter 14: Jesus, the Way: The Gospel of John

1. From the Nicene Creed adopted in A.D. 325 at the Council of Nicea.

2. John 21:24 mentions that the beloved disciple had written down his testimony, so some or most of the gospel may come from a source written by this disciple.

3. Quoted in Eusebius, *Hist*. 3.39.4.

4. Ibid.

Chapter 15: The Story of Jesus in John

1. The name of God, Yahweh, seems to come in some way from the Hebrew word *hayah*, which means "he is."

Chapter 17: Jerusalem, Judea, and Samaria: The Story of the Church in Acts Part 1

1. Those in the Wesleyan tradition may find statements like this one of concern, since the Wesleyan tradition generally relates the day of Pentecost to the experience of entire sanctification. This book does, however, affirm the possibility of victory over sin through the power of the Holy Spirit. See the first three pages of chapter 20.

2. The word *magus*, used of Simon, is the same word used of the wise men in Matthew.

3. The story is also told with minor variations in Acts 22:3–21 and 26:4–23.

Chapter 18: To the Ends of the Earth: The Story of the Church in Acts Part 2

1. While Rome governed the whole Mediterranean world, some special cities were Roman colonies, meaning that they were not under regional control and were granted the same rights as cities located in Italy. As a colony, Philippi would have been a likely city for the descendants of retired Roman troops to inhabit.

Chapter 19: The Life and Writings of Paul

1. See B. J. Malina and J. H. Neyrey, *Portraits of Paul: An Archaeology of Ancient Personality* (Louisville: Westminster John Knox, 1996), 3.

Chapter 21: Unity Problems: The Corinthian Letters

1. In 1 Corinthians 5:9 Paul alludes to a letter written before 1 Corinthians itself. Second Corinthians 2:4 mentions a letter that Paul wrote in great distress and anguish—a letter that does not seem to be 1 Corinthians.

2. See Galatians 2.

Chapter 24: Letters from Prison: Ephesians, Philippians, Colossians, and Philemon

1. E. Goodspeed, *The Key to Ephesians* (Chicago: University of Chicago, 1956), 1–75.

2. Dead Sea Scrolls: *Songs of Sabbath Sacrifice* 1.16; also *Testament of Levi* 3.5–6, perhaps a document of broader Essenism—those from whom the Qumran community split off.

3. Mentioned in the letter from Ignatius, *To the Ephesians*, 1:3.

Chapter 25: Paul's Earliest Preaching: 1 and 2 Thessalonians

1. Some scholars think Galatians was written first.

2. For example, 2 Corinthians 5:3, 6–8; Philippians 1:23–24. Even these comments refer to the intermediate state of the dead between death and their future resurrection. Paul never speaks of an eternity in heaven or hell.

3. Suggestions have included the Roman Empire, the Roman emperor, Paul's need to complete his ministry, the Holy Spirit, etc.

4. The problem with relating it to the events of the preceding paragraph is that we would then have to say that the man of lawlessness has already come. This would contradict the more important fact that the day of the Lord in 2 Thessalonians seems to be the second coming of Christ as Christians have traditionally conceived it.

Chapter 27: Don't Give Up the Race: Hebrews

1. The document known as 11QMelchizedek.

2. In 1 Clement, ca. A.D. 96.

Chapter 28: The General Letters: James, 1 and 2 Peter, 1–3 John, and Jude

1. J. H. Elliott, *A Home for the Homeless: A Sociological Exegesis of 1 Peter, Its Situation and Strategy* (Philadelphia: Fortress, 1981).

2. Ignatius *To the Smyrnaeans* 5.2. The translations of Ignatius are mine.

3. Ibid., 2.1.

4. Ignatius, *To the Ephesians* 9.1.

5. Irenaeus, *Against Heresies* 3.3.4, written in the late 100s.

6. The Greek word for *church* is feminine—it would thus be natural to refer to a fellow church as a sister or woman.

7. Some suggest 2 John is pseudonymous because of its deep similarities to 3 John in style and 1 John in content.

8. Third John seems to mention one—Demetrius.

9. *To the Ephesians* 6.1.

10. Eusebius, *Ecclesiastical History* 3.39.1–11.

Chapter 29: Jesus Revealed! The Apocalypse

1. R. Bauckham, The *Theology of the Book of Revelation* (Cambridge: Cambridge University, 1993), 1–2.

2. Sibylline Oracles 5.93–110 from *Old Testament Pseudepigrapha*, trans. John J. Collins, vol. 1 (New York: Doubleday, 1983), 395.

Epilogue: Where Do We Go From Here?

1. P. Ricoeur, "Biblical Hermeneutics: The Metaphorical Process" *Semeia* 4 (1975): 75–106.